*All
Outdoors*

By Jack Denton Scott

ALL OUTDOORS

YOUR DOG'S HEALTH BOOK

THE WEIMARANER

TOO LIVELY TO LIVE

PUG INVADES THE FIFTH COLUMN

All Outdoors

by
Jack Denton Scott

Hunting and fishing with the author
of America's largest outdoor column

THE STACKPOLE COMPANY
HARRISBURG, PENNSYLVANIA

Printed in the U. S. A.
by
THE TELEGRAPH PRESS
Established 1831
Harrisburg, Pennsylvania

ACKNOWLEDGEMENTS

My thanks to the editors of the American Legion Magazine, Esquire, Colliers, Fishing Waters of the World, Saga, Pageant, in which some portion of this material appeared in somewhat different form—and to Douglas H. Haight whose sincere interest and enthusiasm helped all the way.

Foreword

ON the basis of hard, cold statistics I predict a tremendous success for this book. I don't say this because I've had a chance to sneak an advance look at the contents, nor am I prejudiced because Jack Scott is a nice guy. It's simply a matter of figures. That and my observations as to the kind of books that seem to do well.

Browsing around the neighborhood stationery stores, luncheonettes, and other cultural centers where paper-bound books are sold, I have gotten the distinct impression that love, romance and sex are highly popular subjects with the bookish set. However, it is amazing how little of this reading is translated into down-to-earth, up-and-at-'em, point-of-sale action. In an average year, if there is any such thing, only about 1,500,000 marriage licenses are sold in these United States!

By way of contrast, each year the various States dispense 15,000,000 hunting licenses, while another 17,600,000 licenses are sold to fishermen. From this it is perfectly obvious that Americans are much more interested in the great outdoors than they are in the great indoors, and I for one am delighted that Jack Scott, on the basis of sound statistics, is pioneering in this field. Who knows, but that Hollywood will follow his trail and come up with movies about hunting and fishing starring Marilyn Monroe and Gina Lollobrigida?

If they should do so they may present us with features as interesting as Jack can write them. A long time ago, after World War II, we put him to work writing a rod and gun page for *The American Legion Magazine*. For more than four years he has been keeping 3,000,000 veterans happy every month, and when you can do that you are by way of being a miracle man.

I don't like to give away a writer's trade secrets, but I can give you a clue as to what you might watch out for as you read *ALL OUTDOORS*. You won't find a single chapter about polo. Nor will you find any easy lessons on jai-alai, or helpful hints about steeplechase racing. Such pastimes are of all-consuming interest to some sportsmen, but Jack Scott has never tried to alienate those readers from such esoteric journals as *Sports Illustrated.* After all, Jack is first, last and always a sportsman and doesn't like to poach—especially when there are so many people who don't give a hang about such things.

So you'll find the author concentrating on things that naturally interest the millions who like hunting enough to pay a dollar or more each year to obtain a license, and the additional millions who invest in fishing permits. Also, as a canny fellow, he knows that not many of the 15,000,000 ever go on African safaris, so he has written nary a word about skinning wildebeests and water buffalo. And if any of you want to learn the best way of catching marlin, you'll have to look elsewhere.

I suppose that with that last paragraph I have probably lost fifteen or sixteen sales for this book, but I'm sure that some of you will make up for this by buying a few extra copies to give to friends. And now that we are becoming commercial, why not give a copy of *ALL OUTDOORS* to that farmer friend who lets you hunt over his land or fish in his creek? There's the fellow you really ought to be thinking about. Don't forget, he's as important in the scheme of outdoor things as your hunting and fishing license, *and* a copy of this book.

Joseph C. Keeley

Editor
The American Legion Magazine

Table of Contents

ix

Book 1

THE STREAM

"I envy not him that eats better meat than I do; nor him that is richer, or that wears better clothes than I do: I envy him, and him only, that catches more fish than I do . . ."

Izaak Walton—The Compleat Angler, 1653

CHAPTER 1

No Price-Tag on Pleasure

DURING those hectic hours when the pressures of a modern world force you to withdraw into yourself in escape, I find myself thinking of the outdoors or sports connected with the out-of-door world, and my mind immediately does a sort of celestial transport (with a speed that even today's jet planes haven't been able to equal) and I find myself back in Elmira—a valley town in upstate New York where I spent my boyhood.

Elmira is famous for several things: Mark Twain married a girl from there, spent much time within its limits and is buried in Woodlawn Cemetery. It is also the home of the world's largest fire engine company; it's the gliding center of America, and it's the place where Dan Beard, one of the most famous woodsmen and outdoorsmen America has yet produced, followed Mark Twain (probably because he was illustrating his books at the time) and spent his spare time prowling the heavily-forested hills that rim Chemung Valley.

This was before my time, but with the assistance of that magic appendage, a small boy's imagination, I relived many of the sunlit days Dan Beard must have spent. And although I didn't know him, the small boy's god in older and simpler days, I had a good friend who did.

That friend was my father, Cecil Vivian Scott, a stalwart man with dark hair, bluish-gray eyes the color of a trout stream on a June day, and a full and untethered generosity that was his greatest weakness. Some thought his love of the outdoors was his weakness. To me he was clad in burnished armor and had no weakness of any sort. During long winter nights he would tell stories of the outdoors, talk of Dan Beard, Death Valley Scotty, whom he also knew, and his own boyhood days wandering the wild and dangerous mountains of West Virginia.

He had the true story-teller's gift of simple words and vivid description. He also had the small boy's talent for the world of make-believe and today I sometimes find myself hard put to separate the real from the unreal.

3

But for me it was all real, and as I go back to those days when young character was being put together, I realize that the famed Dan Beard wasn't my hero at all. To me, my father was the complete embodiment of the true outdoor man. He was wise in the way of the wood, knew how to read trails, could catch a wily trout with his bare hands, could talk to dogs and walk all day over mountains without tiring.

When our family finances were at low ebb, a frequent occurrence, he might come home one day with a new hound dog—another mouth to feed. Or he would decide that this was the time to get outdoors, and he'd take that day off. An individual in a world of conformists, he lived life as he saw it and had that rare quality—the courage of his convictions.

He taught me two lessons that I will never forget.

A few houses from where we lived on Hall Street in Elmira, dwelt a magnificent male boxer dog. He was fawn colored, well-muscled, gentle with children and the pride of the neighborhood. True, he wasn't much as a watch dog, mainly because he loved everyone, but he was an animal that definitely impressed me, not only with his handsome good looks, but his nobility of carriage and his demeanor of dependability.

We owned only one dog at that time, a sort of crossbred hound that looked more like a beagle than any other particular breed except that he was long-legged. He bore the name of Spot and he was an excellent hunter and fierce watchdog, though he also was gentle with children. He wasn't permitted the run of the neighborhood like the boxer, but moved on a long length of wire on our back property. He had an insulated dog-house, was given periodic exercise by my brothers and me, and went hunting more often than any dog in our town. He worshipped my father. All in all, I'd say that he was a happy animal.

But I didn't care much for him. The boxer was more to my liking. When I looked at Spot and his long, unglamorous ears and soulful brown eyes, I couldn't envision proud armies of marching men, the clink of armour, and fierce Teutons and their war dogs, the way I did when I dreamed at the boxer.

One night I marched in to my father and said, "Dad, why do we have to have an old hound dog when we could have a beauty like a boxer?"

Red rose in my father's face and I would have to have been a moron not to realize he was angry.

"Sarah," he called to my mother, "I'm keeping Jack out of school tomorrow and taking him hunting." My mother didn't question him. Wise in the ways of small boys and angry fathers, she let nature take its course.

I was only 12-years-old at the time and my father hadn't taken me hunting many times before. Puzzled, I didn't sleep much that night. Excitement and happy anticipation comingled with perplexity and it wasn't until we reached the top of long East Hill the next morning that I realized my father was out to teach me a lesson. He didn't permit me to take my little .410 shotgun he had taught me to use and, strangest of all, old Spot wasn't with us.

It was a bleak December day with low-hanging, dirty-wash gray clouds and it was cold. We were hunting cottontail rabbits.

Suddenly, a rabbit, white flag up, burst out of a laurel thicket and zig-zagged up the hill. My father raised his Winchester 12 gauge and slowly, lead correctly adjusted, completely without excitement, sent a shot after the bunny. And he missed! Another strange thing, for he seldom missed a game shot.

He turned to me and said, "Jack, old Spot was feeling poorly this morning and I didn't think it was fair to take him along. I'm afraid you're going to have to take his place." He pointed up the hill. "Rabbits circle. He's going to the top of that hill. I want you to take off after him as fast as you can, and bark like a dog all the way. That'll fool him and if we're lucky he'll circle right back to the spot where we kicked him out."

I did as he suggested, feeling like a fool. Barking as much like a dog as I could, I raced up the hill. My father kept urging me faster and stood where he was. Making a wide circle, I finally ended up at the bottom of the hill, panting and out of breath. There was no dead cottontail.

"You didn't go fast enough and you didn't bark loud enough," my father said.

Four more times within the next two hours I made like a rabbit dog, and, like a tired hound, tongue hanging out, finally stopped, grabbed hold of a tree and told my father that I was tired. We hadn't bagged one bunny.

My father was quiet as we walked back to the car. And I was doing a little thinking. "Gee, Dad," I said, "that's about the first time you've gone after cottontails in a long time that you didn't come back with the limit."

"Always had Spot with me," my father said.

I laughed a little. "Guess I'm a flop as a dog."

"Yes, son, I guess you are," he said.

He didn't harangue me or make any point. All of a sudden I got it.

"I guess Spot's quite a dog at that," I said. "Not only is he a good rabbit dog, he's swell on pheasants and is a better watchdog than that boxer." Musing, I went on, "And I bet that old boxer wouldn't have been able to do even as good as I did."

My father laughed. "That boxer is all right. He was bred as more of a guard dog than anything else. Civilization and people have even taken that out of him."

"But what's he good for?" I asked.

My father explained that the boxer was a pet, a plaything for his owners, whereas Spot was a pet and a companion, but he was also a hunting dog with a purpose in life.

"Life and nature are teasers, son," he said. "They sometimes slick things up so they look handsome and beautiful. What you've got to learn is that everything isn't on the outside. The things that count are on the inside. And whether you're dog or man you've got to have a purpose in life."

Needless to say, Spot became my chosen dog and even today, if asked what my favorite dog is I'm sure I'd say, "A long-eared hound."

The second lesson began one April evening when my father returned from a day of trout fishing with an empty creel. He was happy, in good spirits, and I couldn't figure out how that could be if he hadn't caught a single fish. I hadn't been able to go with him because it was a school day. And I guess that the taint of sour grapes was evident as I questioned him.

"Dad," I said, "why is it that you can go fishing so often and come back without catching any fish and still feel happy about it? I know when I don't catch any fish I feel like the devil."

He looked at me, the light from the fireplace caught in his blue-gray eyes, twinkled and glowed, and he smiled. "That's a heck of a way to feel," he said.

Then he sat down beside me. "Look, son," he said, "I go fishing to catch the day. If I catch some fish while I'm out that's good fun. But I always catch a dawn or a sunset that makes me glad I'm alive." He paused. "I don't believe I've ever seen a prettier sight than I did today. I spotted a female grouse and her young walking down a dirt road. Such pride, such organization! I didn't catch a fish, but I had a good day."

Poetic, sentimental, corny, drivel? I don't think so, but maybe some of today's sportsmen would. Maybe those 25 people who shot the stuffed deer placed alongside a main highway as an experiment, would think so. Maybe those sportsmen who judge the fun they've had by their watch, and the size of their catch would. I know that the man caught shooting squirrels out of season in Nansemond, Virginia by Warden Shelton Rountree—the man who whirled and shot the young warden, with the result that the boy had to have his arm amputated—would. Yes, he'd think that my father's philosophy was pure drivel.

I hope you don't. This book was put together for people who will appreciate that philosophy. In its pages you'll find simple technique and know-how that may teach you to be a better sportsman. But no book can teach you full appreciation of God's Outdoors. I hope you already have that.

Before you get into a book that I hope will prove helpful, I'd like to leave a couple of thoughts. As you go afield this year, hunting and fishing, try to remember that the magic world of the outdoors is for pleasure—not for profit.

In 1954 the U. S. Fish and Wildlife Service announced that the sale of hunting and fishing licenses amounted to $70,603,207. They haven't yet been able to put a price-tag on the amount of pleasure millions of Americans received.

Don't try to price-tag your pleasure afield. Don't count the hours by the number of trout caught, the full bag of pheasant or cottontail rabbits . . . Go fishing or hunting for the day. Catch that day and hold on to it. It may be a memory that you will cherish in the years to come . . .

CHAPTER 2

Everybody's Fish

FISHING is now reputed to be the most popular of all sports, including the vaunted exercises such as baseball, bowling, football and golf. But given time, the so-called fishing experts will foul it up, creating hazards where none exist. Most outdoor magazines have fishing editors who, feeling their positions demand it, point out the sport's complications, and many general magazines run perplexing how-to articles on how to reap the most from your rod. Technical words and phrases have crept out to fuddle fishing and the simplicity the small boy and Izaak Walton imparted to the sport, is becoming burdened with complexity.

I have the feeling that practically everyone is a born fisherman. Fishing is a sport that takes you into the open on your own terms; it's a sport where you can be alone with yourself and with your maker. A rare occurrence these days. Those who try to burden it with confusing phrases, deck it out in fancy and expensive trappings, confound it with mathematics, the rise and fall of tides, phases of the moon and the temperature of the day, are doing both fishing and you an injustice.

If you've been wanting to go fishing and haven't because of a lack of equipment and experience, this chapter is for you. It's the story of an underdog. Or rather several underdogs, species of fish that the experts don't even admit exist. Fish that have been making millions of people happy. Let's hope you'll be one of them.

Last year some 17,127,896 fishermen got themselves togged up in stream gear, jammed legs into hipboots and waders and went forth. The number who returned with the elegant trio, trout, bass and salmon were in the minority. But those who came home after a day of fun with fish for the pan and the desire to fish again were fishermen who believed that catching the white and yellow perch, the sunfish, the black and the white crappie, the bluegill, the white bass, the catfish and the drum, was as much fun as hooking a trout or a bass. These were

8

the fishermen comprising more than 8,000,000 in the four central geographic regions of the United States; these were fishermen who out of respect began calling the fish they caught by their correct names and not "pan fish."

Even intelligently-skeptical science is beginning to respect the pan fish: It seems that thousands of fishermen complained to conservation authorities about the lack of result in Lake Huron. The catch of white and yellow perch had slipped from 1,345,000 pounds to 41,000 in seven years. Detailed study brought forth the fact that a slimy character of the deep called a sea lamprey (thousands of them) were latching onto the sides of fish in Lake Huron, sucking blood from their bodies and eventually killing them.

The bloodsucking lamprey is a fish classed with the hag-fishes that forms a distinct class of vertebrates, the *cyclostomata*. It looks somewhat like an eel, has a single nostril on top of its head, gill-slits on the neck, no jaws, but a circular sucker equipped with a horny projection. A nightmare creature, it feeds on fish and the blood of fish, rasping away through the scales with its projectile. There are about ten species in North America, of which the sea lamprey is the greatest scourge. They are worthless, although it is said that lumpy Henry I of England considered them his favorite dish and once almost died of indigestion while eating them.

But the lamprey is a type of murderer difficult to deal with. So the authorities in Michigan called for help from the Fish and Wildlife Service in Washington. They, in turn, consulted the Cook Electric Company. A team of Fishery Research Biologists and some of the staff of Cook Electric Laboratories found the answer after long experimentation. They developed an electromechanical weir that would suffocate the adult lampreys as they moved toward their spawning grounds. The experiment took place in Michigan's Ocqueoc River. Reducing it to readable language, a low voltage intermittent DC guiding field led the more sensitive fish such as perch, around the death areas containing the electric charge. Result: less lampreys, more perch.

The various state game and fish authorities are charting the pan fish higher on their popularity graphs every year. J. L. Stearns, Chief of Education and Information for Georgia, says, "It is my estimate that eight or nine out of every ten fishermen are seeking the pan fish, which in our state is called the bream or crappie."

Thomas L. Kimball, Director of the Game and Fish Commission of Colorado claims that his state, long one that concentrated mainly on the stocking of rainbow and Lock Leven trout, is presently engaged in an extensive warm water fisheries' management program that will materially improve the quality of recreational fishing for pan fish. The residents of his state have demanded it, he says.

Lyle M. Thorpe, supervisor of Fisheries Management in Connecticut, is proud of the fact that his state's ponds and lakes are crammed with yellow and white perch, calico bass and crappies. Research has established that over 75% of the fishermen in Connecticut are interested in pan fish.

Ernest E. Mulch, Assistant Chief of the Division of Information and Education of Arizona's Fish Commission, and Frank L. Haynes, Information Specialist for Alabama, both feel that about 75% of their fishermen are interested in pan fish. They prefer the crappies, the bluegill and the redear sunfish to the more esoteric kinds of fish such as trout and bass.

Tennessee with its vast TVA fishing impoundments has a great variety of fish, with bass in the majority. But Louis Clapper, public relations officer for that state feels that the crappie is fast outdrawing bass and other game fish. It is a known fact that both white and black crappie grow big in the Great Lakes of the South. The majority of them tip the scales at well over one pound and are currently being caught on flyrods, by trolling, spinning and casting. They are scrappy and, in many cases, outfight the Tennessee bass.

"In my judgment," says Dan Saults, Chief of the Information Section of the Missouri Conservation Commission, "almost all Missouri fishermen will try for pan fish deliberately, while at least 60% fish for them most of the time." When asked why, he said because the fish are fun to catch, there are more of them and they give the fishermen confidence in themselves.

What these men, all experts in their field, are effectively doing is deflating the out-of-proportion gamefish balloon that certain types of fishermen have blown up over the past few years.

A cross-section study of the Fisheries' Commissions in our states which I have been undertaking not only brought statements from the various officials establishing that the pan fish is unjustly maligned, but proved conclusively that if it weren't for this species, our fishing population wouldn't be well over 17,000,000, but down to about one-tenth of that.

Without exception fishing in America today is the leading participant-sport. I'd gamble the much put-upon pan fish is responsible.

But one of the most important reasons the pan fish makes fishing possible for so many people is accessibility. You can catch a pan fish at the end of any trolley line. Ponds and lakes are dotted in every community and, in most cases, fishing regulations are such that one type of fish is on the open list at practically any time of the year. The lake fisherman, pond dunker, the stream man, the ice fisherman, all can catch pan fish whenever the spirit moves them. This is like saying there is no closed season on pan fish. And it's true. They're really the fisherman's fish. The poor man's trip to Canada.

I talked to one of the large fishing tackle manufacturers. "Every night when I close shop." he said, "I breathe a little prayer of thanks that there is such a fish as this pan fish. Without them I'd be selling flyrods and lures to a few, but the great volume of my business would be gone."

What the tackle manufacturer didn't mention is that the pan-fisherman is three up on the game fisherman. (1) He can fish more often and in many more places. (2) His gear doesn't have to be as varied and as expensive. (3) The legal limit on his fish is much higher.

If you want, you can angle for the crappie or the bluegill with a can of worms and a bamboo pole. And with a little patience you'll come home with fish. Or, if you prefer, you can use a flyrod with wet or dry flies and light monofilament line. Spinning gear with an eight-ounce lure, nylon line, and sixty-yard castability will take the perch and the bluegill. A short stubby trolling rod with trailing line and flashing spinner will take both the black and the white crappie and quite often a nice fat perch or bluegill. You can fish from a dock, a boat, the shore, wade a stream, or take a leisurely river float trip. You, as a panfisherman are no book-of-rule boob. Whatever system you choose will pay off. I personally recommend a $20.00 light flyrod and a cheap single action reel.

And it seems that no matter how many pan fish are lifted from our waters yearly they keep thriving. They are a tough and hardy fish, and contrary to what their derogatators say, are not a panmixia of many species, but are of their own distinct type. Thus they breed and flourish every year healthily and in such numbers that fishermen yet unborn will be assured of fun with a rod, will know the good taste of their own fresh-caught fish.

One day last August, I was standing on the shores of Lake Keuka, in upper New York State, watching a fisherman named Harry Altman standing in a rowboat working the water with a light flyrod. Harry is a well-known, successful fresh water fisherman.

The water was as smooth as a piece of nylon. It was quiet. Harry was flicking his line, working runs in the lake of nylon. One long run started, then exploded. The rowboat began rocking as he fought the fish. The quiet was gone, and, as Harry landed his fish and rowed into shore, his face a little red from exertion, I said, "Let me see that unlucky bass? That was a good fight he put up."

He held up the chunky little fish. "It isn't a bass. It's a bluegill, some call it calico bass. They're scrappy little devils. And they can make a fool out of you if you get too cocky. For my money a bluegill is better eatin' than a bass. Doesn't have that muddy taste."

Fly fishing, the top of the ladder technique in fishing, can be learned in one evening—at least well enough for you to go forth and catch a few fish and have some fun. And, from where I sit, that is the primary purpose of fishing anyway.

Understand that the difference between fly casting and bait casting lies in the fact that when you cast with the fly rod you are really casting the line. Don't depend upon the lure or the fly to take the line out as you do in bait casting. Your line should be out well beyond the rod tip all through your casting. And don't depend upon your reel for anything. On the fly rod it's there to keep your line in a neat little bundle.

Your backyard is the place to start. I'd get a light trout action flyrod either 7½ or 8 feet, and a single action reel. Get what they call the level line and the six-foot, tapered dry fly type of leader. Technically, the leader size would be probably a 5x, .006 inches in diameter. This is the type of gear recommended for panfishing. And as long as you're just starting out and intend panfishing for fun with fly casting equipment, try concentrating on what they call the dry fly. They're more fun than the wet fly. They float on top of the water, and give you more for your money when the fish strikes.

And don't let yourself get lost in the hopeless maze of artificial fly patterns. There's an artificial fly for every fisherman's whim, and number in the thousands. Never buy a fly larger than a number 10 for panfishing. And for sunfish and the like you can even get down to a tiny number 18 if you like.

A few of the patterns you might bring along are the colored hackles, black, white, brown and gray; the Bee, Black Gnat, Royal Coachman, Red Ant, the Alder and the Silver Doctor. That'll be plenty to take any panfish, and it's egg-headed to arrive on a lake or a stream and spend most of your time sorting flies and attempting to make the tremendous decision of which one to use when.

Before you decide to take out after the sunfish, the crappie or the bluegill, give your own backyard a workout. Your handgrip on your fly rod handle can be just a natural closing of the hand over the cork butt-thumb around one side, four fingers around the other. Tie a piece of tightly rolled paper or a small hunk of light wood on the end of your line. Pick yourself an open spot and, if you want to test your accuracy and your eye, mark a circle on the ground and attempt dropping your line with the piece of paper or wood as close to it as possible, conjuring the spot as a sunken tree stump, near which are swimming several very large and handsome type fish.

Once you've got your spot, have the rod gripped in your right hand, then strip off about twenty feet of line. Flip this line to the left with your rod tip, then with a swinging motion of your wrist, move your rod at right angles to the spot you're facing. Now, before your line settles to the ground, and is slightly above the level of the tip of your rod, move the rod quickly but lightly in the opposite direction. Now you've got your line in the air moving free as a bird. Continue to do this —with a rhythm if possible.

You're getting the feel of the rod and realizing what it means to keep the line in the air, in motion and untangled. Do as much of this as you want. It's good practice and will help when you get ready to cast.

Consider that you are standing beside a huge clock; you are not facing it, you are standing sideways to it. Raise your rod up so that you are holding it about ten o'clock on your imaginary clock. Hold arm so that the upper portion is near your body, the forearm horizontal. That line of yours should be stretched out in front of you on the ground.

As you bring the rod back to 11:15 on your guidance clock, using wrist action, flip the rod. This bends the rodtip forward, and assists in throwing the line back over your shoulder. Don't let that rod go back more than 12:00 on your clock, then wait for the line to move back into the air before giving it the forward sweep. The action is *one-two-three;* one to bring it up, two to hold it or check it in position and three for the start of the forward cast.

Don't attempt to use your reel to bring your line in. That's all right at the end of the day when you are through casting, but while practicing on your lawn or actually working a stream, use and practice to perfection the so-called hand-twist retrieve of your line without touching your reel.

It's simple: Just grab the looped line with the thumb and forefinger of your left hand—try to keep your palm up as the line slips through your hand. Close the remainder of the fingers of your left hand tightly over the line which you will feel in your hand. Then turn your hand around, palm down and take another piece of the outstanding line with your thumb and forefinger, and again turn your hand palm up and repeat the same movements until you have retrieved a handful of line.

That's about it. Practice and a couple of trips afield with a man who knows what he is doing will make you a pretty fair fly rod man. To knock the complication out of it, many manufacturers have printed booklets with simple diagrams and black and white sketches showing the exact steps in fly casting. The next time you go to your sporting goods store to buy a few hooks, ask for one of the instruction booklets.

Fly casting isn't the only way. Technique needn't tangle you when it comes to pan fishing.

Last year a friend of mine approached me with a problem. Wife trouble, he said. He couldn't go fishing any more without her constantly carping at him. I suggested that he teach her how to fish and take her along. I thought once she experienced the tug of a fish on the end of her line, she'd have a better understanding of why her spouse wanted to spend so much time trying to outwit the fish. He didn't think it could be done.

One Saturday afternoon I invited her over to my place and suggested that I teach her spin fishing. She was interested; a little intrigued with the strange, coffee-grinder-looking spinning reel and impressed with the lightness of the rod.

In fifteen minutes I taught her the rudiments of spin fishing and had her sending out an eight ounce lure 25 yards without any difficulty. Her excitement in the whole thing made me suggest that we try a friend's pond. The result was that she caught two yellow perch, a crappie and three sunfish, and today is a better panfisherman than her husband.

Spinning, the ancient European type of fishing that is still comparatively new to this country, takes the hazard and backache out of fishing. Many of the experts don't like it and currently are trying to push through legislation to ban it on certain streams. Their objection is that it makes "fishing too easy."

But the pundits notwithstanding, spinning technique is sweeping the country and practically every tackle manufacturer is currently engaged in turning out their own style spinning rods and reels.

Spin fishing really combines fly fishing and bait casting, and is a system of throwing slightly weighted flies, lures, livebait and plugs where you want them. The axis of the reel is at a right angle to that of most other reels; there is no rotating when casting or reeling. The line just falls off the reel at the cast. The line is very light and fine and is of nylon, either in the braided or the practically invisible monofilament. In casting, the weight of the lure (which is seldom over $\frac{1}{2}$ an ounce) takes the line off the reel in small coils which quickly straighten out as the line arcs over the water. When the lure hits your target, the water, the line stops uncoiling.

The fact that the spinning reel doesn't revolve means there is no possibility of tangling the line in a backlash. Great accuracy is possible with spinning in a very few days. The light rod and line give you all the pleasure of fly fishing without any of its complications. It is superior to bait casting because of its accuracy, lack of backlash and the variety of lures that can be used. For panfishing, spinning probably stands at the head of the list.

That's about it for panfishing technique. Remember to keep your hooks sharp and use small ones with small fish. All the pan fish like live baits such as crayfish, worms, freshwater shrimp, frogs, crickets, grasshoppers, minnows and varied kinds of insects. When hooking a worm for a pan fish try to work the worm over the hook in a natural manner, covering the entire hook if possible. Hook the crayfish through the back of the tail and remove his pincers; freshwater shrimp should be tail-hooked; frogs, through the front lips, the grasshopper should have the hook going through the collar on his shoulders, just back of the head. The cricket should be wired on with a fine wire, or a rough piece of thread. Minnows can be hooked in many ways, through the lips, the front portion of the back or the tail. When fishing gets slow with the fly, try tipping the hook with a piece of wiggling worm. In still-fishing, use a split-shot or wrap-around sinker of about ⅛th ounce and a nylon leader. Standard trolling techniques work with pan fish. Small plugs and spinners do a nice job.

There it is, the pan fish panegyric. The song of the crappie, the perch, the bluegill, the pumpkinseed, the catfish, the sunfish and all of their varieties. Good fish who have been sailing under the black flag for too many years.

The figure 17,127,896 has been mentioned as the number of fishing licenses sold in 1954. Clayton B. Seagears, Director of Conservation Education for the sprawling State of New York, brings up a moot point that belongs here: "I believe more fishermen operate on pan fish in New York State," he says, "than they do on the so-called game fish. To make that statement stick I'd like to point out that we can include all the kids under sixteen who don't require a license to fish in our state."

And most states don't ask children under sixteen to purchase licenses. So the 17,000,000 figure can be multiplied; for the youngster under legal age is the greatest pan fish enthusiast in the country. He cuts his fishing eye-teeth on pan fish and learns to respect them at a tender age.

There's the pan fish with the mud rubbed off him and a neat list of his virtues. But there is one important point that wasn't mentioned in detail: the meat of the chunky little characters. They're good to the taste—even their name-callers admit that.

Rex Beach claimed that the natural habitat of a fish was in the frying pan. He was a great respecter of the pan fish.

In that district in New York City, in the upper sixties along Madison Avenue, called "the Mink and Cadillac belt," is a very posh hotel-apartment called the Carlton House. Ruling this many-restauranted dormitory of the dollar-heavy, with delicacy and diplomacy, is the well-known gourmet and hotelman extraordinary, Major Gaston Lauryssen. His fine hand has been felt in many places: Bel Air, Boca Raton, St. Regis, and today it guides the destinies of the best chefs and waiters in the country. For the Carlton House is the natural successor to the old Ritz-Carlton which was razed.

To this royal roost not long ago came trooping some top level sportsmen and gourmets bent on putting their legs under Gaston

Lauryssen's dinner table—R.S.V.P. invitation. The call went out that a special fish dinner was in the offing.

While the guests sat around working up a drool, contemplating what rare and delicious type of fish would be borne out by impeccable waiters, and cooked to perfection by the best chefs in America, Gaston plied them with *hors d'oeuvre* and appetite-whetting tabletalk.

Finally, the fish arrived, two rather small fish per person, sans head, tail and bones. The fish was not swimming in an exotic sauce but was served simply with melted butter and a tiny wedge of lemon.

After they had finished and evinced their delight with small moans and groans, pitched in exactly the right keys of appreciation, the guests began guessing what kind of fish had been served.

Some said Golden Trout, the delicate Dolly Varden, Diamond Jim Brady's old Shepaug River Brook Trout.

To each, Gaston, the gourmet, shook his head and smiled. "No, my friends," he said, his pleasant Belgian accent making the words stand out like neon, "Those fish were white perch, *Morone Americana*. And they were caught by three small boys in Candlewood Lake in Connecticut." Then he twisted the knife, "Probably with worm. Me, I like these so-called pan fish on the table and the pretty trout on the wall." Gaston serves pan fish to the deserving as often as he can, usually at his own dinner table. Sometimes the perch and the crappie will come to the table the French way, gently poached in a fine white wine, sometimes in a special sauce, but often Gaston serves them with nothing except butter and lemon, for he believes that their excellent natural flavor is best accented that way.

"To me," says Gaston the gourmet, "the pan fish is one of the best. Of course I like trout and salmon too, but these people who stick up their noses at America's best, the pan fish, are simply expressing their ignorance."

In the South, the bream or crappie is cleaned and split, rolled in cornmeal and dropped in deep fat and fried. The juices are sealed in by this type of cooking and the fish emerge from the fryer golden brown with the snowy white meat practically melting in your mouth.

Some filet them and dip them lightly in flour and saute in melted butter. I've had a mess of small sunfish poached in the French way that tasted better than any trout I ever ate.

A. J. Fandel, an optometrist from Saint Paul, Minnesota, has a way of cooking pan fish that he dreamed up by himself. Let him tell you about it in his own words. This method appeals to lazy type fisherman like myself.

"Have the pan fish thoroughly cleaned," Mr. Fandel suggests, "fins removed but the head and tail may be left on if desired. And do not remove the scales. Salt inside of fish and pat lightly with flour on the outside. Then place ⅛ inch of vegetable oil in your baking pan and heat. Place your fish in the pan and bake in a 375 degree preheated oven for 30 to 35 minutes depending upon the size of the fish. Bake one side of the fish ten to twelve minutes, turn over and complete the baking.

"This method keeps all the juices inside, the fish does not dry out as in frying and the flesh is more flaky. When you remove the fish from the oven, take a knife and slide it under the skin and scales. The skin with the scales comes off like parchment paper, and you've saved yourself the messy task of scaling the fish."

Scales are probably one of the few things even his most ardent fan holds against the pan fish, but simple know-how can make this chore an easy one.

Pour hot water over your fish until the side fins behind the gills become stiff. Remember to add enough cold water to the hot water to bring it just below the boiling point. After this the scales brush off easily.

Another cute trick is to put a tablespoon of vinegar in the water in which you are cleaning your fish. This will dissolve the scum, make the fish easier to handle and loosen the scales.

An ordinary teaspoon or tablespoon is the best scaler; use the size spoon according to the heft of the fish. Scrape, cross-grain, tipping the spoon back so that *it* catches the flying scales instead of your face, hands and clothing.

Late in 1954 the state of Pennsylvania lifted all restrictions on most pan fish. They call it "liberalized" fishing and will use the results as a yardstick to judge their fishing program for the future. Called by their aquatic biologists, "sound fisheries' management," mainly because of the abundance of pan fish, the Pennsylvania experiment has not only been greeted with enthusiasm by every fisherman in that state, but has been an impetus to start people fishing who have never before dunked a line.

It hardly seems fair to call a fish that means so much to so many by the ignoble "pan fish." This year out of deference, if you can't remember the name of the chunky little devil that gave you so much trouble on the other end of the line and so much pleasure between your knife and fork, how about calling him, "everybody's fish." Being as democratic as he is, he'd like that.

CHAPTER 3

They Hatch, You Catch

ONE April day not long ago a fisherman stood on the banks of the Shepaug River in the state of Connecticut pulling off chest-high waders. Large wet spots were beginning to show through near the armpits: sweat spots from the hard work involved treading slippery pebbles in a swift stream and avoiding a wet and dangerous fall. He was cursing his luck, the sovereign state of Connecticut and fish in general.

Another knight of the reel nearby was slipping into hip boots. He hadn't started.

"Get any?" he said, anticipation running the words together warm and friendly.

"Two lousy fish! Not worth taking out a license for; there aren't any fish in that stream!" Mr. Sweat snarled.

Now, oddly enough Mr. Sweat was wrong. Not only were there fish in the stream but it would even be possible to tell you approximately how many there were. Fishing in the United States has become so tremendous a sport that nature alone and unassisted would not be able to supply the demand. So the 48 states have taken over a part of the job. Millions of dollars taken from fishermen for licenses are literally put back into the streams through state-owned and operated fish hatcheries.

Most states maintain several hatcheries located at strategic points, usually as near the popular fishing waters as possible. A fish hatchery is not unlike any laboratory where scientific experimentation is done. Many of the hatcheries hold brood fish in special ponds for egg production. These fish are selected for their productivity, vitality, and their fast-growing traits. In some ways a hatchery resembles a large poultry farm.

Most hatcheries have three central functioning units: brood fish ponds, egg hatching baskets and rearing ponds. The female fish that are ripe are "stripped" or milked of their eggs. This process merely consists of gently moving the hand from the front of the fish's belly to the rear in an easy, squeezing motion. The eggs squirt out by the thousand. Then the same process is used with the big male fish. His life stream is called milt. Carefully the milt and the eggs are stirred together to insure fertilization. Then they are washed and placed in the hatching baskets, suspended in troughs of running water. Each basket is separated by riffle tins to break the current of the water. The eggs need moving water to make them hatch. A constant temperature is the next step. The water is maintained at 55 degrees. If it varies, the hatching process stops immediately, and all is lost.

Five days after the eggs are deposited in the baskets they attain what is called "the tender stage." The slightest bang or jar will immediately kill thousands of the embryo fish in the delicately membraned eggs. At this stage the hatchery worker starts to remove the infertile eggs. They are white in color and rapidly grow the death fungus which if allowed to spread will destroy all the good eggs.

In twenty-five long and nervous days, the fish hatchery men who are mother-henning the eggs detect two black spots which are large in relation to the egg. They are the fish's eyes and this period is appropriately called the "eyed" stage. Three weeks later the eggs hatch and the cycle has begun—the tiny trout is born.

Now is the most critical time of all: artificial feeding, the nurse-maiding. No two states feed their fish alike, but they all agree that it is difficult and extremely hazardous to the young fish. For example, small fish choke easily and if the food isn't ground finely, put through the smallest grinding dyes several times, soon after a morning feeding it is possible to see thousands of the little guys floating to the surface—choked to death.

Fish eat many times a day. They are fed often but frugally. If too much food is placed in the rearing pond (where the small hatched fish grow to releasing size) it will sink to the bottom and decay, causing pollution of the water and killing the fish. On the other hand if the fish aren't fed enough they become weak and undernourished and remain a dwarf size.

Oregon, under the able guidance of Reino O. Koski, aquatic biologist, has been conducting feeding experiments with gratifying results. Working on the theory that healthy, well-fed fish are able to withstand disease and the usual parasites even when hatcheries are operating at maximum capacity, Oregon has worked out a low mortality rate and spanking healthy hatchery fish for her sportsmen. "Feed 'em high and catch 'em healthy," seems to be Oregon's motto.

Now I suppose you think that all the men at the hatcheries have to do is release the well-fed happy fish in appropriate streams and the lucky license holder dunks a line and comes up with a nice shiny trout. It's not that simple.

Other jobs such as keeping the rearing ponds clean and disinfected, waging a constant battle against death-dealing microscopic parasites, the never-ending task of keeping the food fresh and at the correct temperature, grading and redistributing the fish according to size, weight and state of health—all these routine and wearying tasks are necessary to make the planting of fish in your favorite streams possible.

And how is the actual stocking done? Tank trucks, sectioned fish planting boats, mules and horses, even airplanes are used to get the fish in the proper stream for you to catch. Tank trucks are interesting gadgets: Insulated tanks are mounted on two ton (sometimes larger) trucks. A circulating pump draws water through a carefully screened outlet and sprays it above the water level. This process aerates the water, prevents the loss of oxygen which is necessary to keep the fish alive.

Long ago the men who nurse your fish for you found that distribution was one of the most important facets in planting. In Colorado they found that a whole season's stocking of trout was caught within one mile of the point where the fish were initially released. Consequently, to give all anglers a break, it is necessary to disperse the planted fish.

All this adds up to what? Two words could answer that question: *Work* and *money*. Let me tell you a true story that may help to outline more clearly this picture which we are trying to paint.

Last year a friend of mine decided he didn't much care for the competition in trout stream fishing and determined to stock a stream of his own which ran through his property and ended in a small pond which also belonged to him.

We went to a commercial hatchery, bought 100 fingerlings and fifty 12-inch trout. The small fish cost him 50¢ each and the big trout a buck and a half per pound. Then he had to buy costly feeds and do a nurse-maid job on the fish that brings back nightmares even today. They *had* to be fed several times a day, and they *had* to be fed correctly ground food in a given proportion at a given time. It ended up with his losing half of the fish and catching about one third of the remainder. Roughly he figured that one pound of trout cost him more than three dollars. Of course he could have brought this figure down considerably by buying both fish and food in quantity. But he didn't want that much. Just a few for himself.

Even so, the cost to the states per pound of fish isn't much less. The state of Washington which boasts that its expenditure on fish food is probably the lowest of any western state came up with the figure of $1.25 per pound of hatchery-raised fish! This despite the fact that last year's crop came to 600,000 pounds.

The picture needs a few more strokes of color. We have been cautioned by all of the state authorities to enlighten you fishermen about the complex job of the fish and wildlife or conservation agencies of your states. And the hatcheries are only a part of their program.

John B. Moyle, Research Supervisor of the Fisheries Unit of Minnesota puts the whole thing neatly:

"All of us are basically agriculturally minded, we think in terms of planting corn; corn comes up; corn is harvested. Fine, if we remember that the farmer plows the ground, fertilizes and cultivates it. This is the principle on which fish stocking operated for 75 years. Great success in some places, miserable failure in others. It succeeded where a species of fish was introduced into waters where there was no competition—such as stocking trout in waters that had few fish of any kind. It succeeded where there happened to be space and food in the aquatic environment that was not being occupied—such as stocking wall-eyed pike in large bass-panfish waters."

Get the idea? There's more to this than the mere hatching and planting of fish.

A. B. Cook, Jr., assistant chief of Michigan's fish division claims that "Fish hatching or culture is an important phase of the state's conservation program, but our activities have been broadened to include all phases of fisheries management. The tools are regulatory measures, research, environmental improvement, and a program for securing and developing public access sites on lakes and streams."

Indiana is trying experiments to control by chemical means excessive vegetation in streams and ponds, and has successfully used a combination of black aniline dye and commercial fertilizer.

Kentucky probably operates the largest farm pond fish program in the country. To date they have been stocking bass and bluegill. This state has helped farmers in digging and preparing farm ponds. Today there are 100,000 farm ponds in Kentucky: the state stocked 25,000 ponds with more than 2,000,000 bass in 1951. Conservation officials continue to improve fishing conditions by keeping the ponds clean and placing the fish in aquatic environment where they have a good chance to thrive. They call this program "Fishing in the backyard," mainly because it has given the lucky citizens of that state opportunity to fish in areas where it once was impossible.

Probably one of the most important functions of the fisheries divisions of the conservation agencies of your states is the fish rescue work. In many cases fish really do need rescuing. Often sport fish fight a losing battle of trying to live in ponds and streams where the food is scarce and of the wrong type, or they may be living with other types of fish that are stronger and rapidly destroying them. New Jersey rescued 468,862 of these fish last year—everything from bass to catfish, and redistributed them in waters where they would have a chance for survival.

Ponds, lakes and streams that are located in state parks and are open to public fishing are also the center of much attention and activity these days. The proper fish are stocked in these waters and nature is given a helping hand by the conservation agencies.

Massachusetts posts conspicuous signs pointing out its public fishing ground. Large black letters, NOTICE, PUBLIC FISHING GROUNDS BEGIN HERE, are tacked in hard-to-miss spots. This state publishes a magazine or a Public Fishing Grounds Guide. Most states do. If you're interested in knowing more about the fishing in state parks and the public fishing grounds in your state or in any state, merely write to the conservation agency in that particular state; mark the letter for the attention of the Fisheries Division.*

Now let's get a little heavy. Let's pile up a few facts and figures—some statistics. The big state of Pennsylvania with its shining fleet of 47 tank trucks released 406,408,887 fish of several species in its waters last year. Unlike some states, Pennsylvania's entire fishing program is supported by the fishermen themselves through the purchase of resident fishing licenses.

The comparatively small state of Connecticut poured 286,-205 legal size trout and 639,423 fry and fingerling trout out of

---

*Consult Chapter 5, A Sport Surprise in Every State, for complete state listings.

its three fish hatcheries. Not believing in a large put-and-take system, Connecticut concentrates much of its activity on rescue work and the improving of aquatic conditions for native fish in their natural habitat.

Wyoming, one of the luckier states, with a great natural propagation of fish in the streams and lakes in the park areas, nevertheless believes in the planting system. In 1950, Wyoming planted 3,358,240 fish, of which 3,273,000 were trout or semi-cold water varieties. Fishing pressure has increased tremendously in this state and at present it seems to be the mecca of trout rodmen.

Colorado goes one better. The same excellent natural conditions exist there but even so, in 1951 some 8,898,000 trout were hatched and released; of this number 3,324,000 were catchable fish over six inches in length. Colorado has 120 people engaged in its fish management operation and the yearly budget exceeds one million dollars.

Indiana is getting up a nice head of steam in her program: Last year she dispersed 45,000 brown trout fingerlings, 47,500 brook trout fingerlings, 110,118 rainbow trout fingerlings, 6,492 legal size rainbow and 3,224 catching size brown trout. All of these fish were transported from Neosho, Missouri and Northville, Michigan. No small task.

Wisconsin plunked over 25 species in the total amount of 158,136,376 in her waters and geared up a new watershed management program on her rivers and trout streams.

Tennessee averages about 100,000 out-of-state fishermen a year and has some 600,000 acres of game fish water. Her director of state and game fish division claims most of her warm water fish die of old age. Even though the natural conditions are excellent and the reproduction of fish high, her three hatcheries and two trout rearing stations turned out 50,000 brown trout and 50,000 rainbow trout last year.

This year when you plunk down the three or four dollars for your fishing license do it with good cheer. Those dollars are being well spent and you, personally, are putting a fish in a stream with every nickel of every dollar.

CHAPTER 4

The Fare: Fish

BACK about 1620, even before Izaak Walton wrote *The Compleat Angler,* a fisherman named Thomas Jordon said, "Fish dinners will make a man spring like a flea."

He meant, of course, that fish properly cooked would make a man jump out of his seat in sheer delight. Apparently he was a much wiser man than many present-day fishermen. There are evidences everywhere during fishing season that some think fish are fun to catch but not necessarily worth fussing with after you take them home. Badly hooked fish are thrown back to die, fish are left on the banks for woods cats to eat and the sun to rot. Fishermen who waste fish do so because they probably have never had the pleasure of sinking a tooth into the flesh of a properly cooked fish.

Much ado is made over the types of lures, flies and hooks to use, and countless books have been written on the rods and reels necessary to reap the most from fishing; but scant attention has been directed to what to do with fish after you catch them.

I remember one September day when two friends of mine went bluefishing in Long Island Sound. The blues were running and they had a magnificent day. The crusty five-pounders gave them black-and-blue muscles and a tremendous sense of satisfaction after they had boated over fifty of them. The mate hog-dressed the fish and when they got ashore, the whole bunch of blues were thrown into the back of my friend's station wagon. When the wives of the fishermen saw the catch, they threw up their hands in horror. "What'll we do with *all* those?" they asked.

The next night they gathered and had fried bluefish. The white meat of the fish was dried-out with grease and overcooking and the dinner was something less than a culinary success. So the next day, neighbors were recipients of nice fat bluefish. The two fishermen gave all away except a half-dozen each and their wives sighed with relief.

Two months later, I happened along and heard the story. By that time even the six bluefish they had saved were gone, vanished in deep fat and dissatisfaction. So, to teach a lesson, I took my friend to the fish market, bought two filleted blue-fish at *90 cents a pound* and invited the four of them to my home that night for dinner. When they arrived, I served them golden hunks of meat about the size of a quarter, with their cocktails. They exclaimed over the succulence of the *hors d'oeuvres*. I explained that these were bluefish cheeks that I had cut out in fat little circles and frozen from my last catch. They are a great delicacy and a taste sensation. They are the only part of the bluefish that should be fried.

Next, I took them all out to my kitchen and showed them the bluefish, filleted, laid out in a shallow cookie tin that had been well rubbed with butter. The bluefish were also laved with butter, and salt, pepper and parsley had been sprinkled over them. They were placed in the broiler of my oven which had been preheated to 400 degrees Fahrenheit.

Within a half hour they were crusted a golden brown and ready to eat. I served them with wedges of lemon and a tossed green salad. I can still hear the moans of delight as they ate the juicy, yet flaky white flesh of the bluefish.

"When in doubt, broil! Otherwise, that fish you may spoil!" This is a good dictum for the amateur chef to keep in mind. If you feel that your wife doesn't know or care too much about fish cookery, then man the kitchen yourself. At least half of the thrill of fishing lies in that precious moment when you mate the fish with plate and take up knife and fork.

So good wives, would you kindly go and get a good book to read. We'll call you when dinner is ready.

Fish cookery is uncomplicated. In many cases it is easier to cook the fish than it is to catch it. But, there are a few things to remember and some tools you'll need before you ask the little woman to step out of the kitchen and let you take over.

Most kitchens are equipped to handle the recipes covered in this chapter but anyway I am listing my favorite utensils. I prefer copper pans because they are the best conductors of evenly dis-tributed heat; they are handsome and have added economy of sometimes acting as servers as well as cookers. I also like these new infra-red broilers. You can plug them in and cook right at the table. But any good gauge aluminum over an open gas flame will do the job. You'll need a Dutch oven, a double boiler, a

large, a medium and a small frying pan, a couple of pyrex casserole dishes, one large, one medium; a stainless steel strainer,
one of those little garlic presses that make mashing garlic a
pleasure rather than a hazard, at least three very sharp knives,
a food chopper and accurate measuring devices. At any hard-
ware store you can get inexpensive plastic measuring spoons,
all handily joined together, from tablespoon size right down to
half-teaspoon. Remember, when a recipe calls for a tablespoon,
it doesn't mean the big kitchen size. It means a measuring tablespoon. Likewise, get a glass measuring cup, marked off in
ounces, cups, quarter cups, etc. Inaccuracy has spoiled many a
good fish dish.

It's well to remember that fish cookery differs somewhat from
that of meat. Most people tend to overcook fish. There's a reason for this: All fish have fine and somewhat fragile connective
tissue. Heat breaks this down. Go easy with the flame. Cook
with slow heat, except when broiling.

Even if you do use your own fish, it's helpful to know what
to look for in a fish that is proper to cook. A cookable fish
should have bright, bulging eyes, firm flesh, scales that adhere
closely to the body and little smell. A poor fish makes a poorer
meal. I have found that it also pays dividends to wash the fish
in lemon juice and water. This not only prevents any odor
while cooking but whitens the flesh.

Of course, the first step in any fish cookery is the catching of
the fish. Once you've got him hooked, treat him gently. If they
are freshwater fish, I suggest that you leave them damp and
wrap them in grass or leaves that have also been moistened with
water from their native stream or lake, then place them in your
creel. There are handy little refrigerators that can be filled with
ice and placed in the trunk of your car. Get the fish out of the
creel and into that icebox as soon as possible. If you aren't too
far from the car, make a practice of transferring creeled fish to
refrigerator often and as soon as possible. I don't believe in immediately gutting freshwater fish, especially if you can keep
them cool.

The salt water species should be kept alive in the boat well,
or placed in the ice chest of the boat. These fish should be hog-
dressed and the streaks of blood washed off *before* you transport
them home.

If you are stream fishing and can cook a few of your fish over
the campfire, by all means do it. For freshly caught fish, cooked

on the spot, taste better than those served by three waiters and cooked by a master chef.

Some say bass have a slightly muddy or strong flavor. I contest this. I always make a practice of cooking at least two of my bass right beside the stream. Make sure your campfire is at the right pitch—embers glowing nicely—and then wipe the bass dry. Don't scale them. If you can remember, it's a good idea to bring some foil paper with you, but if you don't have it, newspaper will do the trick. Soak the newspaper—at least three thicknesses—and then wrap the bass securely in it, make certain you wrap them separately, with the ends tucked in. Don't try to cook a half dozen in one wrapping of paper. Then pop the well-wrapped fish into the embers. Ten minutes or fifteen at the most in the intense heat of the embers will complete the cooking. Rake the fish out, remove the charred paper carefully, so as not to break the flesh of the bass. Then simply peel off the skin and scales; turn the bass onto your plate, rub with butter and sprinkle lightly with salt and pepper. If you want to, run your knife along the backbone so that the flesh falls off the bone—remove the bones and sit down to the tastiest fish you've ever sunk a tooth into. Simple?

Another campfire trick I use on trout is to wrap the fish well in bacon, wire it on a stick and broil it over embers, making sure the stick is rotated periodically so that the trout is cooked evenly on all sides.

I've discovered after years of trial and error, that the best way to cook a trout or any small freshwater fish after it has been frozen—especially if you and your guests want it for breakfast and don't have the time to wait around until it is defrosted—is to cook it just as it comes from the freezer.

Take the trout from the package, frozen solid, wash under cold water and then place in a paper bag into which has been placed two cups of ordinary flour, a dash of salt and pepper and a pinch of oregano, an Italian herb that imparts tart but subtle flavor. Shake the trout in the paper bag until it is well-floured. Remove and place in a frying pan into which two tablespoons of vegetable fat have been melted. As I mentioned, I use a copper pan because it is an even conductor of heat and cooks in a balanced way. Cover the pan and cook the fish for five minutes on each side, or until a slight brown crust has formed. Then remove the cover and cook, turning the fish once on each side for ten minutes. When it is nicely browned and has a crusty feel to the fork, turn onto a warm platter and serve with a little dollop of butter riding on top.

Cooking fish frozen does two things. When you pop that frozen fish into the hot grease, especially after it has been well covered with flour, you are cooking the juices right in the fish. If you permit the fish to defrost first, it becomes limp and soggy and doesn't have the flavor the frozen one has. Also, that additional moisture has been frozen into the fish and isn't left on the platter where it would be if you defrosted the fish first. Many will disagree with this, but after several hundred fish and three years of experimentation, I will harbor no contradiction. I've proved it the hard way.

Fish is a good food to get fancy with. No matter what style of cooking you may like, the French have a fish for it.

Take your fish and fool around with it. Don't be afraid to use your imagination. Use wine, use tomatoes, use spinach. Use anything you like—fish will take to it.

In New Orleans they take the lowly blackfish, the flounder or any fish they have and filet them. They are then dusted in flour and cooked until brown on both sides.

The fish is then taken from the pan to another pan. Drop two tablespoons of fat, melt it and add one clove of chopped garlic, cook for about a half minute, then place in thick slices of about four skinned tomatoes (or as many as you want. This is for a serving of four filets). Cook for two minutes, turning tomatoes so that they are slightly cooked and seasoned on both sides. Take the tomatoes from the frying pan and arrange them in a buttered casserole or ovenware dish and place the fillets over them. Over this pour a sauce that you have made from one cup of raw chopped spinach, ½ cup of sour cream, salt and pepper, a pinch of grated Romano cheese and a half teaspoon of lemon juice. Then sprinkle more of the grated Romano cheese over the top, brown under your broiler, and serve.

A few seasons ago in Canada, I had boiled salmon so good that the taste is still with me. The guide prepared a liquid to boil the fish in by chopping a cup of carrots, onions and celery and half a clove of garlic, mixed these all together into a mush, and warmed it in two tablespoons of melted butter. He then placed this in a deep pan with two quarts of water and added a few peppercorns, a bay leaf, some salt, a teaspoon of vinegar, a touch of ginger and let this all boil for ten minutes. Then he cut thick slices of gleaming red salmon, wrapped them in cheese cloth and lowered them into the boiling water for just a little over ten minutes. Next, he took a cup of this stock, added a tablespoon of butter, one of flour, and put it into a little pan. Into this he beat the yolk of an egg. He then poured this sauce over the salmon steaks and served with a side dish of wild rice. He was a Canuck guide and could work magic with a little boiling water, some vegetables—and, of course, a fish.

Swimming in the waters of the St. Lawrence River are many hard-fighting fish called "kings of the chowder"—large, well-fleshed pike. My wife and I caught a half-dozen up in that cold river a few years ago, and I whipped up a specialty of mine: Potato-fish chowder. I also use blackfish and weakfish when I have them.

For a three to six-pound fish, I take ¼ pound of diced salt pork and fry in a deep kettle, until it is brown and the bottom of the kettle is covered with sizzling grease. I add three thinly sliced onions and cook these until they are soft but not browned. I then add four medium-sized, uncooked potatoes (mealy Idahos are especially good) which I have diced into about ½ inch cubes, 3 cups of rapidly boiling water, and my freshly caught pike, which has been scaled and cut into small pieces. I simmer this on a slow fire until the potatoes are soft and then add 2 cups of cream. If you haven't cream on hand, evaporated milk will turn the trick. Season to taste with salt and pepper, and about a tablespoon and a half of finely chopped parsley. In another pan melt two tablespoons of butter and slowly add about a tablespoon of flour. Blend this thoroughly until it is lumpless and a smooth, golden paste. Stir this gradually into the pot of chowder until it is thickened. Cook for about ten minutes longer, very slowly. Then serve over thick, New England soda crackers.

A simple French dish, good even with ordinary American cheese, is Fish Fromage. An onion is chopped and mixed with about ¼ pound of a good grated cheese and spread evenly over the bottom of a pyrex baking wish. Filleted bass, pickerel or pike is then placed on top of this and covered with another ¼ pound of grated cheese. I suggest Parmesan or Romano. Then one teaspoon of Worcestershire sauce, a teaspoonful of ordinary prepared mustard, one of salt, a dash of pepper and one cup of light cream are mixed together and poured over the fish. This is then baked in a 400 degree oven for a half hour.

During the year I spent in Italy, I came to like three fish dishes in addition to pasta. One was a fried fillet. Turn the fillet lightly for about a minute in a frying pan with a tablespoon of butter. Make a batter by mixing a couple of ounces of flour in one cup of milk and a sprinkle of salt. Bring this mixture to a boil, then cook slowly and add a cup of chicken broth and the well-beaten yolks of four eggs. Strain the sauce and place the fish in it while it is still hot. Let this mixture cool, together with the fish, until you can roll it in grated bread crumbs. Then fry quickly in hot olive oil until the fish is browned on both sides. It's simple and delicious.

Fish cutlets are easy to make and tasty as all get out. Cut your large fish, salmon, etc., into nice thick slices, sprinkle with salt and then pound with the blunt end of a knife until they are cutlet size, making certain you do not shred the meat. Place the fish between sheets of wax paper while pounding and you'll get a neater cutlet. Then dip it into beaten egg white. Roll this in grated bread crumbs and fry in butter, making certain that it is well browned on both sides, turning cautiously so that the cutlet holds its shape and doesn't break. Mash three anchovies in a tablespoon of butter, heat until you can mix this into a sauce. Pour this over the cutlets and serve.

Neapolitans have a dish, which I like, called *Cacciucco*. It's a man's dish, hearty, full-bodied. They mince two whole cloves of garlic, one onion, a pinch of parsley and a tablespoon of butter and then add a pound of fresh, cut-up tomatoes, plus generous amounts of salt and pepper. When the tomatoes are cooked, they add a large cup of white Chianti wine and let this entire mixture boil for ten minutes. The resultant sauce is strained and placed over sliced fish in casserole. When the fish has cooked a slow 45 minutes, they mix in a tablespoon of heated olive oil. It is then served in two separate dishes—the fish in one; thick slices of Italian bread, covered with the sauce, in the other. The remainder of the white Chianti wine is served ice cold to wash the whole thing down.

Charter Boat Captain Charles Sebastian, who operates down along the Gulf of Mexico and over to New Orleans, has a way of cooking pompano that brings this delicious fish to the height of its eatability.

Cut up a bunch of green onions, tops and all, two bell peppers, two cups of celery, two tablespoons of chopped garlic and a handful of parsley. In a Dutch oven, melt ¼ pound of butter

and saute the chopped vegetables until soft. Add a can of prepared consomme soup and one can of water. Next, stir in a can
of mushroom soup and a can of water, making sure this mixture
is smooth. Then add a can of button mushrooms (no liquid)
and season the whole works to taste with salt and pepper. Next
to taste, add Worcestershire sauce, paprika and simmer this for
about fifteen minutes. Before you add the cleaned and salted
pompano (as many as will fit into the pot and be covered by the
liquid) throw in a good-sized dollop of sherry. Cover and cook
slowly, until the fish are well done, being careful that they are
not *too* well-done so that they fall off the bones.

A sportsman friend of mine of Danish heritage, Richard
Langseth-Christensen, tells me the Danes are the world's leading
experts on cooking trout. His method is simplicity itself. He
suggests that you take a trout fresh from the water, clean it,
leaving head and tail and fins on, and panfry it in hot melted
butter. He uses a lot of butter, $1/4$ of a pound for two fish, and
browns them quickly, serving them with the browned butter
poured over, garnished with wedges of lemon.

If you want to get real fancy, flounder, flatfish, or any of the
white-meated fish are excellent served with hollandaise and wine
sauce. I always make a stock from a few fish bones left over from
the filleted fish and put them in a pan with a clove of garlic, a
few peppercorns and slices of onion. I add one cup of water
and a half of a cup of a good dry white wine; bring this to a
boil and let it perk along for about a half-hour. Strain this and
pour it over your fish fillets (sprinkle with a few herbs of your
liking) that have been arranged in a glass baking dish. Poach
the whole business gently in a moderate oven for 15 minutes.
Take $1/2$ cup of sliced mushrooms and a teaspoon of lemon
juice, add two tablespoons of melted butter, salt and pepper,
and cook in a covered pan for five minutes, stirring so the butter
doesn't brown. Hold this aside.

Melt two tablespoons of butter, take from heat and add $1 1/2$
tablespoons of flour, stirring mixture until it is smooth. Then
take a cup of liquid from the wine pot, mix it with the butter
and flour mixture until thickened and add $1/4$ cup of milk. Stir
this until it comes to a boil and then put in one tablespoon of
heavy cream. This is the wine sauce.

Now put two egg yolks in a mixing bowl with a tablespoon
of cream, two tablespoons of vinegar, a sprinkle of salt and
cayenne pepper. Place this bowl in a pan of water and beat well

over a slow fire until it begins to thicken, then add two-thirds cup of butter, a little at a time, and a couple of drops of lemon juice. This is your hollandaise sauce.

Take your fish fillets from the dish in which they were poached and add them to another ovenware dish, paint them with the white wine sauce. Spread your sliced mushrooms on top, cover these with the hollandaise sauce and glaze the fish until brown under a grill or broiler. An infra-red grill, plugged in right at the table, is good for this last minute glazing and will have your spouse and friends staring bug-eyed at your expert manipulations.

No article on fish cookery would be complete unless we go in the bag, or try the *fish en papiotte,* fish in paper or paper bags, just for size. For this one, which I learned from an Italian named Gino in Naples, but is a French dish, I usually use about 8 fillets of any kind of sweet-fleshed small fish, even crappie, blue gills, or bream. I first wash the fillets in a combination of water and lemon juice and then dry thoroughly. Then I put two of the fish through the meat chopper and add one clove of crushed garlic, two large chopped mushrooms, a tablespoon of mixed herbs (thyme, rosemary, basil, tarragon), and three tablespoons of sour cream. I mix this up well and spoon a gob of it on each fillet, then fold the fillet over and brush all sides with melted butter. I then place the fish on wax paper and cover with whole mushrooms that have been sauteed in hot butter and two tablespoons of sherry. Over this I spread sliced apples which have also been lightly sauteed in butter. Then sprinkle brown sugar over this very lightly, just enough to cover so that it will glaze when hot. Now, place the fillets and the wax paper in a brown paper bag or brown wrapping paper (cooking paper is available from most grocery stores), wrap well or close the bag end tightly, and bake in a preheated 400-degree oven for a half-hour. Serve in the paper. It's an impressive dish, one that will really mark you as a cook worth following.

Don't get careless with your catch, the next time you go fishing. Take only your limit, but take it. Don't leave badly hooked fish to die, or throw or give them away as something fun to catch, but tasteless on the table.

Fish is the most versatile of food, high in vitamin value and adaptable to any type of dish or cookery. The next time you bring a full string of fish home and hear your spouse say, "What are we going to do with them?" you'll have the answer:

"I caught 'em; I'll cook 'em." It's the mark of the true sports-man and you'll leave your wife and guests at your dinner table dazzled with your dexterity, both on the stream and in the kitchen.

As Rex Beach put it, "The natural habitat of a fish is in the pan." It's a simple matter to put a fish where he belongs. Try it.

CHAPTER 5

A Sports Surprise in Every State

I WONDERED if a half dozen inmates had scooted over the high spiked wall of a nearby nuthatch. These were really crazy, mixed-up characters. Standing beside the Mattawamkeag River in Washington County, Maine, they were catching bouncy, sizeable smallmouth bass, gently removing the hook and letting the fish twist into the sunstruck water. I counted the silver patches of bass bellies as the fish flashed back into the river. Forty in fifteen minutes, with six men fishing! It was like watching pond transfer day at a state fish hatchery.

As the nearest fisherman saw my dumbstruck expression and unhinged jaw, he grinned.

"Don't believe it. We're not goofy. We're members of the 100 Bass a Day Club." He explained as he fished—or unfished.

This is the way it goes: If you'd like to be part of the group that keeps two bass for every 20 they catch and put back into the stream, forget everything you think you know about bass fishing, the Great Lakes of the South, the fabled and famous bass lakes, ponds, and streams. Turn your car toward Washington County, Maine.

Undiscovered Washington County, the bass paradise, is in far eastern Maine, rimmed on the east by New Brunswick and on the south by the Atlantic Ocean. If you drive and come through the southern entrance take the toll route to Portland, then U. S. Route One for the remainder of the trip.

For some unexplained reason most of the tide of tourists in Maine doesn't break any farther than the Acadia National Park, 25 miles to the west. Those who make it a practice of knowing what they talk about say this Washington County section offers the best smallmouth bass fishing in America. And there is a variety of water: lakes, large and small, rivers, ponds, little streams, with fish in all of them.

Again, for some unexplained reason, even Maine doesn't brag about the bass fishing in her state. If you were to write and say you read about the fantastic bass fishing in Washington County and inquire about guides and places to stay, you'd receive polite acknowledgment of your letter plus all the information you requested, with the added intelligence that you probably wouldn't need a guide in the Washington County sector, as all the fishing is near small villages and towns such as Ellsworth, Millbrook, Harrington and Cherryfield, and anyone can point out where the fish are.

The states of Louisiana and Arkansas also have a type of bonus fishing that very few people know about. Along the quiet stretches of the Arkansas River, the White River, the St. Francis and the Red Rivers, laze deadly big fish that tip the scales at 100 pounds and fight like tigers. They are called alligator gar, and 600 well over 100 pounds apiece were taken in one twelve-mile stretch last summer. But don't go after these great gar unless you are looking for a real fishing thrill and a big fight. This is not the lazy fisherman's sport. This is for the strong and the active.

One of the top gar guides is Duane Holloway of DeWitt, Arkansas. He'll take you garing anytime from June straight through to September, and he'll ask you to bring along a rifle, a pistol or a bow and arrow. For once the gar is hooked on salt water tackle in the tarpon class on a 6/0 treble hook baited with buffalo or gou, he'll run with it. The trick is to play him like the crafty creature he is, then when you get him to the boat, shoot him in the head with whatever weapon you have handy. Never gaff a gar and pull him into the boat. That would probably end your fishing days for awhile. It's difficult to fish without fingers.

And take a look at Texas. Never one to be outdone, this state has some of the snappiest and most dangerous game shooting in this country. Roaming her wide territories such as the Black Gap and the Brewster county ranges, are hundreds of small wild pigs called javelinas. They are about the size of a Cocker Spaniel, and they come complete with tusks, teeth, steel-like hides, unlimited stamina and courage, and hearts full of hate. What makes them dangerous is the fact that they travel in packs, and a dozen of these creatures can make it hot and unhealthy for anything that walks, rides or moves, be it man, automobile or dog pack.

Wild boar hunters who have shot those big creatures in Europe, claim that the little javelina is fierce and dangerous enough to test the metal of any big game hunter, even the tiger trackers.

And speaking of wild boars, Tennessee has one of the few
great herds of this giant wild hog. She permits them to be
hunted from time to time on certain dates. With tusks sometimes a foot long, some of the big boars weighing up to 600
pounds, this is a big game adversary that takes clever tracking
and accurate shooting to down. Brainy and brawny, they roam
certain sections of the mountains of Tennessee, lords of everything they survey. All other animals fear them. How about
taking a crack at a wild boar hunt?

Or maybe you'll like it a bit tamer and would prefer stalking
the black bear in Vermont? As this is being written already 40
black bruins have been bagged in the mountains of Vermont,
and the game commission in that state is anxious to issue permits to out-of-state sportsmen to hunt for bear. The black bear
is no pushover. It's big game hunting of the best brand.

Florida will also grant permits to hunt her nightmare creatures, the alligators and crocodiles, in certain areas from June
straight through to January. They don't like you to be a spoilsport though and take beasts under six feet in length, but they
are helpful in suggesting where the saurians are and can recommend guides who can take you on the most unusual hunt
you've ever had, the really different sport.

That is the thesis of this chapter. Rather than sing the song
of defeat, the refrain of no more game in America, why not
pick up a pen and write any state that strikes your fancy and
ask them what sports they have to offer. You'll be in for sur-
prises and bonuses in both fishing and hunting.

Here we are listing alphabetically by state every official concerned with hunting and fishing and conservation in the United
States. All you have to do is select the subject you are interested
in, then write directly to the person who is listed as being in
charge. We'll also wager many of you didn't realize that most
states have conservation magazines featuring articles and valuable information on hunting and fishing. If the state you are
interested in has such a magazine, it will also be listed below.
Perhaps you'd like to join a state sportsmen's club or league,
or would like to know more about conservation clubs and bird
watching societies. This information is collected here for convenience. It was compiled as an index for the sportsminded who
would like to explore new hunting and fishing by-ways in
America. Go to it!

ALABAMA

Department of Conservation, Division of Game and Fish, Montgomery 4

Director: Earl M. McGowin

Chief, Division of Game and Fish: G. C. Hixon

Publications: Game and Fish Laws, Regulations, Division of Game and Fish; Annual Report; Alabama Conservation (bimonthly); Fishing Reports (weekly)

Alabama Wildlife Federation

President: Walter L. Mims, Massey Bldg., Birmingham

Vice-President: S. Brooks Holleman, Bell Bldg., Montgomery

Executive Secretary-Treasurer: Charles D. Kelley, Box 1428, Montgomery

ALASKA

Alaska Game Commission, Juneau

First judicial division: Earl N. Ohmer, Chairman, Petersburg

Second judicial division: Harry O. Brown, Kobuk

Third judicial division: Andrew A. Simons, Lakeview, via Seward

Fourth judicial division: Forbes L. Baker, Fairbanks

Executive Officer and Secretary of Commission: Clarence J. Rhode, Juneau (representative of Fish and Wildlife Service resident in Alaska)

Publications: Regulations relating to game, game fish, land fur animals and birds (annual); Annual Report to Secretary of Interior on operations and status of game species

Alaska Department of Fisheries, 229 Alaska Office Bldg., Juneau

Alaska Fisheries Board members: R. C. Kahlenberg, Chairman, Dillingham; J. H. Wakefield, Port Wakefield; Ira H. Rothwell, Cordova; Kenneth D. Bell, Fairbanks; Henry Denny, Saxman

Director: C. L. Anderson

ARIZONA

Arizona Game and Fish Commission, Arizona State Building, Phoenix

Commission Members: C. J. Mantle, Chairman, Tucson; E. G. Dentzer, Greer; Fred Faver, Buckeye; H. G. Thacker, Yuma; B. Van Voorhis, Superior

Director: J. M. Hall

Land Manager: O. N. Arrington, Phoenix

Chief of Fisheries: Jack Hemphill, Phoenix

Chief of Law Enforcement: Clifford Sorrells, Phoenix

Chief of Information & Education: E. E. Mulch, Phoenix

Publications: Digest of game laws; biennial reports; The Status of Antelope Herds in Northern Arizona; The White-winged Dove in Arizona

Arizona Conservation Club, Inc.
President: B. Ira Judd, Arizona State College, Tempe

ARKANSAS

Arkansas Game and Fish Commission, Game and Fish Bldg., State Capitol Grounds, Little Rock
Commission Members: Armil Taylor, Chairman, Clarksville; Earl Wells, Vice Chairman, Helena; F. H. McCormack, Stuttgart; Charles C. Snapp, Walnut Ridge; Joe F. Shuffield, Little Rock; Ed W. Watkins, Mena; S. C. Dellinger, Fayetteville; J. H. Burge, Lake Village
Executive Secretary: T. A. McAmis
Educational Director: Tom Mull
Supervisor of Game Refuges: H. E. McCracken, Ozone
Superintendent of Fisheries: Joe Hogan, Klonoke
Publications: Annual report; game and fish laws

CALIFORNIA

Department of Fish and Game, 926 J St., Sacramento
Commission Members: William J. Silva, President, Modesto; Lee F. Payne, Los Angeles; Carl F. Wente, San Francisco; Harley E. Knox, San Diego; Weldon L. Oxley, Redding; William J. Harp, Assistant to the Commission, Sacramento
Director: Seth Gordon, Sacramento
Administrative Deputy: Harry Anderson, Sacramento
Conservation Education Director: Robert D. Calkins, Sacramento
Branch Chiefs:
Alexander J. Calhoun, Inland Fisheries, Sacramento
Ben Glading, Game Management, Sacramento
E. L. Macaulay, Wildlife Protection, Sacramento
R. S. Croker, Marine Fisheries, Sacramento
Publications: Fish and game laws; biennial report; California Fish and Game (quarterly); Outdoor California (monthly); fish bulletins; game bulletins
California Audubon Society
President: Paul W. Colburn, 9626 Oak Pass Road, Beverly Hills
Pacific Rod and Gun Club
President: Robert H. Joost, 127 Crespi Dr., San Francisco
Secretary: Charles Goodwin, 171 Desmond St., San Francisco
Quail Preferred
President: Richard F. Jose, 314 Front Street, San Francisco
Secretary: A. J. Richter, c/o Standard Oil Company, P. O. Box 3565, San Francisco

COLORADO

State Game and Fish Commission, 1530 Sherman, Denver 3

Commission Members: Richard G. Lyttle, President, Meeker; Earl H. Mullins, Vice-President, Pagosa Springs; Henry A. Roberts, Secretary, Boulder; Glen B. Clark, Denver; Clair Hotchkiss, Hotchkiss; Henry E. Lague, Monte Vista; John McClelland, Rocky Ford; Harley Rhoades, Burlington

Director: Thomas L. Kimball, Denver

Assistant Director: J. D. Hart, Denver

Fish Manager: R. M. Andrews, Denver

Game Manager: G. N. Hunter, Denver

Chief Game Warden: William F. Hunn, Denver

Educational Manager: Carwin D. Tolman, Denver

Publications: Game and fish laws; biennial report; Colorado Conservation (bimonthly); weekly newsletter; educational pamphlets; scientific reports

Izaak Walton League of America, Inc.

Connecticut Fish and Game Protective Assn.

President: George F. Jackson, Colorado Springs

CONNECTICUT

State Board of Fisheries and Game, State Office Building, Hartford 14

Commission Members: David C. Mahoney, Chairman, West Hartford; Belton A. Copp, Vice-Chairman, Old Lyme; Gordon Lamont, Darien; Daniel Merriman, New Haven; Fred K. Barbour, North Norfolk

Superintendent: Lyle M. Thorpe

Executive Assistant: Roger C. Norling

Chief Conservation Officer: Thomas E. Rose

Acting Chief, Fish Division: Douglas D. Moss

Chief, Game Division: Arroll L. Lamson

Publications: Game and fish laws; Regulations and Annual Report

President: George H. Scranton, Box 1145, New Haven 5

DELAWARE

Board of Game and Fish Commissioners, Dover

President: Austin D. Smith, Dover

Vice-President: C. Parker Wheatley, Seaford

Secretary: Paul E. Wilson

Chief Warden: Thomas N. Stayton

Publications: Game and fish laws; annual report

Delaware Federation of Sportsmen & Conservation Clubs, Inc.

President: John G. Armstrong, Bay View Rd., Middletown

1st Vice-President: Jacob Rebmann, Jr., 2304 Silverside Rd., Wilmington
2nd Vice-President: Walter S. Rapp, Hercules Experimental Station, Wilmington
Executive Secretary: James Godsey, 1503 Bassett, New Castle
Treasurer: Anthony Ferrara, 117 Matthes, Wilmington

DISTRICT OF COLUMBIA

Metropolitan Police, Washington (has jurisdiction over matters pertaining to game)
Chief of Police: Robert V. Murray
Captain, Commanding Harbor Precinct: Otha R. Sanders
Audubon Society of the District of Columbia, Inc., P. O. Box 202, Washington 4, D. C.
President: Irston R. Barnes, P. O. Box 202, Benjamin Franklin Station, Washington 4, D. C.
Editor: Shirley A. Briggs
Secretary: Amelia Hood
Publications: Atlantic Naturalist (published five times a year); miscellaneous pamphlets

FLORIDA

Game and Fresh Water Fish Commission
Commission Members: Miller V. Joiner, Chairman, Jacksonville; E. W. Hinson, Quincy; A. Sterling Hall, Bradenton; Henry M. Jernigan, Ft. Pierce; M. G. Rowlett, Wildwood
Director: Charles W. Pace, Tallahassee
Assistant Director: O. Earle Frye, Tallahassee
Administrative Assistant: Joel McKinnon, Tallahassee
Chief Fisheries Biologist: Barry O. Freeman, Tallahassee
Information-Education Coordinator: Jack Shoemaker, Tallahassee
Division Officers: Clayton W. Mapoles, Panama City; William H. Snyder, Jacksonville; E. T. Heinen, Lakeland; Curtis E. Wright, Okeechobee
Publications: Florida Wildlife Magazine; Hunting and Fishing regulations; miscellaneous pamphlets
Florida Audubon Society
President: John H. Storer, P. O. Box 645, Winter Park
Vice-President: Howard R. Bissland
Secretary: William M. Davidson
Executive Director: Hall Tennis
Publication: The Florida Naturalist (quarterly)

GEORGIA

State Game and Fish Commission, 412 State Capitol, Atlanta 3
Commission Members: Leonard Bassford, Chairman, Augusta;

J. O. Bowen, Vice-Chairman, Decatur; Cason J. Callaway, Jr., Secretary, Columbus; J. D. Pope, Jackson; Ben T. Rawlings, Sandersville; Fred C. Jones, Jr., Dahlonega; W. B. Austin, Douglasville; Fred D. Beasley, Crescent; James F. Darby, Jr., Vidalia; Alva J. Hopkins, Jr., Folkston; Richard Tift, Albany
Director: Fulton Lovell, Clayton
Chief of Fish Management Division: Fred J. Dickson, Chamblee
Chief of Game Management Division: Jack Crockford, Chamblee
Chief of Law Enforcement Division: W. H. Hodges, Watkinsville
Chief of Hatcheries Division: C. C. James, Marietta
Chief of License Division: T. L. Sanders, Atlanta
Chief of Education Division: Joe Stearns, Atlanta
Publication: Georgia Game and Fish (biannually)
Georgia Ornithological Society
President: Dorothy Neal, Demorest
Secretary: Fern Dorris, Box 405, Milledgeville
Publication: The Oriole (quarterly)

HAWAII

Fish and Wildlife Service, Pacific Oceanic Fisheries Investigations, P. O. Box 3830, Honolulu
Director: O. E. Sette
Board of Commissioners of Agriculture and Forestry, P. O. Box 5425, Pawaa Substation, Honolulu 1
Commission Members: Joseph L. Dwight, President, Cyril E. Pemberton; Wilbert Choi; Louis A. Henke; J. Desmond Fitzgerald; Shizuto Kadota; Lindsay A. Faye
Director, Division of Fish and Game: Vernon E. Brock
Executive Secretary: Richard H. Toyoshiba
Wildlife Biologist: J. R. Woodworth
Publications: Fish and game laws; reports
Hawaii Audubon Society
President: Grace Gossard, P. O. Box 5032, Honolulu
1st Vice-President: Blanche A. Pedley
2nd Vice-President: Margaret Titcomb
Secretary: Irma Botsford
Treasurer: Margaret Newman
Editor: Margaret Titcomb
Publication: Elepaio
Hawaii Fish and Game Protective Association
President: Charles T. Tong, Hilo
Secretary: K. C. Law, P. O. Box 967, Hilo

IDAHO
Department of Fish and Game, 518 Front St., Boise

Commission Members: N. F. Raymer, Chairman, 1111 Harrison Blvd., Boise; W. George Moody, Secretary, Calder; O. W. McConnell, 215 S. Hall St., Grangeville; R. J. Holmes, Box 538, Twin Falls; Glenn Stanger, Box 64, Idaho Falls
Director: Ross Leonard
Chief, Game Management Division: Levi Mohler
Chief, Fisheries Management Division: James C. Simpson
Chief, Conservation Enforcement Division: P. J. McDermott, Jr.
Chief, Education and Information Division: E. Kliess Brown
Chief Clerk: R. E. Hoffman
Publications: Idaho Wildlife Review (bimonthly); Biennial Report; Annual Reports; big game map; fish and game laws; regulations pamphlets; Wildlife of Idaho; Mountain Lakes of Idaho

ILLINOIS

Department of Conservation, Springfield
Director: Glen D. Palmer, 121 State House, Springfield
Assistant Director: Lewis E. Martin
Administrative Assistant and Superintendent Division of Fisheries: Sam A. Parr
Superintendent, Game Management Division: Joe B. Davidson, 121 State House, Springfield
State Forester: Eino E. Nuttila, 303 E. Monroe, Springfield
Superintendent, Education Division: Lynn Callaway, 303 E. Monroe, Springfield
Chief Inspector: James Fitzgerald, 121 State House, Springfield
Superintendent, Game Propagation Division: John D. Montgomery, 303 E. Monroe, Springfield

Illinois Federation of Sportsmen's Clubs
President: Ray Johnson, Winchester
Executive Secretary: Royal B. McClelland, 508 West Charles St., Champaign
Secretary: Arthur Mueth, Mascoutah
Treasurer: Walter Maywald, 1400 Church St., Lombard

Illinois Audubon Society
President: Paul R. Downing, 459 Roger Williams Ave., Highland Park

Izaak Walton League of America, Inc. (Illinois Division)
President: Burton H. Atwood, Winnetka

INDIANA

Department of Conservation, 311 West Washington St., Indianapolis 9
Conservation Commission Members: James M. Tucker, Chairman; J. Clifton Hirschman; Rollie Bedwell; Marker Sunderland

Director, Department of Conservation: Harley G. Hook
Administrative Assistant: H. W. Moesch, Jr.
Division of Fish & Game:
Superintendent of Game: Hovey Pritchett
Superintendent of Fisheries: M. O. Scott
Publications: Fish and game laws; yearbook; special bulletins
and findings

Indiana Audubon Society, Inc.
President: Max Forsyth, 4015 Ruckle, Indianapolis 5
Secretary: Margaret Umbach, 2526 East Dr., Fort Wayne 3
Editor: James B. Cope, Earlham College, Richmond
Publication: Indiana Audubon Quarterly

Izaak Walton League of America, Inc. (Indiana Division)
President: George H. Maywald, 105 Beverly Bowl, Hobart
Secretary: James Brahos, 6522 Meadow Lane, Hammond
Treasurer: Harry Johnson, 1630 S. 10th St., Terre Haute
Publication: The Hoosier Outdoors

IOWA

Iowa State Conservation Commission, E. 7th and Court Ave.,
Des Moines 9
Director: Bruce F. Stiles
Assistant Director: J. R. Harlan
Conservation Commission Members: Ewald G. Trost, Chairman,
Fort Dodge; J. D. Reynolds, Vice-Chairman, Creston; C. A.
Dinges, Emmetsburg; George Foster, Ottumwa; Mrs. Emmett
Hannan, Council Bluffs; Floyd S. Pearson, Decorah; Joseph
Stanton, Des Moines
Chief, Fish and Game Division: Raymond W. Beckman
Superintendent of Fisheries: Kenneth Madden
Superintendent of Game: Paul Leaverton
Chief, Division of Lands and Waters: Wilbur A. Rush
Superintendent, Public Relations: George W. Worley
Publications: Fish and game laws; biennial report; Conserva-
tion Notes (weekly); Iowa Conservationist (monthly)

Iowa Ornithologists' Union
President: Edward L. Kozicky, Iowa State College, Ames
Vice-President: Woodward H. Brown, Des Moines
Secretary-Treasurer: Mrs. George Crossley, Farley
Editor: Fred J. Pierce, Winthrop
Publication: Iowa Bird Life (quarterly)

Izaak Walton League of America, Inc. (Iowa Division)
President: Alden J. Erskine, Sioux City

KANSAS

Kansas Forestry, Fish & Game Commission, Pratt

Commission Members: H. M. Gillespie, Chairman, 1307 Union National Bank Building, Wichita; Frank F. Young, Secretary, 17 South Ashby, Chanute; Charles E. Kaup, Box 487, Manhattan; Vern R. Mayo, Box 244, Garden City; Ross Beach, Jr., P. O. Box 270, Hays; Hugh Miller, 106 North Cherry, Olethe

Publication: Fish and game laws

KENTUCKY

Department of Fish and Wildlife Resources, State Office Building, Frankfort

Commissioner: Earl Wallace

Director, Division of Law Enforcement: Frank Phipps

State Ornithologist and Editor for the League of Kentucky, Sportsmen: Burt Monroe

Director, Division of Fisheries: Minor Clark

Director, Division of Junior Clubs: Ed Adams

Director, Division of Game Management: Larry R. Gale

Director, Division of Publicity: Harry Towles

Superintendent, Game Farm: Leon Heiser

Publications: Game and fish laws; game and fish law digests; news releases; radio and television scripts; Happy Hunting Ground (official publication of the Department of Fish and Wildlife Resources); pamphlets on hunting and fishing.

League of Kentucky Sportsmen

President: Al Blum, Irving Cobb Resort, RFD No. 6, Murray

Secretary-Treasurer: Kilian L. Seng, 2603 Broadmeade Rd., Louisville 5

Publication: Happy Hunting Ground (bimonthly)

Audubon Society of Kentucky

President: Alice B. Moran, University of Kentucky, Lexington

Secretary: Eugenia Lair, 409 E. Bridge St., Cynthiana

The Kentucky Ornithological Society

President: Roger W. Barbour, University of Kentucky, Lexington

Vice-President: Anne L. Stamm, 2118 Lakeside Dr., Louisville

Corresponding Secretary-Treasurer: Mrs. W. B. Tabler, 2923 Riedling Dr., Louisville

LOUISIANA

Wild Life and Fisheries Commission

Commission Members: A. C. Glassell, Chairman, Shreveport; J. J. Besson, Vice-Chairman, Baton Rouge; George A. Foster, Pollack; O. A. Lahaye, Eunice; C. H. Brookshire, Meaux; J. W. Doxey, Cameron; A. J. Buquet, Jr., Houma

Commission Director & Secretary: L. D. Young, Jr., 126 Civil
  Courts, New Orleans
Chief, Division of Education & Publicity: John Blanchard
Chief, Division of Fish and Game: George Moore
Acting Chief, Division of Enforcement: John Maghee
Acting Chief Biologist: Harry Schafer
Publications: Louisiana Conservationist (monthly); miscellane-
  ous brochures and pamphlets
Louisiana Ornithological Society
President: Robert B. Moore, 1332 Alfred St., Baton Rouge

MAINE

Department of Inland Fisheries and Game, State House, Augusta
Commissioner: Roland H. Cobb, Augusta
Deputy Commissioner: George W. Bucknam, Waterville
Game Division:
Superintendent of Hatcheries: Gerry Wade, Skowhegan
Chief Warden: Elmer H. Ingraham, Richmond
Advisory Council Members: Maine Hills, Chairman, Belfast;
  Nicholas G. Morrison, Pleasant Island; H. A. Sanders, Jr.,
  Greenville; Elmer J. Melanson, Cherryfield; W. E. Kershner,
  Bath; John C. Page, Jr., Gorham; Arthur MacDougall, Bing-
  ham
Maine Fish and Game Association, Inc.
President: Lewellyn E. Colomy, Maple St., R.F.D. No. 1, Hallo-
  well
Vice-President: William Patch, Kittery
Secretary-Treasurer: Thomas P. Brown, R.F.D., Perry
Federation Representative: Thomas P. Brown
Audubon Society of the State of Maine, Box 592 Brunswick
President: Mrs. John W. Corning
Vice-President: Christopher M. Packard
Publication: Maine Audubon Bulletin

MARYLAND

Department of Game & Inland Fish, 516 Munsey Building,
  Baltimore 2
Commissioners: William B. Holton, Chairman, Chevy Chase;
  W. Desmond Walker, Vice-Chairman, Mitchellville; Charles
  C. Nathan, Grantsville; R. Frank Wimbrow, Salisbury; Roy-
  den A. Blunt, Ellicott City
Director: Ernest A. Vaughn
Assistant Director: Harold Smith Kolmer
Chief, Inland Fish Management: Edwin M. Barry
Chief, Game Management: Chester M. Kerns
Chief Game Warden: George B. Shields

Superintendent, Fish Hatcheries: Albert M. Powell, Lewistown
Public Relations Director: Malcolm E. King
Publications: Fish and game laws; annual report; Maryland
  Conservationist (bimonthly); occasional bulletins on wildlife
League of Maryland Sportsmen
  (National Wildlife Federation Affiliate)
Secretary: J. Hammond Brown, 7 St. Paul St., Baltimore
Treasurer: A. Lee Amoss, 5704 Queen's Chapel Rd., Hyattsville
Executive Director: Russell S. Orr, 18 East Lexington St., Balti-
  more
Izaak Walton League of America (Maryland Division)
Division President: Hubert E. Miller, Hagerstown
Maryland Ornithological Society
President: Chandler S. Robbins, Patuxent Refuge, Laurel
Maryland Sportsmen's Luncheon Club, Emerson Hotel, Balti-
  more 3
President: John C. Kump, 231 St. Paul Pl., Baltimore 2
Vice-President: Morris D. Hyman, 100 E. Lexington St., Balti-
  more 2
Vice-President: Rolfe Pottberg, 3100 Elm Ave., Baltimore 11

MASSACHUSETTS

Division of Fisheries and Game, 73 Tremont St., Boston 8
Chiarman of the Board: Matthew T. Coyne
Secretary of the Board: Frederick A. McLaughlin
Director: Robert H. Johnson
Superintendent of Wildlife Resources & Management: Allan S.
  Kennedy
Massachusetts Audubon Society, Inc.
President: Robert Walcott, 810 Barristers Hall, Boston 8
Executive Director: C. Russell Mason, 155 Newbury St., Boston
  16
Publications: The Bulletin (monthly except July, August and
  September); Records of New England Birds (monthly)

MICHIGAN

Department of Conservation, Lansing 26
Conservation Commission: Lawrence J. Gotschall, Chairman,
  Baldwin; Joseph P. Rahilly, Newberry; Donald B. Mclouth,
  Detroit; Robert F. Brevitz, Battle Creek; Peter J. Calcatera,
  Norway; George A. Griffith, Grayling; Clifford Ketcham,
  Secretary
Director: Gerald E. Eddy
Deputy Director: Wayland Osgood
Division Chiefs:
  Education: F. F. Tubbs

Field Administration: Durward Robson
Fish and Fisheries: F. A. Westerman
Forestry: G. S. McIntire
Game: H. D. Ruhl
General Operations: Gaylord A. Walker
Geological Survey: William L. Daoust
Lands: Charles E. Millar
Parks and Recreation: Arthur C. Elmer
Publications: Biennial report; game and fish laws; Michigan
Conservation (bimonthly)

Izaak Walton League of America (Michigan Division)
Division President: Samuel Stovel, Sault Ste Marie

Michigan Audubon Society
President: Edward M. Brigham, Jr., Kingman Museum, Battle
Creek

Northern Michigan Sportsmen's Association
President: Michael F. DeFant, Negaunee
Vice-President: William Asselin, Norway
Secretary: Allan Ronberg, Norway
Treasurer: Alphonse Peterson, Marquette
Editor: Kenneth Lowe
Publication: Northern Michigan Sportsman (four times a year)

MINNESOTA

Department of Conservation, State Office Bldg., St. Paul 1
Commissioner: Chester S. Wilson
Deputy Commissioner: Clarence Prout
Director, Division of Information: Carl W. Moen
Director, Division of Game and Fish: Frank D. Blair
Supervisor, Bureau of Game: Taylor W. Huston
Supervisor, Bureau of Wildlife Development: Richard R. Dorer
Supervisor, Bureau of Fisheries: Hjalmar O. Swenson
Supervisor, Fisheries Research: John Moyle
Publications: Game and fish laws; Conservation Volunteer (bi-
monthly) special reports.

Izaak Walton League of America, Inc. (Minnesota Division),
1216 Nicollet Ave., Minneapolis
President: George M. Laing, Excelsior

Minnesota Ornithologists Union, Museum of Natural History,
University of Minnesota, Minneapolis 14
President: Lewis L. Barrett, 1930 Lincoln St., N. E., Minneapolis
13
Vice-President: Robert Hanlon, Senior High School, Mankato
Secretary: Joel Bronoel, 1703 3rd St., Duluth 5
Treasurer: Mary Lupient, 212 S. E. Bedford St., Minneapolis
14

Editor: P. B. Hofslund, 36 West Mankato St., Duluth
Publication: The Flicker

MISSISSIPPI

Mississippi Game and Fish Commission, Woolfolk Building, Jackson
Director: Wade H. Creekmore
Commissioners: E. O. Spencer, Chairman, Jackson; Walter Murphey, Vice-Chairman, Hattiesburg; C. L. Huff, Port Gibson; Elkin Jack, Greenwood; Carl G. Tubb, Amory
Public Relations Officer: Rex McRaney
Publications: Press releases; game and fish digests; game and fish laws; Mississippi Game and Fish (monthly)

MISSOURI

State Conservation Commission, Monroe Building, Jefferson City
Commissioners: Frank P. Briggs, Macon; R. B. Clark, 8000 Forsyth Blvd., Clayton; D. L. Pippin, Waynesville; Joe M. Roberts, Gallatin
Director: I. T. Bode
Assistant Director: Jay Morrow
Chief, Fish & Game Division: M. O. Steen
Chief, Field Division: Vernon Bennett
Chief, Education-Information Division: Gordon H. Smith
Publications: Wildlife and Forestry Code; Missouri Conservationist (monthly magazine); Annual Report; bulletins on game and forestry management
Audubon Society of Missouri
President: James F. Comfort, 27 No. Iola Dr., Webster Groves
Vice-President: A. D. Boucher, Jefferson City
Secretary: Mabel James, Browning
Treasurer: Homer R. Bolen, Cape Girardeau
Publication: The Bluebird (monthly)
The Missouri Duck Hunters Association, St. Louis, Mo.
President: C. R. Culling, Mosley Rd., Creve Coeur
Vice-President: E. R. Kropp, 315 North 12th St., St. Louis
Secretary-Treasurer: A. W. Hager, 139 Victor St., St. Louis 4

MONTANA

State Fish and Game Commission, Helena
Commission Members: Walter Banka, Chairman, Conrad; Manson H. Bailey, Jr., Glasgow; H. W. Black, Polson; Ralph D. Shipley, Miles City; William T. Sweet, Butte
State Fish and Game Warden: A. A. O'Claire
Chief Deputy: Walter J. Everin
Superintendent of State Fisheries: Walter M. Allen

Director, Wildlife Information and Education: W. K. Thompson
Publications: Fish and game laws; Montana Wildlife; Biennial
  Report

NEBRASKA

Game, Forestation and Parks Commission, State House, Lincoln
  2
Commission Members: W. O. Baldwin, Chairman, Hebron; Don
  F. Robertson, Vice-Chairman, Box 837, North Platte; Frank
  P. Button, 609 West 4th St., Ogallala; Bennett Davis, 1646
  North 53rd, Omaha; Harold H. Hummel, Rt. 1, Fairbury;
  LaVerne P. Jacobson, 325 Sheridan, St. Paul; Floyd Stone,
  Alliance
Executive Secretary: Paul T. Gilbert, Lincoln
Supervisor of Fisheries: Glen R. Foster, Lincoln
Supervisor of Game: Lloyd P. Vance, Lincoln
Supervisor of Information: Wallace F. Green, Lincoln
Publications: Game and fish laws (annual); Outdoor Nebraska
  Magazine (quarterly); P. R. research periodicals (reports);
  P. R. trappers guides
Nebraska Council of Sportsmen's Clubs
President: H. C. Zellers, 915 Sharp Bldg., Lincoln
Secretary: Merritt Pedersen, 1700 South 24th St., Lincoln
Treasurer: H. W. Jesperson, Rt. 1, Lincoln
Izaak Walton League of America, Inc. (Nebraska Division)
President: Ray Beggs, Fremont
Nebraska Ornithologists' Union
President: W. E. Eigsti, c/o Hastings Museum, Hastings
Vice-President: Mrs. G. A. Spidel, 2840 North 56th, Lincoln
Secretary: Doris Gates, 4 South Willow St., North Platte
Treasurer: Mrs. F. J. Patton, Blue Springs
Editor: William F. Rapp, Jr., 430 Ivy St., Crete
Assistant Editor: Henry E. Baumgarten, 3135 N. 60th St., Lincoln
Publication: The Nebraska Bird Review (quarterly)

NEVADA

Fish and Game Commission, Box 678, Reno
Commission Members: Wayne Kirch, Chairman; Earl Branson,
  Secretary; Jewel Turner; John Etchart; Warren Monroe; Herb
  Carter; Lloyd Boone; Hobart S. Leonard; Tom Papez; Ned
  Kendrick; Alex Glock; Dod Quilici; Tom McCulloch; Owen
  Walker; Art Biale; William Kottke; Art Champagne
Director: Frank W. Groves
Assistant Director: Morley W. Griswold
Chief of Fisheries: Thomas J. Trelease
Chief of Law Enforcement: James C. Negley
Information & Education: M. E. McDowell

License Department: Grover C. Freeman
Superintendent, Hatchery: Lester E. Nicholas
Publications: Fish and game laws; Biennial Reports; Departmental News Bulletin; news releases
Nevada Federated Sportsmen, Inc.
President: William Gravelle, 120 East Pueblo, Reno
Vice-President: Earl Crouch, Austin
Secretary-Treasurer: Merton Mickleson, Wells, Box 388

NEW HAMPSHIRE

Fish and Game Department, State House Annex, Concord
Director: Ralph G. Carpenter, 11
Assistant to Director: William D. Beal, Jr.
Commission Members: Charles E. Smart, Chairman, Center Ossipee; Herbert W. Hill, Secretary, Hanover; Nelson E. Ramsdell, Portsmouth; Edmund Albec, Andover; William Zimmerman, Keene
Education Division: John Dodge
Supervisor of Fish Propagation: Harry Hubbard
Chief of Fisheries: Bernard Corson
Publications: Fish and game laws; biennial report; technical papers
Federated Sportsmen's Clubs of New Hampshire, Inc.
President: William Smith, Nesmith Hall, Durham
Vice-President: Waldo Sanborn, RFD, Nottingham
Secretary: Harry D. Dufresne, Wilson Rd., Kittery, Maine
Treasurer: Frank N. Bucklin, 42 Adams St., Laconia
Audubon Society of New Hampshire
President: Tudor Richards, 289 Pleasant St., Concord

NEW JERSEY

Department of Conservation and Economic Development, Division of Fish and Game, State House Annex, Trenton 7
Commissioner: Joseph McLean
Commission Members: Frank J. Valgenti, Jr., Chairman, Madison; James C. Salvato, Paterson; Herman S. Johnson, Neptune; Charles A. Campbell, New Brunswick; William R. M. Long, Haddonfield; George C. Onkst, Penns Grove; Henry W. Jeffers, Jr., Plainsboro; Roderick D. MacDougall, New Vernon; Lawrence Bohm, Eldora; David H. Hart, Cape May; Charles M. Cubbage, Port Monmouth
Director: A. H. Underhill
Secretary: Anne E. Sullivan
Superintendent of Game Management: L. G. MacNamara, Pittstown
Superintendent of Fish Hatchery: Charles O. Hayford, Hackettstown

Public Relations Assistant: Jules W. Marron, R. D. No. 3, Newton

Publications: Fish and game laws; annual report

New Jersey State Federation of Sportsmen's Clubs

President: W. Stanley Applegate, 212 Union Ave., Neptune

Vice-President (North): Walter Mooney, Andover

Vice-President (Central): E. J. Humphries, R. D. 2, Box 173A, Rahway

Vice-President (South): Benjamin Thomas, Sr., 241 W. Graisbury Ave., Audubon

Secretary: Daniel D. Warfield, 201 Midland Ave., Metuchen

New Jersey Audubon Society, 796 River Rd., New Milford

President: Frank P. Frazier, 424 Highland Ave., Upper Montclair

Vice-President: Roger Barton, 22 Arlington Ave., Caldwell

Secretary: Mrs. Chester A. Burt, Jr., Bear Brook Rd., Park Ridge

NEW MEXICO

Department of Game and Fish, Santa Fe

Commission Members: C. M. Botts, Chairman, Albuquerque; Angus Evans, Espanola; George Turner, Cimarron; Paul Wright, Silver City; Henry Brown, Carlsbad

State Game Warden and Secretary to Commission: Homer Pickens, Santa Fe

Publications: Game and fish laws; reports; New Mexico Magazine (monthly)

NEW YORK

Conservation Department, Albany

Commissioner: Perry B. Duryea

Deputy Commissioner: J. Victor Skiff

Secretary: Robert A. Wells

Director, Division of Conservation Education: Clayton B. Seagears

Director, Division of Fish and Game: Justin T. Mahoney

Chief, Bureau of Game: E. L. Cheatum

Chief, Bureau of Fish: W. Mason Lawrence

Superintendent of Game Farms: Earl Holm

Superintendent of Inland Fisheries: A. P. Miller

Superintendent of Fish Culture: Sumner M. Cowden

Chief Aquatic Biologist: John R. Greeley

Publications: Conservation laws, including forest, fish and game laws; maps; annual report; bulletins on forestry, fish and wildlife; Conservation Department magazine, The New York State Conservationist; New York Fish and Game Journal (technical publication); The Fish and Game News

Izaak Walton League of America, Inc. (New York State Division)

President: Harry W. Learner, 840 Chestnut Hill Rd., East
Aurora
Secretary: Mabel H. James, Holland
Treasurer: Smith Y. Hughes, 125 Oxford Rd., New Hartford
Conservation Consultant: Kenneth A. Reid, Sabattis

NORTH CAROLINA

Wildlife Resources Commission, Raleigh
Commission Members: R. Floyd Crouse, Chairman, Sparta;
H. C. Kennett, Vice-Chairman, Durham; E. D. McGougan,
Secretary, Lumber Bridge; Charles T. Wilson, Biltmore;
Robert Sadler, Bayboro; James A. Connelly, Morganton; O.
L. Woodhouse, Grandy; G. E. Beal, Red Oak; Thurman
Briggs, Lexington
Executive Director: Clyde P. Patton
Assistant Director: Eugene E. Schwall
Chief, Game Division: Frank B. Barick
Chief, Fish Division: J. Harry Cornell
Chief, Wildlife Protection Division: W. C. Bumgarner
Chief, Education Division: Rod Amundson
Publications: Wildlife in North Carolina (monthly); game and
fish laws and regulations (seasonally); wildlife bulletins
(occasionally)
Carolina Bird Club
President: Robert Overing, Rt. 4, Raleigh

NORTH DAKOTA

Game and Fish Department, Capitol Building, Bismarck
Commissioner: H. R. Morgan
Deputy Commissioner: Charles Cadieux
Chief, Fisheries Division: Dale L. Hennegar
Chief, Public Relations Division: Pershing Carlson
Chief, Enforcement Division: Irvin Reidman
Publications: Game and fish laws; annual report; North Dakota
Outdoors (monthly); Game and Fish News (biweekly)

OHIO

Department of Natural Resources, State Office Building, Columbus 15
Natural Resources Commission: George S. Wenger, Chairman,
Port Clinton; D. D. Blubaugh, Danville; Bryce Browning,
Dover; C. L. Dow, Athens; John Lyon Rich, Cincinnati;
Milton Ronsheim, Cadiz; Leo L. Rummell, Columbus; John
A. Silpher, Columbus
Director: A. W. Marion
Chief, Division of Wildlife: Charles A. Dambach

Members Wildlife Council: Emory R. Beetham, Chairman, Cleveland; Louis Bromfield, Lucas; John Halliday, Gallipolis; Maurice Kocher, Toledo; Baldwin Rice, Greenfield; John Hellebush, Cincinnati; B. K. Jones, Cambridge; Leonard Yochum, Sabina

Enforcement Section: Lester Bailey
Information and Education Section: Randall Guthrie
Game Management Section: E. D. Martin
Fish Management Section: E. L. Wickliff
Publications: Ohio Conservation Bulletin (monthly) miscellaneous pamphlets

League of Ohio Sportsmen
President: Ira L. Porter, Deshler-Hilton Hotel, Columbus
Vice-President: G. B. Montgomery, The Signal & Times Recorder, Zanesville
Secretary: P. M. Jones, 847 West Main St., Ravenna
Treasurer: Ben Drayer, 44 West Longview Ave., Columbus 2

Audubon Society of Ohio
President: Victor Coles, University of Cincinnati, Cincinnati 21
Vice-President: J. Herbert Heger, 3969 Lowry Ave., Cincinnati 29
Secretary-Treasurer: Irene Lammers, 3530 Epworth Ave., Cincinnati 11
Publication: The Chat (spring and fall)

Central Ohio Anglers' & Hunters' Club
President: Clark Longstreth, 1298 Wilson Ave., Columbus
Vice-President: Walter Lauffer, 1921 Summit St., Columbus
Secretary: Kenneth E. Crawford, 262 E. 19th Ave., Columbus
Treasurer: Maurice Shaver, 355 E. Hudson St., Columbus
Chairman of Board: Ben Drayer, 44 W. Longview, Columbus

Izaak Walton League of America, Inc. (Ohio Division)
President: Kent Shoemaker, 209 North Campus Ave., Oxford

OKLAHOMA

Game and Fish Department, Room 118, State Capitol Building, Oklahoma City 5
Commission Members: Maurice Finklea, Chairman, Warner; Louis M. Burtschi, Vice-Chairman, 310 Chickasha Ave., Chickasha; Raymond Lucas, Secretary, Howe; George W. Schultz, Box 64, Medford; James W. McMahan, Okemah; C. C. Morgan, Fairfax; Arthur Hall, Elk City; Dan Tankersley, 1st National Bldg., Oklahoma City
Director: E. W. Dahlgren, Oklahoma City
Assistant Director: A. D. Aldrich, Oklahoma City
Publications: Biennial Report of the Oklahoma Game & Fish Department; Oklahoma Game, Fish & Fur Laws; law digests; Oklahoma Game & Fish News (monthly except August);

numerous other pamphlets, leaflets and bulletins on fish and game management activities

Oklahoma Outdoor Council
President: E. E. Torbett, Box 1388, Enid
Executive Officer: Harold Cooksey, 102 Security National Bank Bldg., Norman
1st Vice-President: E. E. Townsend, Box 201, Stillwater
2nd Vice-President: Charles Cobb, c/o O.C.A.A. Railway, Shawnee
3rd Vice-President: S. R. Ellis, Duncan
Secretary-Treasurer: Bess Smith, Box 337, Arcadia
Federation Representative: E. E. Torbett

Izaak Walton League of America, Inc. (Oklahoma Division)
President: George Knapp, Jr., Tulsa

Oklahoma Ornithological Society
President: Joe C. Creager, Drawer 1267, Ponca City

OREGON

State Game Commission, P. O. Box 4136, Portland 8
Commission Members: J. H. Van Winkle, Chairman; D. Gildersleeve; Elmer Balsiger; Kenneth Denman; Don M. Mitchell
State Game Director: P. W. Schneider
Assistant State Game Director: C. B. Walsh
Chief of Game Operations: John McKean
Chief of Fisheries Operations: John Rayner
Publications: Game laws; biennial report; Oregon State Game Commission bulletin (monthly)

Izaak Walton League of America, Inc. (Oregon Division)
President: L. C. Binford, Portland

Oregon Audubon Society
President: Earl A. Marshall, 1172 S. E. 55th, Portland 15

PENNSYLVANIA

Pennsylvania Fish Commission, Harrisburg
Commission Members: R. Stanley Smith, President, Waynesburg; Albert R. Hinkle, Vice-President, Clearfield; Wallace Dean, Meadville; Gerard Adams, Hawley; Charles C. Houser, Allentown; John W. Grenoble, New Bloomfield
Executive Director: William Voigt, Jr.
Administrative Secretary: H. R. Stackhouse
Director, Publicity-Public Relations: Robert Glover
Publication: Pennsylvania Angler (monthly)

Pennsylvania Game Commission, Harrisburg
Commission Members: Col. Nicholas Biddle, President, Bethayres; H. L. Buchanan, Vice-President, Franklin; Ross L. Leffler, Pittsburgh; John C. Herman, Dauphin; B. K. Wil-

liams, East Stroudsburg; Andrew C. Long, Shamokin; Tom L. McDowell, Bradford; C. E. Huffman, Marshalls Creek
Executive Director: Dr. Logan J. Bennett
Director, Bureau of Administration: Rollin Heffelfinger
Public Relations Director: Robert D. Reed
Publications: Game laws; bulletins; educational pamphlets; biennial report; Pennsylvania Game News (monthly)

Pennsylvania Federation of Sportsmen's Clubs
President: Joseph H. Barkley, 437 Indiana St., Punxsutawney
1st Vice-President: Raymond H. Armstrong, Guys Mills
2nd Vice-President: Steve Emanuel, 421 River Rd., Wilkes-Barre
Secretary: Charles H. Nehf, 1038 North 21st St., Allentown
Treasurer: Glen C. Dodds, R.F.D., Smiths Ferry

Izaak Walton League of America, Inc. (Pennsylvania Division)
President: William D. Henning, 501 Berger Bldg., Pittsburgh 19

Pennsylvania State Sportsmen's Association, Inc.
President: Frank Dissinger, R. D. 1, Lebanon
Secretary: Andrew C. Long, 660 Center St., Shamokin

RHODE ISLAND

Department of Agriculture and Conservation, Veterans Memorial Bldg., 83 Park St., Providence 2
Director: John L. Rego
Assistant Director: Edward C. Hayes, Jr.
Chief, Division of Fish and Game: Thomas J. Wright
Publications: Fish and game laws; commercial fisheries laws; annual reports; special publications of fish and game (PR and DJ)

Audubon Society of Rhode Island
President: William B. Dean, 282 Lake St., Seekonk, Mass.
Executive Secretary: Roland C. Clement, P. O. Box 31, Providence

SOUTH CAROLINA

South Carolina Wildlife Resources Department, Columbia
Director, Division of Game: A. A. Richardson
Publications: Game and fish laws; open seasons for hunting; digest of general state fishing laws

South Carolina Wildlife Federation
President: Charles Brice, 1220 Huger St., Columbia
Vice-President: F. Bartow Culp, 69 King St., Charleston
Secretary-Treasurer: Mrs. W. E. Griffin, 55 Arcade Bldg., Columbia

SOUTH DAKOTA

South Dakota Department of Game, Fish and Parks, New State Office Building, Pierre

Commission Members: R. D. Albaugh, Chairman, Winner; A. M. McKay, Vice-Chairman, Orient; E. J. Kahler, Sioux Falls; Walter H. Burke, Pierre; Newell E. Krause, Lemmon; Mancel W. Peterson, Waubay; Leonel M. Jensen, Wall; Cecil W. Duncan, Mitchell
Director: Elmer Peterson
Assistant Director: N. E. McEachron
Chief Game Warden: Virgil R. Johnson
Superintendent of Fisheries: Harold J. Horrigan, Woonsocket
Fisheries Biologist: William D. Clothier, Woonsocket
Publicity Director: Gilbert W. Zieman
Publications: Game, Fish and Forestry Laws (bi-annual); annual report; South Dakota Conservation Digest (monthly)

South Dakota Wildlife Federation
President: Bern Dickinson, Box 121, Aberdeen
Vice-President: DEA Baldwin, Lead
Secretary-Treasurer: Larry Woodman, Jr., Box 1082, Aberdeen
Izaak Walton League of America, Inc. (South Dakota Division)
President: Carl E. Sundahl, Webster

TENNESSEE

Tennessee Game and Fish Commission, State Office Bldg., Nashville
Commission Members: Milburn C. Jolly, Chairman, Jackson; A. D. Huddleston, Vice-Chairman, Alcoa; Edwin Crutcher, Secretary, Madison; John H. Webb, Sparta; Enoch Brown, Memphis; J. A. Williams, Kingsport; Broadus Maples, Murfreesboro; Will S. Roper, Covington; LeRoy Rymer, Cleveland
Director: Hayden W. Olds
Administrative Assistant to Director: Louis S. Clapper
Chief of Game Section: Albert E. Hyder
Chief of Enforcement: Frederick A. Williams
Chief of Fish Section: Glenn Gentry
Public Relations Officer: Donald Pfitzer

Department of Conservation
Commission Members: George R. Mayfield, Chairman, Nashville; Russell Stadelman, Vice-Chairman, Memphis; Mayland Muse, Secretary, Johnson City; George G. Thomas, Nashville; N. E. Fitzgerald, Knoxville; James C. Durdin, Camden
Commissioner of Conservation: Jim McCord
Director, Division of Information: Earl L. Shaub
Educational Supervisor: James L. Bailey
Tennessee Ornithological Society
President: Mrs. Robert A. Monroe, 1424 Tugaloo Dr., S. W., Knoxville 16

Vice-President for East Tenn.: Mrs. E. M. West, 1625 S. Clayton Ave., S. E., Chattanooga 4
Vice-President for Middle Tenn.: Jennie Riggs, 3313 Fairmount Dr., Nashville 5
Vice-President for West Tenn.: Nelle Moore, 275 Palisade St., Memphis 11
Secretary: Mrs. Robert J. Dunbar, 106 Glendale Lane, Oak Ridge
Treasurer: Lawrence C. Kent, 1896 Cowden Ave., Memphis 4
Editor: James T. Tanner, Department of Zoology, University of Tennessee, Knoxville
Publication: The Migrant (quarterly)

TEXAS

Game and Fish Commission, Austin
Commission Members: Walter W. Lechner, Chairman, Fort Worth; Herman F. Heep, Buda; Frank M. Wood, Wichita Falls; W. T. Scarborough, Kennedy; J. W. Elliott, Mexia; Henry Coffield, Marfa; Herbert J. Frensley, Houston; Henry LeBlanc, Sr., Port Arthur; Hal Peterson, Kerrville
Executive Secretary: H. D. Dodgen, Austin
Editor, Game and Fish: Townsend Miller, Austin
Publications: Game, fish, oyster, sand, shell, gravel, and pollution laws; annual report; bulletins; Texas Game and Fish (monthly); Principal Game Birds and Mammals of Texas
Texas Wildlife Federation
President: Jack Austin, 409 First National Bank Bldg., Wichita Falls
Vice-President: Don Maxwell, 806 W. 2nd St., Odessa
Secretary: A. A. Werlla, Wichita Falls
Treasurer: C. C. Parfet, Wichita National Bldg., Wichita Falls
Texas Ornithological Society
President: Charles H. McNeese, 2916 Revere, Houston 6

UTAH

Fish and Game Commission, 1596 West North Temple, Salt Lake City
Director: J. Perry Egan
Commission Members: K. E. Bullock, Chairman, Provo; Golden G. Sanderson, Fairview; J. Allen Browne, Price; W. Rulon White, Ogden; Robert B. Mitchell, Parowan
Chief, Fisheries Division: M. J. Madsen, Salt Lake City
Chief, Division of Game Management: Harold S. Crane, Draper
Chief, Law Enforcement Division: Golden B. Peay, Salt Lake City
Chief, Public Relations and Education Division: Lee Kay, Salt Lake City

Publications: Fish and game laws; Biennial Reports; Fish and Game Bulletin (monthly); numerous other technical publications

Utah Wildlife Federation
President: D. Keith Barnes, 48 N. State St., Kaysville
Vice-President: Dean Andrus, Richmond
Vice-President: Ralph Williams, Kaysville
Vice-President: Alvin Kay, Vernal
Secretary: Herb Smart, 430 Judge Bldg., Salt Lake City 1

Utah Audubon Society
President: Rex B. Snow, 602 East Fifth South, Bountiful

VERMONT

Fish and Game Commission, Montpelier
Commission Members: Samuel A. Parsons, Chairman; William S. Preston, Sr.; Earl Yeaw; J. Malcolm Colton; George K. Sprague, Jr.
Fish and Game Director: George W. Davis
Publications: Fish and game laws; biennial report; Hunting and Fishing in Vermont

Vermont Federation of Sportsmen's Clubs
President: Robert W. Crowe, Sheldon Springs
Vice-President: Andrew Pitonyak, Montpelier
Vice-President: George Plumb, Bennington
Vice-President: R. C. Nadeau, Brattleboro
Secretary: Solon Vail, Woodstock
Treasurer: Jules Chicoine, 311 Lake St., St. Albans

VIRGINIA

Commission of Game and Inland Fisheries, 7 North Second St., P. O. Box 1642, Richmond 13
Commission Members: B. W. Stras, Jr., Chairman, Tazewell; Charles D. Andrews, Suffolk; Homer G. Bauserman, Sr., 4211 16th St., So., Arlington; Frank P. Burton, Stuart; William C. Gloth, Jr., Redart; Thomas G. Herring, R.F.D., Dayton; E. C. Nettles, Wakefield; Warren B. Rains, Warsaw; T. D. Watkins, Midlothian; Holman Willis, Jr., Mountain Trust Bldg., Roanoke
Executive Director: I. T. Quinn
Assistant Executive Director: Miss E. M. Paris
Chief, Division of Game: C. F. Phelps
Chief, Division of Fish: G. W. Buller
Chief, Division of Education: J. J. Shoman
Chief, Division of Law Enforcement: Webb Midyette
Publications: Game and fish laws; annual report; Virginia Wildlife (monthly); Educational Bulletin (semi-monthly)

Virginia Society of Ornithology
President: Jack E. Perkins, Back Bay Refuge, P. O. Box 269, Virginia Beach
Izaak Walton League of America (Virginia Division)
President: Paul O. Peters, Arlington

WASHINGTON

State Game Commission, 509 Fairview Ave. North, Seattle 9
Commission Members: Walter Failor, Chairman, Aberdeen; W. R. Bernard, Cheney; Edson Dow, Wenatchee; J. A. Loudon, Yakima; Richard S. Seward, Seattle; Claude C. Snider, Vancouver
The Department of Game, 509 Fairview Ave., North, Seattle 9
Director: John A. Biggs
Assistant Director: Carl N. Crouse
Chief, Division of Education and Information: Wesley A. Hunter
Chief, Division of Enforcement: Walter Neubrech
Chief, Division of Fishery Management: Clarence F. Pautzke
Chief, Division of Game Management: Burton Lauckhart
Chief, Division of License: Albert V. Bertucci
Publications: Seasons and bag or catch limits for game, migratory waterfowl, migratory game birds, fur-bearing animals, and game fish; biennial report; quarterly bulletin
Washington State Sportsmen's Council, Inc.
President: Ransom Minkler, 521 E. First St., Aberdeen
1st Vice-President: Frank Bunker, Amber
2nd Vice-President: David A. Botting, 905 Fourth, N.E., Auburn
3rd Vice-President: W. C. Vickerman, Ellensburg
Secretary-Treasurer: Fred N. Mintzer, 1004 Okanogan St., Wenatchee

WEST VIRGINIA

Conservation Commission of West Virginia, Charleston
Commission Members: Jay L. Kidwell, Points; Raymond J. Lambert, Kenova; R. H. Miller, Jr., Charleston; M. V. Fisher, Sissonville; R. O. Raine, Lewisburg
Director: Carl J. Johnson
Chief, Division of Game Management: Charles O. Handley
Chief, Division of Law Enforcement: Arthur C. Bachman
Chief, Division of Fish Management: Harry Van Meter
Chief, Division of Education and Publicity: Harold Lambert
Editor: Robert R. Bowers
Publications: West Virginia Conservation; annual report; hunting and fishing regulations; numerous bulletins
West Virginia Sportsmen Unlimited
President: Paul Rusk, Box 908, Charleston

Regional Vice-Presidents:
  Region 1: Chester Bourne, 802 Beech Ave., Charlestown
  Region 2: Bert Honaker, 4331 Route 60, Huntington
  Region 3: W. R. Clinger, 645 13th St., Parkersburg
  Region 4: M. W. Cooper, 1035 Jefferson Ave., Moundsville
  Region 5: Maxwell H. Smith, 314 Center St., Bridgeport
  Region 6: H. Paul Stewart, 214 Maple Ave., Bridgeport
  Region 7: Leo Young, Box 103, Durbin
  Region 9: B. H. Barnett, Box 269, Logan
  Region 10: R. L. Thacker, Franklin
  Region 11: Earl H. Orndorff, Box 33, Route 1, Keyser
Secretary: Harold Powers, 401 Tennessee Ave., Charleston 2
Treasurer: Leo Young, Box 103, Durbin
Izaak Walton League of America, Inc. (West Virginia Division)
President: W. R. Clinger, Parkersburg

WISCONSIN

Conservation Commission, Madison
Commission Members: Guido R. Rahr, Chairman, Manitowoc;
  John O. Moreland, Secretary, Hayward; Douglas Hunt,
  Wautoma; A. W. Schorger, Madison; Leonard J. Seyberth,
  Eau Claire; Charles F. Smith, Wausau
Assistant Secretary: Lydia S. MacKenzie, State Office Building,
  Madison 1
Conservation Department, State Office Building, Madison 2
Acting Director: L. P. Voigt
Assistant Directors: H. T. J. Cramer, G. E. Sprecher
Chief, Division of Fish Management: Edward Schneberger
Chief, Division of Game Management: William F. Grimmer
Chief, Division of Law Enforcement: George S. Hadland
Chief, Division of Information and Education: W. T. Calhoun
Publications: Hunting, fishing, and trapping laws; forest, field,
  and marsh fire laws; Wisconsin Conservation Bulletin
  (monthly); recreational literature; numerous terminal and
  popular publications on various conservation subjects
Wisconsin Federation of Conservation Clubs
President: Kenneth Christensen, 4543 Winnequah Rd., Madison
Vice-President: B. Shearier, Wisconsin Rapids
Executive Secretary-Treasurer: Les Woerpel, 411 E. Lincoln,
  Stevens Point
Izaak Walton League of America, Inc. (Wisconsin Division)
President: Arthur Molstad, Milwaukee
Wisconsin Pheasant Breeders' Association
President: Elliott Parker, Route 5, Eau Claire
Secretary-Treasurer: Don Mac Farlane, Route 3, Janesville

WYOMING

Wyoming Game and Fish Commission, Cheyenne
Commission Members: Nels H. Smith, President, Sundance;
   T. Seddon Taliaferro, III, Vice-President, Rock Springs; Gus
   Fleischli, Cheyenne; Ed Von Korsigk, Riverton; Wesley
   Bircher, Wilson; William H. Underwood, Gillette
State Game and Fish Commissioner: Lester Bagley
State Game Warden: Norbert C. Faass
State Bird Warden: George R. Wells
Information & Education: James E. Grasse
Publications: Wyoming Wild Life Magazine (monthly); game
   and fish laws and regulations (annual); biennial report
Wyoming Federation of Sportsmen's Clubs
President: Carrol Noble, Cora
Vice-President: Otto Stevens, Afton
Secretary: John Borzea, 1313 Clark, Rock Springs
Treasurer: George W. Bird, Box 396, Rock Springs

Izaak Walton League of America, Inc. (Wyoming Division)
President: Fred A. Thompson, Laramie

CHAPTER 6

Try Trolling

THE boat cuts through the water making singing waves; the sun gleams; your reel screams a little as the line plays out; the sound of the motor goes back across the water in contented growls. One hundred yards behind you the bright silver of your lure shines and leaps like it is alive. Everything seems alive: the water, the boat, even the fishing rod in your hand. Trolling does that to one: It's a relaxing yet exciting sport that combines the best features of boating and fishing.

Ever since Izaak Walton's book, *The Compleat Angler,* appeared in early 1653, men with warm blood have been trying to devise schemes, methods and ingenious lures with which they can catch bigger fish.

As any worm dunker can tell you, if a fish is not feeding, no matter what tempting and exotic morsel you flaunt before him, he just won't take it. If his belly is full, the fish is beyond temptation.

But there is one stubborn school of fishermen which claims it can catch fish under almost any conditions. These are the trollers, the men who like to combine the soft chug of an outboard motor or the creak of oars with the strike of the fish and the whine of the reel.

A fat Universal Dictionary of 1,440 pages that I turn to when less complete books fail, has this to say:

"Troll—to fish by trailing or spinning a revolving or wobbling lure behind a boat."

A fisherman I've swapped lies with, who concentrates on trolling, gave me a somewhat different definition. "Troll—a method by which wise fishermen, who have failed to get fish, go deep where the big ones are and come home with a boatload of fish."

Candid Bud Benoit of Sandpoint, Idaho, does it more completely: "I had been trying for the big trout in Lake Pend Oreille (Idaho's Big Hole) for the past four years and not having any degree of luck until last year, when I hit upon a

64

method that is successful for me. Trolling. And I believe this system will work well in any large freshwater lake with depths of several hundred feet.

"The big rainbows, which we call 'kamloops' here in North Idaho, like a certain low temperature of water to lie in. When the top water is still warm and, as a consequence, the old ones are hugging the cool of the bottom, then you've got to get where these fish are.

"In order to reach such depths, so that the plug or spoon will have a natural action, it is necessary to use tackle that will go deep and still pull the lure at the proper angle. Some fishermen use metal lines. They do get the depth but pull the plugs at an undesirable angle. It is true that some of the big fish are fooled with this method. But I've never been able to get away with it.

"I've found that a 20-pound test braided nylon line with about six feet of 10-pound test leader will give the lure a chance to work normally, without the weight and stiffness of a metal line. Depths are obtained by placing a four- to five-ounce lead weight or sinker (clip type) on the line 200 feet from the lure.

"I took a 20-pound rainbow on September 23, 1952, on 450 feet of braided line, with a Lucky Louie Pearl Pink plug. The following day I took a six-pounder, and the following week-end a ten-pounder. All from Lake Pend Oreille."

Trolling, the technique that takes the big ones, is a system of fishing that must be adapted to the nature, habitat and size of the fish. Fish that are regularly pulled into the boat with the tempting line of the troller are: all the panfish, long-ear sunfish, crappies, bluegills, perch, basses, steelhead, cut-throat, lake, rainbow trout; muskellunge, northern pike, walleyes, pickerel and bass. Saltwater fishermen also find trolling most efficient. Striped bass, tuna, marlin, tarpon are taken with the trailing line and the splashing lure. But the freshwater fisherman is in the majority, so let's concentrate on that facet of the fine art of trolling.

Your casting rod, about 5½ feet, of medium weight and sturdy action is the best all-around trolling rod. If you use a lighter rod such as your fly rod you'll have difficulty setting the hook. If you really want to get deep don't use the fly rod. However, for a new fishing thrill I've found that fly rod trolling *can* be fun. I use it for surface bass or land-locked salmon trolling. Their strike, I'd say, is usually terrific.

Let's take the fish and name the tackle to get him.

Bass. Rod: select the 5 to 5½-foot casting rod and a reel medium heavy, with capacity for at least 100 yards of line. The line should be a 15-pound test with a three-foot nylon leader. Lures: for water not over six feet, without weed growth, take the lure that won't travel downward over three feet. Bucktails, spoons, plugs, pork-rind and bait with spinners. Ask for the floating-diving variety of lure. The lure should run straight out from the boat. When fishing for bass adapt your gear to the depth of the water and aquatic conditions. For example, say you are fishing for bass in a weedy area ten feet deep, using a sinking type lure. This should go down about eight feet and move just above the underwater growth. And use a weedless lure. They come in all shapes and sizes, sometimes equipped with weedless hooks. If you are fishing in deep water use a large collared deep diving lure. The large collar or neck makes it dive, attaining the always-necessary depth.

Pike and Pickerel. Use your 5½-foot rod and a 12-inch wire leader; these fish have teeth. I suggest at least a 20-pound line. Any sturdy reel which will hold 100 yards or more of heavy line will do. Red spoons and June bug spinners are effective. Weed beds, sunken logs, tree stumps are the target areas. *Troll slowly;* strike hard to set the hook fast once the pike or pickerel hit. Carry a gaff or landing net to avoid cutup fingers when you boat these characters.

Muskellunge. This is the big guy, dream catch of the troller. Use the 5½-foot, stiff-type rod. Your reel should hold 100 yards or more of 40-pound test line. Use an 18-inch wire leader. Large bucktails and spoons work best. Troll over deep-hole weed beds. Set your hook hard on the strike. Play the fish from the back of the boat. Stop the motor when you begin to fight the musky. If he seems to be a big one, the experienced troller sometimes follows him with the boat until the fish tires, then the final boating of this prized fish of trollers takes place.

Lake Trout. This fish might be considered the glamour puss of the trolling tribe. It's a deep, deep dweller, 'way down with Davy Jones, and some of the sport or fight is lost because of this fact. Good, heavy rods, the variety with long butts which give extra leverage; wire leaders are preferred, and the jumbo trolling-reel with 200-yard capacity of a 50-pound test line. Heavy sinkers (the sport killers) are necessary. The line should run down until it is just above the bottom. Lakers are unpredictable and take a wobbling spoon or live bait. Sometimes they like a fast sometimes a slow-moving lure. It's a matter of changing the technique to suit the mood of the fish.

Rainbow Trout. Sometimes called steelhead and kamloops, both are large rainbows.

The kamloops, famous in the Idaho lakes, likes a fast-moving bait or lure and is usually taken from motor-driven boats trolling in the 5 horsepower speed range. The metal leader is not ordinarily used, for the kamloops is a wary fish. They are fished with deep wobbling lures. They fight in the acrobatic manner and are prized highly by trollers. Steelheads take to plugs and favor deep holes. Use medium trolling speed and fish the deeper area well. At least a 25-pound test line is recommended for both these fish. The short, stiff rod is also favored.

Walleyed Pike. These fish like to feed at night and take kindly to June bug spinners, commotion lures. The combination of live bait and small spinners has been known to get the limit in record time. A 12-inch wire leader is used, and you should troll reasonably deep. A 100 yards of 15-pound test line, on a medium casting type reel will turn the trick. If you fish for them at night, head for the shallow bars and shoals and use a white, easy-motioned plug.

Panfish. Contrary to general belief, the gamy little fish known categorically as the panfish can also be taken by trolling. An automatic reel, or the smooth hazardless spinning rod and reel can be beautifully adapted for panfish trolling. Live bait behind small spinners is effective; even the small, active plugs bring good results. An outboard trolled slowly increases the pleasure of the catch.

Unless you have a weak-minded companion who doesn't mind using oars for several hours at a stretch, an outboard is a must. Three to five horsepower is sufficient. You can buy a trolling plate which will permit you to slow the motor to any desired speed. Some motors are effectively constructed with the trolling fisherman in mind, and the plate isn't necessary. But it is necessary for you to learn to handle the boat and your trolling rod and line as a unit. For example, the speed of your boat should always be timed with the depth of your line and the length you have trailing so that your lure or bait is always just temptingly above the bottom or weed-bed.

With an outboard it is also possible to troll two rods, thus increasing your chances. Say you are trolling along, motor hum-

ming and you get a strike. First thing you should do is to stop
the motor and tilt it out of the water so that the fighting fish
can't tangle your line and stop your fishing for the day. Play
your fish from the stern of the boat. Both you and the boat are
better balanced that way and you have a wider area to swing
the fish in.

If the hooked fish moves into heavy cover such as a weed bed,
move your boat directly over the spot and pull your line easily
in various directions until it comes free. Don't sulk back in
your boat and mule the line until you've snapped it and lost
the bait, your temper and the fish.

The outboard also helps fatten your catch. Note the spot
where you've just landed the big one, swing your boat away,
circle and troll through the same area. Many fish are gregarious
and come in schools. Your powered boat makes it a cinch to
fish out an area until you are sure there isn't any more business.

Your motor will come to your aid if your line becomes twisted
while trolling. Remove the lure and let the line trail behind
the boat; keep your motor at medium speed and the water and
forward movement will take the twist out of your line nicely.

The Shakespeare people drop pearls of wisdom. The one
fundamental requirement of good trolling, they say, is that the
trolling rod be balanced to the weight of the lure you are using
and the speed at which you troll. Time will tell you about the
right amount of shimmy at the rod tip when correct boat speed
is reached. A rod that is too soft in the butt section will bow
so far that there is no strength or backbone left to set the hook
and absorb the shock of the fish. The ideal trolling rod should
have just enough bow in it at trolling speed so that when the
fish strikes, the rod can naturally arc far enough to absorb the
shock and set the hook. The thing to avoid is having so soft a
rod the line has to take the entire blow of the striking fish,
rather than having the resiliency of the rod absorb it. Then,
again, if the rod is too stiff, it fails to bend in response to the
strike of a fish and the line takes the beating.

With the spinning rod and reel a normal cast will put your
lure as far out as you want.

When you feel that you have enough line out, engage the
pick-up finger simply by turning the reel handle. This will stop
the line from going out, except for the obvious fact that the
handle can still turn backward. To prevent this, on most spinning reels you engage the anti-reverse clutch. Now the line will

only run out under drag control and the reel handle will not turn in reverse. But it is also necessary to keep the drag tension tight enough to set the hook but not so tight that the fish can snap the line when he strikes. When you get a strike, you'll hear the drag click in the spool as the line starts out.

Men who go to school to learn how fish think, the aquatic biologists of the various states' conservation departments, have ideas about trolling.

Richard H. Stroud, Chief Aquatic Biologist of the Massachusetts Department of Conservation says:

"Trolling is practiced in most of Massachusetts' waters for chain pickerel, largemouth bass, smallmouth bass, and certain panfishes particularly white perch and, to a lesser degree, yellow perch. Many rainbow and brown trout are taken by trolling in such of these waters which are annually stocked by the state (55 ponds in 1952). Most trolling is shallow trolling with cloth line in depths of water seldom over 15 feet. Deep trolling is occasionally practiced with good results for trout. Recently opened Quabbin Reservoir (Central Mass.) provides new opportunities for deep trolling and has produced interesting results in the form of big strings of both white perch and yellow perch ranging from 1 to 3 pounds in weight. At the same time a generous sprinkling of large pickerel and bass is an ever-present possibility."

Edward J. Longtin, Aquatic Biologist of the Fisheries Research Unit of the state of Minnesota, offers this lore:

"In Minnesota trolling is applied mainly to three types of fish—northern pike (and musky), walleyed pike and lake trout. Depending on the species sought, the gear and techniques differ.

"Northern pike are found during the fishing season in shallow water, generally associated with weed beds. Trolling is done back and forth parallel to the bed and close enough so the lure can attract pike lurking in and about the weeds. As to lures—almost anything with hooks. However, as a guess, I would say that the daredevil takes more northern pike in Minnesota than any other one lure. One thing we have observed in our work about the lakes is that most fishermen seem to troll too fast.

"Trolling for walleyed pike is done at a medium depth near rocky or sandy bars as the walleye is generally found associated with this type of lake bottom. For this species trolling should be slow. Good results are obtained fishing close to the bottom. I often troll for walleyes using windrift as the only means of moving the boat. It is my impression that live baits are best for walleyes, but artificials of the flat-fish type have become quite popular with walleye fishermen in recent years.

"Trolling for lake trout has developed into a particular brand of fishing all its own. During most of the season the fish are caught in very deep water and copper or monel lines with heavy rods and reels are required to stand the strain. In Lake Superior and other larger inland trout lakes this type of fishing is often called 'Deep Sea Fishing.' During certain periods of the year the trout are in shallow water and can be taken on lighter trolling gear with a great deal of sport involved. Spoon and spinners are the principal types of lures used."

New Jersey's Fisheries Biologist Roland F. Smith says his state is well adapted for trolling:

"Contrary to popular opinion, large pickerel in our New Jersey lakes will not usually be taken in shallow, weedy areas. They are fished deep, fifteen to twenty feet of water—sometimes deeper, and in areas that one would usually fish for small-mouth bass. This is why most of the large trout that are caught in New Jersey lakes are caught by pickerel fishermen—those who know where to fish for the big ones. Live bait is used for the most part, although the common pickerel lures will be effective, depending on the season.

"Bass anglers in this state fall into two categories—the 'buggers' and the bait casters using artificial lures. In many of our lakes that appear to be more suitable for smallmouth bass, the largemouths seem to have taken over and will be caught in areas normally considered smallmouth habitat—along with big pickerel.

"We have few 'open' lakes that can be considered good small-mouth waters. Trolling with a panfish master (weighted a little so it hits bottom occasionally) has been found effective. Alternate between the light and dark model. I would like to see more people using leeches (blood suckers) around here. They make excellent bait up north and are obtained by dropping horse-meat into water near a weedy area.

"It is my belief that more trout should be taken in lakes during the summer. In general, our lakes become deficient in dissolved oxygen during the summer and trout are found in the 'intermediate' level. This is where people should troll for them —not on the bottom."

Reino O. Koski, Aquatic Biologist for Oregon, is helpful:

"The chief fish angled for by trolling in my state is the salmon. We have just completed a survey of the catch the past year, and the data indicates a catch of over 111,000 salmon of a size greater than twenty inches.

"The salmon are taken in all the major coastal streams as well as off shore. The Columbia River provides the greatest amount with as many as two or three thousand boats on the river each day of the Astoria Salmon Derby, which is held annually over Labor Day. Trolling is the method by which almost all the fish are taken. The most effective lures vary from time to time and stream to stream, but wooden or plastic plugs are mainly used. This is true for the ocean and bays, but when the salmon ascend the streams for some distance, spinners and flashers are used.

"Some ten to fifteen thousand spring chinook salmon are caught annually in the Willamette River near Portland from March to May. Single or double-headed spinners of many sizes and finishes are the accepted lures. Some anglers swear by the wobbler type.

"The tackle is quite heavy. Steel, glass, and bamboo rods are all used in many sizes. The most common length is around five feet. Star drag reels are in favor. From 150 to 200 yards of line is necessary, and it should test to 36 pounds. Several salmon exceeding 60 pounds were caught last season.

"Trolling is one method employed in taking the coastal cutthroat trout or 'blueback' as it is known in some localities. These trout are caught in coastal bays and streams including the Columbia River, where they are referred to as 'harvest trout.' Favorite lures are double spinners with a trailing bait of night crawlers, flatfish, or similar types.

"In the Cascade Mountain Range there are large lakes and rehabilitated reservoirs. Large rainbow trout, eastern brook, and brown trout are taken from these waters. Trolling is practiced to a great degree. A variety of lures is used with spinner and worms in greatest favor. Streamer flies are trolled in some lakes with success. The coachman and caddis bucktails seem to be the favorite choice.

"Mackinaw or lake trout can be taken in several large lakes in the Cascades. This fishery is just developing and much experimenting with lures attends this development. Weighted lines are generally used with pearl finish wobblers as the most favored lure."

The Fish Management Supervisor for Ohio, Robert Cummins, Jr., paints a pretty picture of trolling possibilities:

"There are numerous methods used for angling in Lake Erie, but since the trolling season comes at a peak in the vacation season, it is perhaps more popular than most other methods.

"The two predominant species of fish to be taken by trolling are the yellow and blue pikeperch. As the water becomes warm during the summer months the fish move into deeper water. This is when trolling begins, in about thirty feet of water along rocky or ledge bottoms. The more successful anglers fish their baits among the rocks. There are various systems of weights and spreaders used which take the baits to the required depth in an untangled condition.

"A flatfish baited with worms seems to be the most widely used. Since many baits are necessarily lost while fishing close to the rocks, a combination of hook, inexpensive spinner (resembling a June Bug spinner) and common sinker is used.

"Ordinarily the artificial lures are baited with worms or a hook baited with a large minnow is attached two or three feet above the flatfish. In this way it is not uncommon to hook the fish 'following up,' thereby making a double catch."

Most of the states will give you trolling information if you ask for it. Address your letter to the Department of Conservation, Fisheries Division, to the capital city of the state you are interested in and enclose an addressed, stamped envelope for return. See chapter, A Sports Surprise in Every State, for complete listings.

Here is lead-off information which may give you the push you need.

There is a great deal of trolling in Missouri, particularly in the summertime, on such as Lake of the Ozarks, Clearwater Reservoir, Lake Wappapello, Lake Taneycomo and the two lakes they share with Arkansas—Norfolk and Bull Shoals. Deep lake trolling during the hot Missouri summer is usually the best way to take fish.

Trolling is an important aspect of fresh water fishing in North Carolina. In eastern waters there is year-round trolling for striped bass. This is not for the migrants of the Atlantic coast, but for the resident population which remains in brackish and fresh waters the year 'round. Trolling continues during their spawning run up the Roanoke River. With the exception of Chesapeake Bay, one of the largest concentrations of this species may be found at Weldon, N. C. about April 1st.

Trolling for black bass is good in power reservoirs in the Catawba and Yadkin river systems, and the TVA reservoirs in the western part of the state. In western lakes where walleyed pike are found, trolling takes 'em.

One unexploited aspect of sport fishing is trolling for rainbow trout in two of the western reservoirs. In the power reservoirs there is no closed season on trout, and ultra-light tackle is not advisable.

Louis S. Clapper, Administrative Officer from the State Game and Fish Commission of Tennessee, fills in:

"I would estimate that of fishing from boats, which is the principal method, more than half is trolling. More game fish probably are caught in Tennessee by trolling than by any other method. When the TVA and Army engineers created the 'Great Lakes of the South' and the 500,000 acres of water, they skinned the impoundment areas. All small vegetation was removed and trees were cut down to stumps. This resulted in waters free of obstacles. Only those stumps and rocks hinder fishermen who wish to troll.

"Largemouths, smallmouths, Kentucky bass, rock bass, white (or striped) bass, walleyes, sauger and crappie all are caught by trolling methods. At Dale Hollow Lake, where the walleyes often come in 15- and 16-pound weights, anglers troll up to 200 yards with wire or wire-filled line. This, in fact, is about the only method by which the national championship walleyes are taken at Dale Hollow."

Always helpful, Clayton B. Seagears, Director of Conservation Education of New York State, breaks his state into trolling territories for us.

"*Muskellunge.* Chautauqua Lake and the St. Lawrence in the Thousand Islands region and east beyond Ogdensburg. Very large spoons and wired suckers are most popular.

"*Great Northern Pike.* Sacandaga Reservoir, many of the larger Adirondack lakes and Lake Champlain.

"*Bass* (both largemouth and smallmouth). Saranac; Lake Champlain, especially the northern part; the Finger Lakes, Lake Ontario and the St. Lawrence.

"*Lake Trout.* Many Adirondack lakes from Lake George north, the Finger Lakes (particularly Seneca and Keuka).

"*Rainbow Trout.* Seneca and Keuka in the Finger Lakes, using surface streamers and wobblers in the early spring and Seth Green rigs later.

"Walleyed Pike. Oneida Lake and northern Lake Champlain, using spoons and minnows."

Alabama has substantial trolling waters as the result of several large impoundments in central Alabama by the Alabama Power Company. These impoundments offer hundreds of miles of trolling waters.

Most successful Alabama trollers use a slow rate of speed with a river runt or some small deep running lure followed by a small spoon, Colorado spinner or barracuda on about two feet of leader.

There are miles of good trolling on the Tennessee River in north Alabama as a result of TVA lakes on the Tennessee and its tributaries.

Arizona has varied fishing conditions. In lakes such as Lake Mead (which it shares with Nevada), where largemouth bass seek a depth of from 30 to 70 feet, a special technique in trolling is accomplished by using hell divers, Paul Bunyan or lures of similar type. Trolling is begun by a long cast of 50 feet or more and the lure is allowed to sink until the line is in a vertical position. Letting out a fairly short amount of additional line and drifting with the wind will usually keep the lure at sufficient depth.

Lyle M. Thorpe, Supervisor of the Fisheries Management of Connecticut, is encouraging:

"Rainbow trout are most often taken by trolling in lakes. Wononscopomuc Lake, Salisbury; East Twin Lake, Salisbury; West Hill Lake, New Hartford; Compensating Reservoir, Barkhamsted; Cream Hill Pond, Cornwall; Crystal Lake, Ellington; and the Quassapaug Lake, Woodbury, are well suited for trolling for rainbows.

"Lake trout are taken from Lake Wononscopomuc and East Twin. Trolling with fly and spinner is a successful way of taking smallmouth bass. Waramaug Lake, New Preston; Candlewood Lake north of Danbury; Gardner Lake, Salem; Waumgumbaug Lake, Coventry and Lake Pocotopaug, East Hampton are best suited for this type of fishing. Yellow perch, white perch and calico bass are readily taken by short-line trolling with fly and spinner combinations. Most anglers do not seem to know the possibilities of this method. Pickerel which are widely distributed in Connecticut can be taken by trolling where weeds are not thick."

There are thousands of lakes in Wisconsin where trolling for muskellunge and northern pike may be carried on providing such trolling is not done by the use of an outboard motor or other means of propulsion than paddle or oars. This regulation applies to inland waters only, and in certain sections of the Mississippi River and in the Great Lakes trolling may be done with the use of an outboard motor or launch.

The use of outboard motors and small boats is on the increase in Florida, but a good deal of Florida fishing is still the deep sea, charter boat type of fishing. Much of this is trolling, and a guide who knows the waters and the method helps get the big ones. Captain Jimmy Albright, member of Keys Memorial Legion Post, who operates between Key Largo and Key West in the upper Mattecumbe region, is one of the best. He specializes in shallow water bonefish and tarpon fishing, in addition to trolling.

Freshwater trolling is popular in Florida's central and southern lakes, which seem to be weedless. A deep running plug turns the trick.

Georgia boasts 24,000 lakes and ponds. When the fish are deep, anglers use deep-running plugs such as the bomber. Most of them troll with medium running plugs. Some of the outstanding bait used are the trix-o-reno, reefer, Paul Bunyan 66, L. & S. bass masters and the usual assortment of live bait.

This is just a sampling of trolling's possibilities. A boat load of information will cost a three-cent stamp, five minutes of your time and a walk to the post office.

If you want to catch a fish as big as a lie, try trolling.

CHAPTER 7

Underwater Fishing

GOGGLE fishing, skin diving, spear fishing, call it what you will, is the science and the sport of men who go down to the sea in rubber flippers and splash about like giant fish to meet the scaly creatures in their own element—under the surface of the water.

It can be as dangerous as playing footsie with a blood-scented shark, or as pleasant and relaxing as cavorting in the old swimming hole. It all depends upon how you go about it.

Actually, almost any shore will do. To prove it, we took Gustave Dalla Valle, Italian champion diver and founder of the International School of Spear-Fishing at Port-au-Prince, Haiti, out to the cold waters of Great South Bay, Long Island, New York, and dumped him in. He did nobly.

The general technique of underwater fishing seems to have been developed by the Japanese, back in the days when they founded their cultured pearl business. From the Japs, it spread to Europe, as a sport, and now here.

Underwater fishing can be commercially practical—in fact, schools of fishermen operate underwater in the Mediterranean and in the waters around the Philippine Islands, making large catches. But here it's predominantly regarded as a sport, and with the price of fish what it is on the open market, we don't advise anyone to try and compete with the professionals.

Spear fishing is a lot of fun, requires skill and provides plenty of excitement—both in observing the beauties of the deep firsthand, and in outwitting the fish on his own ground. Fighting fish are found in any water, and the colder and murkier it is the greater the sport and the challenge. Goggle fishing doesn't require much equipment—a mask, some rubber swimming fins, a knife and a spear gun. Technique improves a catch, but it's great fun always, and the beauties and mysteries of the ocean deep more than make up for the one that gets away.

Choice of the right gun or spear is the most important task for the beginner. If you're planning a simple venture to begin with, the five-tined spear will be about right for you. It'll do for halibut and most of the medium-sized game fish. If you're going out for heavier game—like the steel-skinned sea bass, groupers and other deep-water types, you'll need the heavier artillery of a .38 caliber spear gun, or one touched off by high tension springs like the slip-pointed spear. The lower section of the spear gun is fitted with a trigger mechanism to release the spear, or harpoon. When it's sprung, the spear at the end of the gun shoots out of the hollow lower section and at your game. The harpoon is retrieved by a length of line attached to the lower section.

Spear guns originated in Italy, where spear fishing is practiced with a passion. An Italian holds the underwater dive record in the sport—125 feet! Many weights are sold on the market, the lighter ones capable of harpooning at tremendous distances. The lightest model will make a land throw of 800 yards. But the spear of such a light gun will generally go right through the resilient body of a five-pound fish. A heavier weight gun—unless you intend to hunt only small game fish—is more practical.

Beginning goggle fishers, after hunting medium-sized fish in the grouper and sea bass class, should choose the jet gun for an attempt at swordfish, yellowtail and the other fast, deep-water fish. It's powered with C12 cartridges. But in general, remember, as in archery, the heavier the gun, the heavier the game you'll get.

A face mask is next on the equipment list. The mask consists of a simple glass circle housed in rubber which fits over the face to improve vision and equalize pressure underwater. It fits over the entire upper part of the head, leaving the mouth free for a full intake of air before diving for the bottom, and is completely air- and water-tight.

At first, eye goggles were worn for underwater spear fishing—hence the name. But, as swimmers advanced into deeper and deeper waters, seeking game, they found that pressure caused the goggles to crush against the eyeballs, causing them to pain and bulge. The face plate or mask was developed and has proved successful in correcting the faults of the goggles.

The snorkel is an improvement on the face mask and is most useful for those fishermen who take a five-foot submersion seated on the ocean bottom, awaiting fish with pronged spear in hand. It's a clever invention that brings oxygen to you underwater by means of a soft rubber mouthpiece, inverted tumbler intake, and exhaust valve.

A good sheathed hunting knife and rubber swim fins complete the necessary equipment. The fins slip over the feet, giving you underwater jet propulsion. You'll need the power, drive and maneuverability they'll give you. Even skilled, fast swimmers find themselves no match for a fish in a dive without them.

There are several techniques for under-water spear fishing. The simplest, of course, is the tined-spear method mentioned, in which you pick a spot in shallow water where the fish go by, seat yourself—either with or without a snorkel—and spear them as you can. The rock-bound coast of Maine is becoming popular among Easterners, and fishermen seek out lobster and other crayfish that hide in crevices in Maine waters, as well as dodging for small game fish from the ocean floor.

Dalla Valle advises one of two other methods for novices. In his school in Haiti he takes a group or "caravan" of fishermen out in waste-deep water, places them face down on inflated rubber inner tubes, and tows them or bids them paddle round till they spot a fish in the clear blue of the tropical water. Spearing from that position, of course, is easy.

Here are the essentials of this method. First, you should practice in shallow water until you get used to breathing with the mask. You'll find it difficult to stay underwater for more than 60 seconds. That means you have to know what you're looking for, travel fast when you see it and be able to get in a thrust within a matter of a few seconds after spotting it. Before your first dive in a mask, practice filling your lungs with air and breathing through your mouth. Water pressure squeezes the air out of your lungs and equalizes pressure in the face plate.

Seek the clearest water possible—providing there are fish in it —and keep it shallow, from five to 15 feet. From a face down swimming position, using either the breast stroke or crawl, and keeping your strokes as quiet as possible so as not to disturb the fish, go after your game. As soon as the prey is sighted, dive deep and strike quickly.

You won't find your catch exciting the first few times at this. Your quarry will be quicker than you are. But take the whole business in stages. Start off by going for the smaller species of the sea.

In southern California they have as much fun and good eating from concentrating on abalone, which is a mollusk said to be tastier than anything in water.

The abalone latch onto rocks and are difficult to pry off. If touched, they clamp down on the rock and are impossible to pry loose. So the trick is to approach with the least splashing and noise possible and pry them off with a quick, easy motion. And don't attach your prying iron to your wrist with anything except rubber. One goggler had his attached to his wrist with a leather thong and an abalone latched on and clamped it to a rock formation. He nearly drowned.

Lobsters are also a neat prize. These you can catch with your hands from their lodgings in crevices and rock formations. Be careful going in after them. Some fishermen have misjudged and dived under such crevices to be caught and held there by a strong current until they drowned.

In goggling you are not limited in varieties of fish. You may run into anything from a bullhead shark to a quitar fish—both weird, nightmarish-looking creatures.

The most common are sheepshead, black sea bass and groupers. Off La Jolla, California, some black sea bass and broomtail and gulf grouper have been taken that exceeded 100 pounds in weight. The coast of southern California and and the Florida Keys are the spots that attract the largest number of spear fishermen after really big game fish. The Keys are the most beautiful of the underwater garden spots, with myriad coral reef formations and rare species of gorgeous tropical fish to seek. Half the popularity of spear fishing is due to the excitement of exploring marine life.

It's wise to have a floating base of operations if you intend working in deep water. Take a rubber raft along, or a boat with extra gear and an extra person aboard to help in case of emergency. If you can, work in pairs. Then, if trouble breaks, you can help one another.

With practice, and the development of a steady sense of timing, you're ready to master the technique of the experts. All the things you learned in living from the surface will stand you in good stead now. After finding a spot you judge good for hunting, fill your lungs with air and dive all the way to the bottom. Stay there and let the fish come to you. They will—out of curiosity. A 25-foot dive at first is safe. As you perfect your technique, you'll find yourself able to go down farther and stay under longer. Dalla Valle has gone down 80 feet. In deeper waters better take the spear gun. It's no fun being attacked by an angry barracuda. Be assured of your kill as much as possible.

Another caution. Don't ever carry your catch on your belt the way you'd carry quail or partridges. One swimmer did once and found himself circled by barracuda. One fish charged him and snapped his game in half with a single bite. The barracuda was only interested in his catch, but it was a little close for comfort.

Trouble can come in the form of your own carelessness or the sting of a sea ray or the bite of a nasty-tempered moray eel. Morays are vicious, six-foot strings of slime, muscle and sharp teeth. They will attack if provoked and have been known to follow gogglers for long distances gnashing their teeth in rage. They seem to love abalone and will attack if alarmed while feeding. Cruising shark are always a hazard but the moray and sting rays seem to personally resent underwater fishermen. There are many species of rays in California and Florida waters. They carry a sharp, poisonous barb in their tail, and when stepped on or annoyed, whip the tail in the same wink-quick motion that the rattlesnake has and bury it in the exposed leg or calf. If you are taken to a hospital immediately after being lanced by a ray it is possible that nothing worse than a sore leg will result. The sting can become dangerous if not properly cared for and in some cases has caused death.

There it is: method, kind of equipment, type of fish available and a brief picture of what you may find while swimming underwater after fish. They say the fun lies in shooting your spear into a big fish, hanging onto your end of the 30-foot line while the fish plunges madly about at his end, attempting to throw the barbed spear and drown you at the same time. The trick is to battle the fish until he is tired or gives up and then tow him to shore or to your floating base of operations.

They say gogglers get together after a long underwater day and tell each other tales of what they have seen in the briny. Lost jewels, valuable equipment, guns, knives, money belts, all kinds of expensive fishing gear have been found in the sea.

So it can be a combination adventure-treasure hunt and, at the same time, aid to science—that goggling expedition of yours. If you're planning a winter vacation in Florida or California, goggling can make your trip exciting and uncover a new world for you. The land under the sea.

The underwater adventures also make important contributions to marine biology and some of their prized specimens are contributed to experts at the Scripps Institution of Oceanography at La Jolla, California. Gogglers have discovered that morays are not the five-foot speciments science thought, but some of them go as long as seven feet. Textbooks say sheepshead weigh as much as 25 pounds. Gogglers have brought them in at over 27.

An organization to promote and protect this relatively new sport has sprung up. It is called the International Underwater Spear Fishing Association and has its headquarters at the Los Angeles County Museum, Exposition Park, Los Angeles, California. For complete details on joining or finding out good spear fishing spots and correct equipment, you might write the president, Ralph N. Davis. The executive board of the association includes Dr. Howard Hill of the museum staff, Dr. Carl Hubbs of the Scripps oceanographic institute, Johnny Weissmuller, and Earl Warren, Jr., with Ralph N. Davis serving as president. This is probably the first time the organization has hit print. It was set up in May, 1950, and has already received pledges of cooperation from France, Spain, Italy, Mexico and Australia.

Here are its four major purposes:

1. To encourage the sport as a recreation and as a potential source of scientific knowledge.

2. To contribute scientific data to institutions and individuals.

3. To maintain standardized rules for the sport.

4. To keep an attested and up-to-date chart of World Record catches for the sport of underwater spear fishing.

Every year spear fishermen or gogglers gather from all over the world at Laguna Beach, California, to enter and enjoy the National Underwater Championships. Nearly every year they are attended by over 5,000 people, with 15 spear fishing clubs entering three-man teams to compete for the coveted silver trophies and awards.

Individual recognition is given by the Spear Fishing Association for record catches, comparable to that given rod and reel enthusiasts. The biggest fish taken in the United States by gogglers or spear fishermen are a 440-pound southern jewfish, a 310-pound black sea bass and a 56-pound white sea bass. Three enormous hunks of fish in any man's language.

If you decide to give goggling a try, you might keep your eye on a membership in the world's most exclusive fishing club, the San Diego Bottom Scratchers Club. So tough are the trials for membership that only nine men have qualified in 15 years.

Here are the simple rules:

You must swim alone through heavy surf, over a reef covered with stiletto-sharp coral which is hidden by white-capped combers. When you reach the designated spot you must dive in 30 feet of water and bring up three abalone with one plunge. Next you go down 20 feet for a spiny lobster, a scissor-handed creature that has been known to grow over three feet. The last feat is a 20-foot dive to capture a shovel-nose shark by the tail and bring him to the surface. This little number you must do twice.

If you want to have some splashing good fun and maybe become a Bottom Scratcher you'd better get started. They're still looking for that tenth member.

CHAPTER 8

On the Ice

U NDER its covering of darkening snow the ice groaned and
the noise, they say, could be heard miles away on the other
side of Candlewood Lake. Most of the iced lake had been swept
clear of snow by the December winds that howled out of the
north and seemed to make a game of skating the white stuff
across the surface of the sleeping lake and onto the land beyond,
forming small geometrically spaced drifts. But this one spot on
the far northern edge of the lake was still crusted with snow and
when the jeep and the three men drove on it the cracking groan
became a scream as the ice splintered and the jeep went down
into deep water.

Two of those ice fishermen died in the water of Lake Candlewood near New Milford, Connecticut, that winter of 1954. The
one who survived said, "I can't understand it. We've driven that
jeep on the ice this time of year for years. What could have
happened?"

Experienced ice fishermen know that when solid ice is made
colder it contracts. This causes the squealing, creaking, cracking noises heard in the early morning or evening hours. But
the great, cracking noise the men in the jeep heard was caused
by the ice actually breaking because of weakness. When snow
has lain on ice for any appreciable length of time, it can make
it unsafe by creating an air-ice condition that forms during
alternate thaws and freezes. This snow the doomed men had
driven across was also discolored. It was later discovered that
the ice had been thin under the dark snow; swirling water had
prevented it from thickening properly.

The story of the jeep fishermen is not used to frighten away
potential ice fishermen, but to point out that ice fishing like
most other sports also has its hazards and requires a certain
amount of know-how.

Fishing in the "water that sleeps" was originated by the In-
dians well over one hundred years ago. The redmen couldn't
trot down to the corner sports store for canned baits and the

newest items in hooks and lines, so they used spears, bows and arrows and a neat little gimmick they dreamed up called a gorge. This was chipped out of stone or bone. Some kind of tempting bait was placed on it and when the fish swallowed it the gorge was constructed in such a way that it turned sideways inside the fish, acting as a gullet hook so that the Indian could then easily pull the fish up through the hole in the ice.

Ice fishing has progressed a long way since the gorge and today the man who trods the slippery stuff goes prepared for a comfortable stay. Fleece lined boots, pants and jackets, heated miniature houses that the initiate call shanties, fancy equipment and beautiful baits that will make even the most lethargic fish jump in delight.

It's difficult to definitely state the number of men and women who are interested in ice fishing. They don't buy a special license, and there is no space on the regular license for them to write in their interests. But it is estimated that the shake-and-shiver brigade checks out at well over a million.

Not long ago the Conservation Departments of New York and Vermont got together and made a count of ice fishermen on a certain blustery January day unfit for any living creature to venture out. On Lake Champlain alone, they counted 1,203 shanties, with 1,941 fishermen hard at work sitting in their chairs, holding their hands over the little oil stoves many of them carry, keeping an eye on their lines as they sipped hot coffee, and solved the world's problems. In 8,010 hours they yanked 33,243 fish up through holes in the ice. Sixty-six per cent were smelt, 30 per cent yellow perch, the balance walleyed pike and herring.

If you are traveling a bleak winter road one day and suddenly see a settlement of small houses appear on the horizon of a familiar lake, houses that hadn't been there the day before yesterday, don't be alarmed. This astounding age of ours still hasn't been able to figure out how to build a village overnight. But the ice fisherman has, and he has slid his castle on the iced lake probably in the dark hours while you were sleeping.

I sat in a friend's ice shanty last winter and marveled at what he had been able to do in a floor space of about six-by-eight. This one was constructed of plywood so that it would be easy to push or pull, and lined with regular asbestos insulation. It was built on runners so that it could be slid to any desired spot on the ice, and it had a trap door in the floor center that could be raised over the target hole in the ice. The roof was slanted not unlike a Cape Cod cottage to prevent snow piling. There was a window on each side and built-in bunks that could be lifted up and hooked out of the way when not in use. Comfortable canvas camp chairs were in use the day I was there. In the center of the room, not more than a few inches from the hole in the ice over which this hut on runners had been pushed, that hole that is the focal point of the entire business, was a Coleman stove of the newest and most effective design.

Around this stove which was serving the double duty of giving heat and simmering a mouth-watering beef stew, were gathered four fishermen, which made for pretty cramped quarters. But as the thermometer hanging on the side wall testified, 10 below zero makes even the most cramped conditions seem snug-as-bug-in-rug rather than over-populated.

Beside the thermometer on the wall hung a calendar (why I can't imagine unless the blonde who wasn't dressed for ice fishing and who sprawled on the leopard rug, kind of cheered up the place), and on neat pegs all across the wall hung fishing gear and extra clothing. On the opposite wall built-in shelves held books, canisters of coffee, sugar and flour. Below this was a small refrigerator chest which held milk and beer at the correct temperature. While they were waiting for the walleyes to bite, these ice fishing friends of mine solved several of the knotty international problems that President Eisenhower and Secretary Dulles hadn't been able to handle.

Probably this camaraderie and the male-manufactured food help make ice fishing what it is. That terrible January day with the wind howling like a mad wolf outside our door, we sat comfortably fishing in the little snow-banked hut, polishing off the beef stew and dunking crisp Italian bread in the gravy, manners that would be frowned on in normal society, and after that was finished we cleaned and panfried three nice walleyes. The ice water from which they had been lifted made their flesh firm and sweet, and popping them into a buttered pan no more than five minutes after they were caught made them taste more delicious than any fish I have ever eaten. Fish, as you know, unlike beef, fowl, and other meats is best eaten soon after it has been lifted from its native water. And winter-caught fish are the best, so good that I can't even begin describing the fine flavor of their flesh.

So maybe ice fishermen aren't so crazy after all. If you are interested in joining the ear-muff clan, in addition to the shanty which can be made from anything, from castoff lumber to spanking new aluminum, you'll need a "spud," or an ice chisel to cut holes, a strainer to clean the chopped ice out of the holes, fish poles and lines—and don't forget the license. Most ice fishermen use poles about ten inches in length made from any kind of wood. One end is notched so that line can be wound, the other end has a hole cut through it for the line to pass through. A sinker about the size of a well-smoked cigarette butt is tied to the end of the line, and, for perch and medium-sized fish, a No. 2 hook on a gut leader is attached. That's basic. Some use the stubby glass, steel, or bamboo trolling rods and inexpensive reels that actually aren't much use except for storing the line and keeping it untangled. A good many of the shanty fishermen just drop ordinary hand-lines in the hole. That's another asset of fishing through the ice: Neither the fish nor your companions are impressed with expensive equipment. Frankly, you can use about anything with a hook, as long as you can get deep enough in the water and have the line weighted so that it can take your baited hook down to the fish.

Bait is important though. In the winter fish slow down with the result that they eat less food, move around with less vigor. A good yardstick is to use what the other successful ice jockies are—anything from doughballs and minnows to fish entrails and worms. Live minnows seem to attract most winter fish, but caddis worms, sawdust worms, the grubs that you find in hardwood when you are splitting it into fireplace lengths, are considered fine fare. Corn borers, and the so-called meal worms also take winter fish.

The "ice fly" made of soft hackles and a lead shot is the best of the artificial lures. Spoons with some flash to them also sometimes turn the trick. But the veteran ice fisherman nearly always swears by the active live minnow. The old timers scoop out a shallow hole in the ice, not cutting through into the water, and it soon fills up with slush, then ice water. Here your live minnows keep bouncy and healthy until you are ready to send them down into deep water to tempt the perch, pike, or lakers you are scheming to outwit.

There are four types of ice fisherman: the tip-uppers, who use a set line attached to some kind of signal which indicates by popping up or falling down when a fish has taken the bait and run with it. There are those worthies who fish out in the wild, blowing open with hook and line; the elite who huddle in huts, probably the smartest and most comfortable of the lot, and the spearfishermen who also sit in dark shanties and attempt to spear fish as they glide under the hole in the ice.

No matter what group you fall into, make certain that you dress warmly enough. Try to use everything fleece-lined, even boots and mittens, and bring along extra gloves or mittens, for they are bound to get soaking wet when you pull fish up through the hole. Handwarmers are handy things to have in your pockets, and dark glasses to reduce the glare of the sun on ice and snow are a must. Boots or shoes that grip the ice will keep the spills at a minimum, although most ice fishermen don't go in for much walking. Your sporting goods stores can furnish ice cleats that will keep you on your feet rather than your posterior.

If the tip-up method appeals, you can either make your own or buy it. They are generally made of a slot of wood which fits across the hole in the ice. On the center of this hunk of wood is the signal, a red flag, a bell or another piece of wood that is jerked erect or falls when the fish makes his grab. Some use three or four tip-up sets to insure a fatter catch.

Unless you are an experienced hand better stick to the conventional methods of fishing with hook and line, and leave the spearfishing to those who like it. It can be fun, but it really isn't fishing in the sense that we know it.

Don't cut a big hole in the ice. Make it of a size so your foot won't go through, and make certain that you skim all of the ice out of it so you won't louse up your leader. If you're after walleyes, I'd recommend a No. 0 hook and at least six inches of wire leader. They're tough fish and can snap ordinary leaders. Always give the fish a chance to really get into the bait before you set the hook.

Rays of light entering the water through ice in the winter trigger fish into different reactions. If the ice is mostly covered with snow, the hole you chop in the frozen stuff will pour light into the dark water underneath and usually bring fish to you. Light always makes fish more food-conscious. But remember, that if the ice is clear and light is penetrating it generally, then the fish will fin toward the darker weed beds and underwater growths. The constant light through the ice makes them wary, and if you chop a hole permitting a larger entry of light, then suddenly stand beside that hole and your shadow falls into the water, the fish will scatter and leave your vicinity. You can fool them sometimes by lying down beside the hole in the ice, covering your head with an extra coat or something to shut out the light, and then actually peering through the water to discover what the underwater conditions are.

But let's face it. Ice fishing is the same old thing. The eternal problem—man trying to outwit the fish. Sometimes he does, and sometimes he doesn't. Go fishing with that philosophy and you'll have fun.

CHAPTER 9

Think Like a Fish

ONE day a few summers ago near Mt. Shasta, California, a warden-pilot, named Al Reese, placed 30 trout in a metal milk can containing three gallons of water. Then he popped in half-grains of sodium amytal per gallon of water and watched, delighted, as the drug dissolved and the trout promptly went to sleep.

A couple of months later two men were wading a trout stream in upper New York State. One carried a bucket, the other had a pack strapped on his back and a paddle resembling a tennis racket in each hand. They would stop suddenly; the man with the paddles would place them in the stream. Shortly after he did this a fish would float to the top of the water, and the man with the bucket would plop it in. The paddles actually were electrodes and the fish, caught between them, would be immobilized by electric shock.

In northern Michigan, three men were recently observed dropping chopped beef liver, a fish food, in a pond. As fish approached the food, two of the men stuck long, slim electric rods in the water shocking them. Although the shock was slight, the fish flinched, spun in the opposite direction. While two of the men continued their underwater torture, the other calmly took notes.

Not far from Hartford, Connecticut, six men were seen stealthily dragging a net through a pond. Some of the netted fish they kept, others were placed back in the water.

In nearly every instance observers reported these actions to the police or local wardens. Although they were breaking the law, none of the men was arrested. To the consternation of the conservation-minded people who made the reports, the warden or policeman arriving on the scene would go into a laudatory routine, actually walk over and congratulate the men for doing the very things that every fish and game syllabus warned against.

Somewhat sheepishly the informers learned that the men fooling with the fish were aquatic biologists doing their jobs—

89

fisheries scientists who had gone to school to learn the ways of the fish for the benefit of the American sportsman.

The man with the milk can in California was conducting an experiment which involved putting fish to sleep so more of them could be transferred to points of release. The drug, sodium amytal, was used because it quieted the trout, permitted at least 50% more fish to be transported in the same amount of water, and no ill effects were suffered once they were released in the streams of their destination.

In New York State the biologists were electrically shocking trout into submission so they could be studied for rate of growth, physical condition, and tagged so when they were caught by fishermen later their life story would be a matter of record.

The cruel men in Michigan teasing the fish with the electric rod were working on a psychological experiment to increase the fish's longevity. It has long been believed that hatchery-reared trout released in native streams are not wary enough to survive for any length of time. Michigan is pioneering in experimenting with this psychological conditioning of trout prior to planting in streams. Working with a Psychological Research Service, the aquatic biologists are using electric shock, underwater feeding, and other stimuli to learn more about the reactions of trout and whether conditioning methods may be employed which result in a higher survival and better physical condition of planted fish.

Those men netting the fish in Connecticut were trying to clear out stunted, "rough" fish, the species sportsmen weren't interested in, so that game fish, bass, crappies, pickerel and their ilk, would have a better chance for survival. They were bringing a balance to the pond, a balance nature was unable to provide.

The majority of America's fishermen, most of the 17,127,896 who bought licenses in 1954, have never heard of the aquatic or fisheries biologist. To them he is just a complicated word. Yet, without him, fishing wouldn't be the greatest participant sport in this country—it would probably be on its way out. The aquatic biologist is one of the big values received for your fishing license dollar.

Lest you think that he is a lucky character who sits in the back of a boat all day with a fishing rod in one hand and a book on the habits of fish in the other, it might be prudent to

give you a picture of what he does and how those actions benefit you.

Consider first that the aquatic biologist usually must have
spent four years in an accredited college, graduate with a
bachelor's degree with a major in zoology and a minor in
chemistry. He usually follows this with a master's degree, with
extra course work in several of the natural sciences and a thesis
on some phase of aquatic biology. Quite often this man who is
going to devote his life to seeing that you have a healthy fish
on the other end of your fishing line will go on for a Ph. D.
degree, with a certain amount of additional work plus a lengthy
thesis—an original contribution to knowledge on some facet of
fisheries biology. Before the aquatic biologist received full time
work in his field, he will have spent from five to nine years in
college.

Generally his vacations are spent in the field, working under
the direction of a professional fisheries man. Since the winter
months are the most critical in the life of a fish, the period
when field observation is most important, the biologist spends
many of his days in the cold and the wet.

Because this fellow with the cinch job must have competence
in both field and laboratory he must take a wider range of
courses than most professional biologists—advanced studies in
physics, chemistry, physiology, parasitology, genetics, and mathematics as well as field courses such as plant and animal ecology,
limnology, geology, and geography. And, since he must constantly deal with you, the public, he must develop skill in
speaking and writing at the popular as well as professional level.

John B. Moyle, research supervisor for the Fisheries Research
Unit of the Department of Conservation of Minnesota, is con-
cise in his concept of the aquatic biologist.

"It appears to me that the most important job of a fisheries
biologist is not thinking like a fish, but thinking for him," he
says. "Man is peculiar among the inhabitants of this planet in
that he can modify the environment to favor himself and co-
incident with such changes often makes the environment un-
suitable for other animals such as fish.

"It is up to all of us to be advocates for the fish. This involves
first of all an understanding of what fish need in the line of
living quarters, food and social relationships. It is our job to
provide as large a fishing harvest as can be taken without injury to the population that provides the fishing. The size of

this harvest is going to vary from water to water, depending upon natural fertility and climate and can be expected to vary somewhat from year to year since the biological system is very complicated and a failure in the food supply at any level is apt to be reflected in future fishing."

In short, if you want the fish to care for you, you must care for him.

You can see there's much more to this fishing business than simply buying a license and dunking a line. For instance, do you know why tackle manufacturers produce lures in practically every color? From fishing experiments conducted by aquatic biologists they know that fish can distinguish colors—quite easily between widely separated colors. Many species between closely related colors.

Recently largemouth black bass were used in an experiment proving definitely that fish can intelligently discern colors. In the beginning it was found that red was the bass' favorite. Every bass used seemed to prefer it. (Fishermen, take note). Tested bass were fed on daphnia (water fleas) and mosquito larvae which were presented to them in opaque eye-droppers— of different colors. The red would contain food; yellow, or another color would not. When the bass approached for food, he got it if the color was right, if it wasn't, he got a slight electric shock. Interchanging of colors conclusively proved that the feeding fish really knew their color spectrum, could remember it for days at a time.

Those fishing stalwarts who clump along the bank of a stream, or clank their oars when rowing a boat, quite oblivious to the noise they are making, evidently aren't aware that fish can hear. They should have spent a short session with the aquatic biologist before sallying forth. It would have meant more fish in the creel. Fish haven't any external ears, but the sounds they detect are picked up through their bodies. In some fish, the air bladder is connected by a series of bones to the ear capsules. Our men who have gone to fish school believe that this acts as a resonant room for vibrations.

In one test a dinner bell was rung every time the fish were fed; another used a telephone instrument placed in a balloon and immersed in water. The scientist produced on his instruments a series of tones beginning with 43 double vibrations per second, and going up through 86,172, doubling the number each time. He found that fish responded to all vibrations from 43 to 2,752.

Other questions that may have bothered you about fish have all been answered by the aquatic biologist. Fish can see above water. Because of tricky light refractions sometimes fish can spot you on the bank of a stream long before you see them. There are tropical fish that rise to the surface of water, squirt a stream at hovering insects, then gobble them as they drop. Fish don't drink water—only that which they take in with their food. The exception to this rule is the salt water varieties. They do drink, because the water in which they live draws out the less salty fluids in their bodies, and they must constantly take in water and excrete the salt through special cells in their gills. Scales are not shed. They grow with the fish, develop rings which can be counted to determine the age. Fish can smell. Their nostrils open into sacs lined with the organs of smell. And fish do talk. Some made sounds by forcing air through their bladders; others gnash their teeth; some vibrate their gills covers against the sides of their heads; others have special muscles which vibrate as they move. Although fish have no eyelids it has been proven that they do sleep. Some even lie on their sides on the bottom, others just remain motionless for long periods of time, many of the so-called schooling fish disperse at night for individual rest then reassemble the following morning. Do fish feel pain? Some, but slight compared to what we know as pain. Lacking a cerebral cortex, the fish hasn't a home for the conscious association of an idea—therefore robs pain of an imagination to work on. One fisherman recently reported that he had caught a fish, hooked it in the eye, and found it necessary to remove the eye with the hook. He then decided that he didn't want the fish and put it back in the stream. Being something of an experimenter, he then decided to use the fish's eye as bait. He dropped it in the water and in a matter of minutes recaught the fish that had lost its eye. It had such slight pain after losing the eye that it almost immediately began grubbing for food. The sense of hunger was far greater than that of pain.

But our aquatic biologist isn't merely a scientist who studies the habits of fish, then expounds on his findings in a learned manner. He's a hip-boot man with mud on his hands.

John Hewston, district fisheries biologist for the North Dakota Fish and Game Department, gives the following report to set you straight on that point and help with a few fishing facts:

"A typical day in my job might be as follows:

"A very early start in the morning in order to get out on a

lake before the fisherman. A creel census is taken of the fisher-men on that lake. From such information, we can determine how long the sportsmen fish each trip, how long it takes to catch each fish, how many fish are caught, what species are caught, which species are most sought after, what type of fish-ing and what tackle is used, the weather conditions, the age groups and sex of the fishermen, where they come from (to determine if a lake is of local importance only, or is popular over a large area). While taking a creel census, a bit of enforce-ment work is carried on at the same time by checking licenses. The person who does not pay his share of the freight, is not entitled to a share in the profits, exclusive of those not required to buy a license.

"After checking all or a fair sample of the fishermen, we would set to work removing a gill-net from the lake being tested. From the catch an idea of the condition of the fish population, the species present, species composition, growth rates, reproduc-tion, can be obtained. Having done this, we sound the lake and make a map of it for future use in water level manipulation, eradication, determining the per cent of the lake in the various depth classifications and such. Then we take water samples at various depths and run them through chemical analysis to deter-mine the amount of dissolved oxygen present—and to find alka-line content. Various species of fish require different amounts of oxygen (minimum requirements) for best growth and condi-tion. Different layers of water hold different amounts of oxygen during winter and summer months. The degrees of hardness or softness of the water will determine the fertility of that water and also the species of fish best suited to it. (This work is car-ried on during winter months, too. That is our critical period as far as oxygen content is concerned in this state. This winter work requires cutting holes in the ice, taking water samples, and getting the bottles of water into one's pocket before they freeze and break. Then getting them into a warmer place of operations quickly.)

"The above jobs usually take up most of a long day, so we head for home. After supper we attend a wildlife club meeting to explain our fisheries program in this state and to answer questions, as well as to listen to gripes, and get acquainted with the people of that area.

"It has been my experience that test-netting in this state would indicate that we always catch more fish in shallow water than we do in deeper water. Aquatic vegetation grows mostly in comparatively shallow water, particularly in muddy waters. Small organisms that live upon the plants and hide among them attract small fish and other things that live upon them. Small fish that feed upon plant matter will also be found here, and the plants also shelter these smaller fish. Therefore, the larger fish that feed upon vegetation and those that feed upon other fish will do their feeding in these shallow areas. Some of them feed actively throughout the day. This list would probably include the minnows, carp, suckers, bullheads, perch, drum. Most of the more desirable sport fish move into these areas to feed at night, and may be caught in the evenings and early mornings. This is particularly true of the large trout and the walleye, in this state. The black bass and northern pike feed more at this time, but may be taken at any time throughout the day.

"Catching fish is much more difficult during the summer months than at any other time. This we believe to be due to the heavy production of food organisms in the lakes in this time of long, warm days. The fish are well-fed at all times and are not fooled as easily as when they have to hunt around a little for a meal, as they do in the other three seasons. Winter fishing here is much more productive in number of fish per hour of effort, than it is in the summer.

"A few years ago the most popular method of fishing here was that of cane pole, bobber, live-bait, still-fishing. It is still nearly the only method used by the older fishermen. However, the casting rod has replaced many of the cane poles for live-bait fishing. Bait casting (or plug casting) is the most widely used artificial lure fishing carried on and is becoming more and more popular for the large northern pike and walleyes. Since these two fish and the black bass are all sight feeders, fishing with artificial lures of any kind is much more productive in clear water. The more turbid the water, the harder it is to catch these fish on artificials. Therefore, if these lures are to be used, those that send out strong vibrations (such as wobbling types or spinners) should be used. Live bait fishing is more productive in muddy waters.

"Fly tackle or spinning tackle is best suited to our new trout fishing, for bass, and for pan fish. Spinning tackle appears to be the most versatile and is used for these fish as well as the northern pike and walleye. Most of the fishing here is done from the bank or still-fishing and casting from boats. Trolling is productive for the huge walleyes and northern when they are out in the deeper water during the daytime.*

"The northern pike is by far the most popular game fish in this state. This is due to its rapid growth and growing to very large sizes, its tremendous appetite (thus it can be caught fairly easy, and by most types of fishing), and its excellent eating qualities.

"Carnivorous fish (large trout, northern, walleye, bass, perch) are most readily caught on lures that resemble other fish, whereas, the bug-eaters (smaller trout and perch, crappies, bluegills) may be caught on flies or nymphs."

Another doctor of the deep waters, A. S. Hazzard of the Pennsylvania Fish Commission, has a scientific observation that may improve your trout fishing:

"Trout are cold water fish," he advises. "They require a certain minimum of oxygen, so the angler will do much better if he keeps his lures or bait in the cold water zone where there is enough air for the fish to breathe. Most trout lakes become depleted of oxygen in midsummer and the surface waters are too warm. Midway between this warm surface and the bottom is a zone of cold, well-oxygenated water, and that is where the trout will be."

In Michigan fishermen are benefiting from the work of this aquatic biologist in the following ways. Most of our states have similar projects designed to improve your fishing.

1. *Prepare bottom contour maps of lakes as a basis for fish management.* Michigan has mapped about 2400 important lakes to date, and copies of the maps are distributed at cost to anglers. These are helpful in determining deep water areas, weed beds, and other shelter for fish and have proven of great assistance to fishermen.

2. *Lake inventory.* Crews of biologists examine lakes, mostly during the summer months, determining fish populations, growth rate, and need for improvement such as addition of brush shelters, trout stocking or introduction of other important game or forage fish.

3. *Stream inventory.* Crews determine conditions in streams and the need for additional shelter, spawning places, food improvement, stocking, etc.

4. *Planting experiments.* Marked planting of trout, walleyes, bass and other species are followed from the hatchery to the

---

*For trolling details see Chapter 6, Try Trolling.

angler's creel to determine the best time to plant, the best size, and the proper numbers to give good results.

5. *Control of aquatic vegetation*. Experiments are now underway to determine how extensive plant growths can be reduced in certain lakes and how plant beds may be developed in others where desirable vegetation is lacking.

6. *Studies of fish pathology*. A trained pathologist is studying hatchery diseases and ailments of natural fish populations and is working out methods for improved disease control and nutrition of hatchery fish. His studies of natural mortalities and disease of fish in nature are of interest to anglers and explain fish mortalities which might otherwise be alarming.

7. *Growth rate studies*. Determining the normal growth rate of the different species, mostly by scale examination, enables us to tell the conditions for fish life in waters which are inventoried. Experiments in stream and lake fertilization or other modifications of the environment to improve the growth naturally follow.

Here are some off-the-cuff findings of the men who go to school to learn to think like fish—findings that will improve your fishing and your knowledge of what makes good fishing.

Fish in the backwaters and whirlpools: The scaly characters lie in wait for food moved about and circulated by them. The mouth of a stream is always the best place to start. This also seems to be the apex of the fish's highway and aquatic traffic is heavier there. If fishing a lake try casting off the long points of land that angle off into the water. The spit of land continues right into the water for some distance and fish will often be found in these places. Remember that fish live in shallow water in spring and autumn; winter and summer they move to deeper water. Nearly every distinct species of fish has its own water temperature—and at that point in the lake or stream is the best place to find them. Check with the aquatic biologist in your state for the answers to the habit patterns of your favorite fish. We are listing as many as we can here but yours may not be among them.

People like a sterile lake with a sandy, weedless bottom. Fish like a fertile lake that supports a weed growth. The tendency is to fill in the marshy margins of a lake although the margins are an important factor in a lake's fish production. The results of any lake rebuilding should be determined in advance. It is useless to expect fish in a lake that we have made unproductive.

When fishing, try the water areas where there is underwater growth and natural food to attract fish. Weedless spinners, wobbling surface lures will usually take fish in these waters.

Sometimes fishing mysteriously becomes poor in a pond or lake. Years of study by biologists have shown that the three most common causes for this condition are: (1) over-abundance of one or more species of pan or game fishes; (2) siltation which destroys fisheries habitat; and (3) effect of the presence of large populations of less popular species of food fishes, such as carp and buffalo.

If your pet lake used to produce fish and now seems barren, check with your state Conservation Department in the capital city. They'll see that it produces again.

Ever since the 14th Century and Izaak Walton's time, fishermen have been plagued with a passel of problems. Does a full moon improve fishing? Do the rise and fall of tides, phases of the moon, and changes in weather affect a fisherman's luck? Are fishing calendars, tables, barometers and thermometers helpful?

Edwin L. Cooper, sage among the aquatic biologists in Michigan, sums up the scientific attitude on these questions:

"There are many factors that influence the quality of fishing, and it has not been possible as yet to obtain information on many of them. It is obvious that atmospheric pressure changes and lunar periods are perhaps the least in importance of any that we have studied. Since most game fishing is a highly individualized sport, the psychological attitude of the angler is an important consideration. Consequently anything that gives the angler more confidence in his own ability to catch fish very probably actually increases his fishing success. If you want to catch fish, there is no substitute for "know-how" and that includes much information which the fisherman is loath to divulge. It is perhaps in this field of black magic that the fishery biologist has no right to explore for fear of being labeled a meddler or spoilsport. The best time to go fishing apparently is when you have the opportunity."*

But regardless of Mr. Cooper's intelligent comments we were able to cage some black magic jottings from the notebooks of those savvy guys who go to school to learn to think like fish.

Here, for your memory book, are some character sketches of America's popular fish—how they live, what they like to eat,

---

*To increase your fishing confidence read Chapter 2, Everybody's Fish.

their favorite lounging spots.

Lake Trout

A lover of deep-water lakes; seldom found in water less than
40 feet in depth, the laker thrives in water temperature that
doesn't go above 65 degrees F, prefers it chilled down to 40
degrees. Noise doesn't seem to bother him. He is often found in
lakes which are heavily surfaced with active motor boats. Gadget-
happy, he will strike a flashing silver spoon if it goes deep
enough in the water to attract his attention. During warm
months he lives only in the deeper water of lakes and can only
be reached with heavy trolling methods. In early spring he
frolics around reefs, ledges or rocky shoreline where the water
may be only 8 to 10 feet deep. Fond of his brethren, whitefish,
herring, smelts and minnows of all kinds, he chaws them with
teeth located on the roof of his mouth and attacks viciously
if the object such as flashing spinner or hooked minnow is moving vigorously. A stay-out-late, he is a night-feeder and takes
happily to midnight snacks.

Brook Trout

Endowed with a good appetite the brookie likes flies and insects in season, worms appeal as an appetizer just about anytime and as the trout grows larger he will take to the table
smaller fish of many kinds, crawfish, sometimes even the mol-
lusks. If he finds his way into streams where the water goes
much above 70 degrees, he becomes sullen and lazy, loses his
appetite. He prefers swift creeks and streams, sometimes can be
found in the trickle of a brook. In the morning hours he appears
for meals in the mouths of streams and in riffles. Learning that
an obstruction in a current, such as a rock, affords an excellent
place to hide and lay in wait for a meal, he is often found in
places like this when the sun is overhead. Later he takes to
congregating in pools and collecting insects and other winged
things that gather on the surface. Sensitive to noise, he will dart
away if startled by loud bankside noises or overhead commotion.

Rainbow Trout

A pugnacious no-good, never settling down to one home, he
wanders from lake to stream, sometimes even gypsying into the
ocean, changing into a Steelhead. Zig-zag rows of teeth on the
roof of his mouth, the strength and ability to leap well out of
the water trying to shake a hook or snag a meal, make the rainbow a tough customer. Although he takes to lakes easily enough,
he really prefers swift-flowing streams and cold water, but

warmth doesn't bother him. In streams he is nearly always found in rough water, at the perimeter of strong currents and at the apex of boiling rapids. A meat-and-potato man, the rainbow likes any of the smaller fishes providing they are lively members of their breed; big flies, catawba worms of the juicy variety. It is rare when a rainbow turns down a salmon egg, his filet mignon. To him a salmon egg, even tied to a hook and gently floated down a stream with the fisherman's line clearly visible, is hard to resist. When he moves into the water of lakes, the rainbow feeds deep-down, almost exclusively on small blueback salmon who have somehow made it through the egg stage. Your time is his time: he will eat when he can get it.

Largemouth Bass

Terror of pond, lake or stream, the largemouth prefers rather still even warm water. He begins his reign from the moment the water begins to warm up in the spring until late fall. He will strike at practically anything that moves on the surface of the water and has been known to pull ducklings under and swallow them whole. Early morning or dusk is his breakfast and dinner time, but he can be prodded into striking at a smartly moving lure as a between-times snack. He likes frogs, crawfish, field mice, even snakes, and lies stealthily in wait for his food near underwater weed beds, under a lily pad, or any section where there is underwater growth. The aquatic growth attracts smaller fish who come in to feed, and the largemouth in turn feeds on them. He will leap well out of the water after food, and will fight like a bulldog when hooked or out after a meal that decides to defend itself.

Smallmouth Bass

Choosier than his largemouth cousin, the smallmouth will not eat anything that swims, walks or flies, but concentrates on small minnows of bright hues, crayfish, hellgrammites, large worms known as nightcrawlers, and some of the bigger insects. Red seems to be his favorite color and he can be tempted to strike at a small, fast-moving red plug or spinner when other lures fail. Tested by aquatic biologists over a long period, it was definitely proven that he had an affinity for red, sometimes even attempting to eat a piece of red flannel. He prefers rivers and streams to ponds and lakes, and likes his water cold. He can lick his weight in anything that moves and is a better fighter than his glutton cousin. He likes to eat in the postdawn, mid-

afternoon and dusk. Large rocks, almost submerged, are good
spots to meet him. He can also be found fanning his fins at the
tail end of a pool, a rapid, or a riffle, waiting for a meal to
drift. If he strikes your lure or fly, you'll know it's a smallmouth
bass by the elbow jar.

Muskellunge

A conscienceless character, the muskellunge's (largest member
of the pike family) favorite food seems to be his own kind.
Smaller pike and pickerel, next come perch, suckers, any kind
of minnow with a fin; then if he is hungry enough, just about
anything that moves: squirrels, snakes, rats, mice, frogs—and if
you're a small man don't swim in muskellunge water. He'll
tackle just about anything with a wiggle. He's a lone ranger,
keeps to himself, and, like a traffic cop, is fond of waiting in
hidden places for his victim. Fickle, he sometimes will not touch
any food at all, will catch it, mouth it, then release it. Often
he will take the food into his mouth, hold it for a long while
before swallowing. Thus, if you are after Mr. Musky, let a little
time elapse after the first strike before you set the hook. Catlike,
he seems to delight in stalking his prey, even to enjoy the competitive game of fishing almost as much as man. Large, sometimes tipping the scales at 75 pounds, he likes big water—large
rivers or lakes. A weed bed, edges of sand bars and channels,
underwater growth and reefs are likely spots. The best time
to go for him is when he is hungry. And no one seems to know
just when that is. Whenever the spirit strikes. But early morning and dusk when other creatures are abroad scrabbling for
food seems the best fishing time. Daybreak is the time most
record catches have been made on this clever, unpredictable
fish.

Northern Pike

Smaller than the muskellunge, found all over the world, the
northern is much like the bigger fish in eating habits—hungrier
if anything. It is said that he consumes one-fifth of his own
weight in food daily. Smaller species of food the musky likes,
is also his dish. Where the musky takes a squirrel, the northern
likes a small, juicy mouse or immature frog. He's fond of hanging around sunken logs and underwater obstructions. He's also
a pouncer and can be depended upon to leap at anything moving near him. He also keeps his own company, but there is
nothing fickle about his eating habits. Anytime, morning, noon

or night, if approached with the right combination (fast-moving plug, feathered lure, spinner, minnow, imitation frog) he's likely to decide it's mealtime. He's mean-tempered, seems to hate anything and everything in his underwater world. Daybreak is his favorite feeding time.

Walleye

Large eyes with a glassy cast give this favorite of yours his name. A liking for lakes, rivers and streams, places him high on your hook parade. A gregarious, happy-go-lucky sort of guy, he likes to get together with his own kind. Walleye can be found in schools in deep water to feed. He likes flats and sandbars, takes kindly to silver-hued minnows, large insects, crustaceans, even worms. As with other members of his clan, he likes his meals lively, served up about midevening, from 7 o'clock on. He will sometimes take food in the daytime, if you get it deep to him and make it attractive. In streams he sticks to deep bends and twists, in small pools beneath falls and water drop-offs.

Chain Pickerel

Largest member of the pickerel menage, smallest of the pikes, the chain pickerel, is a tricky character who grabs his living meal with his small canine teeth at the middle of the body, crippling it, then rapidly turning and swallowing it head first. He favors small pickerel, has even been known to feast on members of his immediate family. He likes good protection in the ponds, rivers or lakes which he inhabits, underwater growths, sunken stumps, old boats that have gone to the bottom. He doesn't go for fast water, likes it quiet. You'll never catch him hanging around riffles or rapids. The long, flat, silent stretch of water is his meat, and usually where he finds it. Small frogs, anything that seems to be vigorously alive, smaller and slower than he is his dish. He'll eat anytime he is hungry, which is all the time.

Atlantic Salmon

Versatile, much respected, the Atlantic salmon is really four fish: The young guy called a parr likes larvae and all kinds of insects in season; the high-school type, the smolt, prefers minnows, sand fleas, shrimp and tiny crabs; grilse, fish which have not quite matured, and the grownups like all the crustaceans, smelt, herring and minnows—especially while they are at sea. Tagged with the fancy, "anadromous" handle, which simply means that he has two homes: salt water and fresh, the Atlantic salmon is found in streams during his spring migration. He moves in from the sea to spawn, traveling clear, fast streams, to reach his spawning grounds. While he is making this trek is the time to tempt him with hook and bait. He doesn't eat food at this time, but strikes in a fast, reflex motion. Look for him only in clear, fast-moving streams, the far end of deep pools, the spray-edge of eddies, near big rocks that break the current. An unweighted fly drifted slowly on top of the water takes the Atlantic salmon better than any other lure.

King or Chinook Salmon

Largest of the Pacific salmon, the king, also migrates to sea. But before he takes off for salt water he's a game fighter, laps up with pleasure flies, practically any lively insect, all the worms that wiggle. At this stage he eats all the time. He's small though and doesn't reach any size until he gets into the ocean. Once there he develops a liking for anchovies, small squid, shrimp, herring, minnows of all kinds. From a peaceful sort of fellow he converts into a killer and preys on most fish smaller than himself. Fishermen like him best at the early stage in fresh water, or the migrating stage when he moves from ocean to stream to get to his spawning grounds, lays eggs, and dies. Although he goes on a diet when entering tidewater, he'll strike a moving lure or take a natural bait into his mouth—but won't swallow it. He has gained plenty of strength in the sea, puts up a big battle once he's grabbed your bait. He'll strike anytime you annoy him or make it tempting enough—morning, noon or night.

Shad

The biologists say he's a salt water fish, but the fisherman knows him as a river scrapper. He moves to fresh water to spawn; no one knows anything about him at sea and although he also goes on a diet when he moves up rivers toward the nursery, he has been striking at and feeding on objects such as other small fish, minnows, all kinds of insects and larvae for so long at sea, that a rapidly-moving lure placed in front of him at practically anytime will cause him to strike. Hooked, he makes a businesslike fight of it. When the water begins to warm up to about 60 degrees in the spring is the time to take out for shad—when the dogwood blossoms. Anytime of day will do. Make certain by asking the natives that it is shad river and you're in business.

Catfish

With more relatives than Gracie Allen, some 1,000, the catfish comes in all sizes and in several colors, but basically he's one fish. He likes mud-bottomed, slow-streamed rivers, quiet ponds and lakes. He's a scavenger, likes anything at all to eat, the more age to it the better. Anything that moves (or even most things that can't) of a size that will fit into his mouth is his meat. Because of his kingsized appetite, he will feed during the day but he really prefers meals after the sun goes down. During the day he hangs out in deeper water, but as soon as the moon comes out he fins into shallow water close to shore. Homemade gooey doughballs, pieces of salt pork, any meat that has a rancid touch, even the usual minnows, worms, crawfish, and other natural fishing baits tempt him. He's a good natured slob and others of his kind are usually with him.

Crappie

Largest of the panfish, both black and white in color, also called calico bass the crappie probably gives more people fun than any other fish. His favorite food above all else is the scrappy, inch-long minnow. He'll also munch the fish's staff of life: worms and varied insects and crawfish. Small flashing spinners, reeled to imitate a wounded minnow will excite him no end. He's a school fish which means if you find one there are bound to be others nearby. Some fishermen catch him, tie an inflated balloon or a cork to his jaw, release him, then row the boat to where the signal floats, knowing that he has rejoined his pals. He likes lakes above all, spends most of his time close to shore, or near growth like water lilies. But sometimes he breaks habit and will school out toward the middle of the lake. He doesn't seem to have any particular feeding time, has no respect for fishing skill (being caught in great numbers by young anglers without know-how) and is all things to all people.

Perch

There are other perch, but the popular one is the yellow or ringed. He's all over the place and is generally considered to be the first fish to be caught by fishermen everywhere. He's a lake fish, but can also be found in the slower rivers and streams. Has firm liking for quiet water, deep holes. Many of his kind often school in 25 feet of water. His spirit is good; he fights lustily when hooked. He likes morning meals best, prefers small minnows, worms and grubs, but will strike a fast lure if it is running deep. Like the lake and brook trout he will also take to the flash of silver from a spinner late at night.

Bluegill

Bluegill is a happy fellow who delights in crickets, grasshoppers, worms, flies, small worms and wiggling insect life of all kinds. He's a sunfish, but a scrappy one who grows to more than 2 pounds. Also a schooling fish he likes plenty of company and the competitive spirit when on the grub for food. Rivers, streams, lakes, all are home, but like the crappie, he would prefer a lake if the choice were up to him. Favorite lounging and lunching spots: deep holes, around docks, bridges, stumps, dead underwater vegetation, weed beds. He likes something nearby he can dart into or behind. He really prefers feeding in the morning and evening, but being inclined to overeat he can be tempted at other times. He is somewhat allergic to noises, and fins it out of there quickly if he thinks things aren't just right.

Bluefish

He can be found in Florida most of the year, and in the eastern and western Atlantic from spring straight through until fall. Small blues called "snappers" can be caught from docks, in inlets in the fall. But the big blue is caught in the ocean or bay while chasing his favorite food: menhaden. He is a school fish, likes to move after the tiny menhaden which also travels in school formation, snapping them voraciously with his sharp, barracuda-like teeth, until pieces of the fish rise to the surface of the water. There seagulls pounce on the torn menhaden, eating what the blue doesn't surface and gulp. From May to September on Long Island Sound and all along the coast, you can spot the feeding schools of blues by the screaming, diving, flocks of gulls that follow as long as the blue is feeding. Said to be one of the strongest and gamest fish, pound for pound, that swims in the ocean, the blue puts up a mighty battle when hooked by trolling on a turkey bone rig, a feathered jig, or jigged for with your line heavily weighted with large sinker and flashing metal jig, resembling a menhaden, as close to the bottom as you can get. The blue has been known to take worms, squid, and crustaceans, but his great favorite is the menhaden. When the menhaden are on the move is the time to fish for blues, other than that there is no set rule of thumb for this vagabond.

Bonefish

He is sometimes called "Quail of the Sea," because he often feeds in shallow water with tail up, and seems to be able to detect the sight and sound of fishermen from some distance. When he does, he "flushes" fast. He must be approached with caution and tempted with food he likes: crabs, sand fleas, worms. He feeds on the bottom, likes to have his meals in shallow water on an incoming tide. Mud flats, inlets and sand bars are also favorite eating spots. Fly rod and spinning gear, with the usual techniques, spinners, flies, feathered lures will often take him. Sometimes he travels in small schools, but the larger he grows the more independent he becomes, finally deciding to keep his own company. Early morning and late afternoon are the best times. Keep your voice down, all noise at a minimum, if you want to take this sensitive fish.

Striped Bass

He spawns in rivers, flees to them when it gets cold, but he's a salt water fish and can be caught as such along the Atlantic from May until late fall. He has been transplanted in the San Francisco area and is caught there usually in the spring. He's a lusty fish, eating and fighting, and likes all the crustaceans: small lobsters, shrimps, crabs, wood lice, water fleas, barnacles. He also moves in schools, grows as heavy as 70 pounds. He prefers to feed at night, from sundown on is the best time, although he often can be caught just after daybreak. He can be tempted to strike by trolling, using an eel skin, trolling fast, and jerking the rod to give the eel skin the "wounded" motion. Feathered jigs with long strips of pork rind, and Barracuda jigs also attract him. Casting from the surf use a top-water plug such as a popper, atom or mullet; metal jigs tipped with feather, or the weighted eel skin are also good. He is an inshore fish, likes to work behind the first breaker of the surf, on rocky or sandy shorelines; at low tide bay channels are good places. Sometimes he feeds near the bottom, others he is near the top hunting for food. Gulls also tip off a school of stripers that is driving smaller fish to the surface by feeding on them. The striper is everybody's game fish. He can be caught from a rowboat, from a dock or a bridge, from the surf, or from a fancy-rigged, special trolling job. He is the poor man's tarpon and as game a fish as swims in the sea.

Book II

THE FIELD

"I saw old Autumn in the misty morn stand
shadowless like silence . . ."

Thomas Hood

CHAPTER 10

Duck Dementia

WHEN it gets around the middle of November, the Dolan brothers of Guilford, Connecticut, get kind of a glaze in their usually bright Irish eyes, and the word goes around that the craze is upon them again. They forget their families, don't do justice to their large commercial fishing business, and stand around staring at the sky and praying for bad weather.

Some people in Guilford, an Ethan Allen picture postcard sort of a town, lying on the Connecticut side of Long Island Sound, believe that Joe and Frank Dolan actually do go off their rocker at this time of year. If true, there are hundreds of thousands of Americans in the same sad condition.

The Dolans are avid and fanatic duck hunters. They have been ducking on the Connecticut coast for over thirty years, and know the habits of most kinds of wild fowl better than the average American knows what is in his wardrobe.

Last year the Dolan brothers proved to me that the supposedly wary black ducks, *anas rubripes,* are really boobs if you catch them with their knowledge down. Most hunters speak of the black duck in hushed, reverent tones, and without exception say that this bird is the wisest and most intelligent of all the feathered clan.

The Dolans don't agree. They know when and where the blacks come in for feeding on mussel beds, and have proved to me that the black duck's belly is his weakest point. I have sat upright on a sea wall and watched blacks come within fifteen feet of me, oblivious of everything except the mussel beds. And some of the old respect I had for them began to dribble away.

I have also crouched on a small rocky island with the Dolans, and stared in disbelief as four or five thousand broadbills would settle in to the clever Dolan decoy stools.

Duck hunting is like that. It's a sport that sweeps away little knowledges and beliefs that have been built up over a long period of years. Duckers like the Dolans are rare, and you're

109

indeed lucky if you can catch a ride on their boat *THE WILD DUCK* on a bleak and cold November or December morning. They take two parties a day for the short season and are usually booked up three years ahead. They are duck guides for fun not for hire. The fees they charge scarcely cover boat costs for the day.

Last year evidences began to show that ducks were on the increase. From Currituck and Pamlico Sounds in the South to the prairies of Saskatchewan, Manitoba and Alberta, wildfowlers sent back enthusiastic reports that the day of duck shooting is still with us.

There are those who argue that duck shooting is the fastest and most difficult, thus the most interesting of all game shooting. Others put dove shooting on the same level. It is a fact that the duck is a speedy, tough bird and you really have to be "on 'em" to bring them down. A few stray pellets from your shotgun shell string won't knock a duck in the water. Their feather construction is such and their speed so extreme that a direct hit is necessary to make them stay down.

On the debit or discouraging side of duck shooting is the arising at 5:00 a.m., and sitting in pouring rain, or cold and windy weather. But most duck shooters don't seem to mind this. The sight of a black, a mallard, or pintail pitching into a well-set decoy, swinging your shotgun in exactly the prescribed lead arc, and following through on the swing, then staring in disbelief as the duck flares and flies on unscathed, makes duck shooting fascinating and never dull.

One of the most important steps is the selection of a good guide, a man who knows ducks and their habitat. Men like the Dolans. It is also intelligent to hunt ducks with a retriever, a Labrador, Chesapeake or Golden. Quite often your guide will take you to your blind or even small rocky island, stool the decoys, then row away and leave you for a couple of hours. During this time you may have shot at several ducks, killed a couple and wounded one or two. If you had a retriever, the cripples wouldn't get away before your guide gets back. Thus, using a dog is humane and makes good conservation sense.

A few facts on decoys may help. Set the decoys (providing you don't have a guide to do it for you) so the ducks can get to them easily, by flying slowly upwind. Ducks are smart. They'll move into decoys this way because it gives them a better chance to wheel to the right or left, and swing downwind. A little trick some wild-fowlers use is the placing of two outsize decoys at the head of the string or set, a space away from the main body. These are called tollers or teasers. Ducks can see these for some distance, are reassured by the appearance of the teasers and cup their wings, ready to plane in and sit down.

The size of your decoy set or stool depends almost entirely upon the type of duck you're hunting. If you're after canvasback, broadbill, or redhead, it is wise to have a large decoy setting, flocked close together. These species of duck usually travel in large groups and feed in rather tight groups. Mallards, blacks, pintails, teal can be decoyed with anything from a pair up to a dozen. Except in bad storms, these ducks feed in smaller numbers. About the only duck you can call in is the mallard. Some geese can be brought in by calling, but the smartest way to bring duck or geese within gunshot is with a well-placed decoy set.

Diving ducks should be decoyed in at least five feet of water. This type of duck can be listed in three groups: (1) sea ducks: scotters, coots, eiders; (2) bay ducks: canvasbacks, redheads, ruddy ducks, scaup, goldeneye, buffleheads; (3) the fish-eating sheldrakes or mergansers. Although most of these ducks feed on small shellfish, crab life, and some water grasses from the bottoms, one of them, the canvasback, is considered the choicest of all ducks. Some wild-life specialists claim that the canvasback feeds almost exclusively on wild-celery buds and claim this is why the canvasback is such a superior table bird.

Shallow-water ducks on the whole are better as table fare. The mallard, the black, cinnamon, green- and blue-winged teals, and the beautiful wood duck should be decoyed in water one inch to two feet in depth. Of these the mallard leads as the tastiest. For our money he is the best of all ducks.

Geese don't seem to have the brains that the duck has. They will decoy to almost anything: hunks of mud, pieces of white paper. Sometimes profile decoys are made by roughly cutting the shape of a goose from cardboard. These are placed so that the sun strikes them and throws a shadow which attracts the geese. They are also known as shadow decoys. The Canada goose, Blue, White America, Snow, White-Fronted or Specklebelly are the favorite species of geese. Geese may be a little slower in the air (and some think dumber), but they are tough babies and carry a lot of lead.

We've seen a goose expert shoot three times at a Canada, not over thirty yards away, and watched the goose sail grandly away to freedom. It is very difficult not to get overconfident on the big fellows. They look as large as a house and you forget all about lead and the speed of their wings—and shoot behind.

Always remember that a duck or a goose can spot movement miles away. So sit tight in that blind. When they cup their wings and start in toward your decoys, don't stand up and start blasting. If you want to get ducks, wait quietly until they are pitching in. Then as their wings do a buzzsaw motion, just before they sit down among the decoys, blast away. This is a tough rule to follow. It takes years of experience to harden yourself to watch and wait while they come buzzing in. Six out of ten shooters will leap to their feet when the ducks are about fifty yards off. The sudden motion flares the ducks. And when they are flaring and wheeling for a getaway, they are the world's toughest targets.

Don't feel that you are good enough to hunt ducks with a .410 or 20-gauge shotgun. Even if you are an expert shot, it is brainier to stick to the reliable 12. The 12-gauge shell has more powder, more shot. Use either size 6 or 4. Six is the better all-around shot. But on windy, rainy days the 4 is superior. It has a tighter, heavier pattern. The pump, over and under, side-by-side are all good. But the three-shot automatic is fast gaining high favor with wild-fowlers.

Most of the arms companies now put out a magnum shell with Winchester leading the way, that contains more powder and lead—a shell designed especially for duck shooting, for fewer cripples. If you can't think of the word magnum, just ask your sports dealer for that new duck load that is supposed to do away with misses and messy shooting.

One of the props the Dolans have on their boat THE WILD DUCK that never fails to start a conversation, is an old Winchester 12 gauge, mottled with rust, looking as if it had lain out in the wind and the storm of the Atlantic for years. One of the neatly, Abercrombie-and-Fitch-attired sportsmen never fails to ask, "What's *that*? Part of a sump pump?" as he unsheaths his own Browning over-and-under or gleaming Winchester side-by-side. Joe Dolan usually grins and remarks that he also has brought along a license and would like to point the sump pump at a bird or two just for the heck of it. Frank usually says, "Man, that's a shootin' iron. We don't pamper guns 'round here."

The first time I fell into the trap was a late November morning in 1949. Gordon Carroll and I sat in the stern bundled to the teeth, talking to Frank when I made the classic observation about the rusty old gun. Hours later, when we were trying to fill out our limit before sundown and a cold wind was beginning to come up, making the pointing and swinging of a gun a bit of a chore, three broadbills decided to wing into our decoy set. We had agreed that Joe Dolan should take the next birds that dropped in. At forty yards Joe started swinging the rusty old pump, and with three shots laid the three birds in the water as if they had dropped of a sudden mysterious disease. From that day I've had a great respect for *any* gun in the hands of Joseph Dolan. He never wastes a shot and has such an easy, natural follow-through, the whole thing looks pie easy.

"The gun's rusty," Joe said after the last shot, "because of the salt water spraying on it for years, but the bore's clean. We don't bring along fancy guns for duck shooting, the salt water makes 'em mighty unsightly in no time."

A lesson learned. Don't pack your best gun into a duck blind. If you can, make one of your guns your "ducker" and keep it for that purpose, for no matter what part of the world you decide to shoot ducks in, you'll find that it will always be either on or near salt water or water of some kind and you will be banging the barrel on the rocks of small islands on the gunnels of boats, always giving the gun a bad time. It's something that just can't be helped.

The Dolans had some other advice they passed out that gray November day as we sat munching cold roast beef sandwiches and holding cups of hot coffee. Joe Dolan, who can almost fly like a duck, did the talking:

"Never shoot blindly at the flock. Select ONE bird. Swing on his line of flight, and as it passes in front of him squeeze the trigger. Swing as you fire—don't jerk to a halt and shoot. How far in front of him depends on the speed of the bird, the direction of flight, and how fast you swing. You learn this only by experience. At 30 yards, if you are a fast swinger maybe 3 feet is enough. If you swing slowly, 10 feet may not be sufficient.

"Decide whether the ducks are winging in to settle with your decoys or taking elevation to pass over your blind. If they drop altitude, draw a bead just a few inches below the leader. If they've seen you and have started climbing, then take them high by at least three bird lengths.

"When the duck is going away from you, the collision point is somewhere ahead of the leader, but it depends on how fast you've tracked them, how far they are, and how fast they're traveling. Shoot low. Swing on line of flight and fire about four bird lengths, slightly under the leader—while your gun is swinging. Follow-through is all important in duck shooting.

"It's unnatural to make an over head shot. Swing on their line of flight and get out ahead plenty far—9 bird lengths, more at 40 yards. Your shot column strings out quite a ways, and if you can plant it ahead so they'll fly into it, you'll get hits. Keep both eyes open in this kind of shooting.

"You'll have to learn how to calculate distances, both horizontal and vertical. If your duck is quartering left, moving away from you at a diagonal, he's covering more ground than it seems because your sight line is 'foreshortened.' Make this one a long lead, a shotgun barrel at least. It's better to err on the long side than the short. The short side is a sure miss while the long side still gives you a trailing shot cone that he can fly into. Try leading 8 bird lengths at 35 yards.

"In all bird shooting remember to swing your gun on his flight line and keep swinging as you pull the trigger. At least 95 percent of the misses on ducks is caused by the shooter stopping his gun (or slowing it down) at the time he pulled the trigger. Guessing the right lead comes with experience but even the right lead doesn't help if you stop the gun as you shoot.

"As a good wild-fowler, make every shot count, but above all, recover everything that drops. It's wrong to cripple ducks and then not make an attempt to recover them."

Thank you, Joe Dolan.

Below are some estimated speeds and leads that may help fill out your game bag.

TYPE	FLIGHT SPEEDS— feet per second	AVERAGE SPEED— feet per second	PRACTICAL LEAD— at 40 yards
Teal	75 to 95	85	5 to 6 feet
Canvasback	90 to 100	95	6 to 7 feet
Canada Goose	80 to 90	85	5 to 6 feet
Brant	80 to 90	85	5 to 6 feet
Mallard	50 to 90	70	4 to 5 feet
Spoonbill	50 to 90	70	4 to 5 feet
Pintail	60 to 90	75	5 feet
Widgeon	70 to 85	77	5 feet
Redhead	80 to 90	85	5 to 6 feet

Although duck hunting is always pleasantly adventurous, it can also be dangerous as all worthwhile adventures sometimes prove to be. Two duck safaris that I took in the past few years point up one lesson: always go out with an experienced guide, a man who knows the terrain you are hunting, is adept at handling boats, knows how to stool decoys, rewind them and pack them in the boat.

About five years ago Gordon Carroll and I went out after broadbills with the Dolans. As usual we started off in *THE WILD DUCK* about 4:00 a.m. from the dock at Guilford, Connecticut. It was a cold December morning with a fine rain falling and the wind blowing it around in great, driving sheets. Frank Dolan, still sleepy, said, "Perfect duck weather." When he is wide awake, Frank never uses cliches. He has a clever Irish tongue. But he was right. We shot well all day, got our limit and Frank and Joe expertly scooped up the 100 decoys in their small motor boat, threw them in *THE WILD DUCK* where Gordon and I hunkered down and, with numbed hands, helped rewind the weighted cords around the wooden bodies as we started back to Guilford. Darkness was coming in on us fast, and Joe Dolan had just got the motors on *THE WILD DUCK* revved up and moved us out of the little cove, skillfully maneuvering around the tiny rocky islands that seem to be a natural part of the landscape in that part of Long Island Sound, when it became completely dark. It was one of the blackest December nights I have ever seen, and the rain started again, this time coming down hard, pelting us like hail as we stood on the open deck watching the dim lights on the far shore glow and fade like fireflies in a mist. The only dry thing on the boat was Joe Dolan's classic wit.

I guess we had moved two hundred yards from our shooting cove when something went wrong with the electrical system and the running lights and the big searchlight *THE WILD DUCK* carried to hunt out the tricky channels and juts of rock, blanked out. Frank climbed up on the roof of the cabin, and Joe, the rain masking the window of the pilot house, cut the motor down and squinted into the dark night and we started a slow, inching, crawling trip for homedock.

Soaking wet, cold, trembling a little both from cold and the harrowing experience of moving slowly along the invisible but rock-laced shore of Long Island Sound, Gordon Carroll and I stood silently on the open deck, the rain walloping us in

the face, peering into the darkness trying to help Frank and
Joe spot the dangers in our watery path. Silently, we looked
at each other, but the look said loudly, "We're in the hands
of the Dolans. Let us pray to God that they know the Sound
well enough to navigate it blindfolded!" For that was exactly
what they were doing.

Two hours that seemed like ten years later, we hoved quietly
into harbor and tied up at the dock at Guilford. We had gone
duck hunting with two experienced boatmen, two intelligent
men who knew their trade, knew the waters of the Sound
like you know the wrinkles on the palm of your hand. We
were alive because of that.

I'm not suggesting that I wasn't a little weak-kneed when
we clambered out of *THE WILD DUCK,* but I got out with
respect. Gordon Carroll and I, and my wife Mary Lou who
also is my frequent duck hunting companion, have never lost
that high respect for the dexterous, ducking Dolan brothers.
They are men of merit.

The next ducking adventure started off with a telephone
call from a friend, a colonel in the Army who was then stationed
in Maryland. He invited us for a weekend of duck shooting
on Chesapeake Bay.

With the usual duck shooting protocol we started off in the
predawn hours the day after our arrival. Our friend had
arranged for us to shoot with a young lieutenant we'll call Art.
We drove to the shore to get our small rowboat, then Mary
Lou, Art and I lugged about fifty decoys out of the car and
transferred them to the boat. Our blind was one mile away,
surrounded by water, the Bay before us, a small inlet behind us.
We rowed to the blind, got Mary Lou set, then Art and I
stooled the decoys in a large bunch, with two teasers or tollers
about ten yards farther out than the main group, the usual
procedure when hunting bay ducks or mallards.

Art didn't seem to know much about putting out the decoys
and I am no expert, so it took about twice as long as it should
have. It was late November and cold. After we got in the blind,
Art said, "You two do the shooting. I'll peel an eye for birds."

It began raining and blowing, but the ducks detoured our
decoys. After we had sat in the rain for two hours, one lone
mallard winged over the farthest teaser, and Mary Lou made
a fast 45 yard shot and brought him down. We sat there for
another half-hour and a strong wind came up and seemed to

be moving the duck farther out in the Bay. Art said that if
we didn't pick up that duck pretty soon, it would be too far
out to get and the way things were shaping up we'd end up
going back skunked.

"How about the two of us going out and getting it?" he
finally asked. I said okay and we got in the boat. Mary Lou
was against it. "It's raining too hard and I'm afraid of that
strong wind," she said. "Besides, it's my duck and I don't want
it. What can anyone do with *one* duck?"

Art laughed. "I think that bird died of a broken heart. We
want to get it to prove a point." I sat in the stern of the small
boat and he rowed, putting plenty of muscle in it. Too much.
About fifteen feet from the duck he lost an oar. The wind was
driving us out into the open Bay and the rain was increasing.
Now I could barely see Mary Lou back in the blind, but I
could tell by the way she was waving the gun that she saw our
predicament. We took turns trying to reach the other oar, but
it was on its way, moving much faster than we were. Art stood
up and tried to use the one oar like a canoe paddle, but the
boat was a big, clumsy flat-bottomed affair and the wind and
the water pushed us back four feet for every foot we made
toward shore. I tried the oar for awhile, but it was no good.
Mary Lou was firing her gun trying to attract help, but I
knew that too was hopeless. If there was anyone around they
would think she was shooting at ducks. It began to rain harder
and by now we were about three miles straight out from the
duck blind and I suddenly had that helpless, hopeless feeling
that fear sometimes brings. It looked like we really had it. Art
started cursing himself for his clumsiness in dropping the oar,
and I told him to forget it, it could happen to anybody.

I thought longingly of the Dolans. No matter how I tried
I couldn't imagine either Frank or Joe ever dropping an oar.
I told myself I should have asked if Art knew how to handle a
boat. But I couldn't blame him. He had done the best he could.
The dropping of the oar was an accident.

We were drifting faster now and moving away from even
the familiar landmark of the duck blind, and I looked back
and saw the little, lonely figure of Mary Lou getting smaller
and smaller and a sadness came over me. I wondered how she
would get back. She, too, was surrounded by water.

Now we could see that it was hopeless to even attempt rowing with one oar and we just sat silently praying that the rain

would stop, that the wind would switch and start driving us toward shore not the Bay where we would be sure goners. I looked at my watch and saw amazingly that we had been out in the boat for three hours.

We both saw it and both said, "A point! Maybe we'll drift close enough to get ashore." Off to our right a long finger of land poked out into the Bay. We were about three or four miles from it and much too far out to reach it. But as we drifted, the wind veered a little and brought us parallel with the point of land. I got the oar and started paddling. Then all of a sudden we could see the bottom and the water was shallow. We got into it and pulled the boat after us to shore. There was a building and three soldiers came out when they saw us. We told them what happened and asked if they could give us a ride back in their truck to a spot opposite the duck blind. I thought the small inlet behind the blind might be shallow enough to wade. They said it was but that we couldn't get to it because the land on this side of it was heavily mined. It was an explosive testing area. They would take us to a motor boat. We'd get Mary Lou out the way we went in.

All the way there I prayed that she would sit tight and not try to wade that water. Then up the road I saw a familiar figure trudging toward us. It was Mary Lou, soaking wet and exhausted, but carrying the three shotguns we had left in the blind.

"How'd you get out?" we all shouted as soon as she recognized us in the truck cab. "Jack, Jack, thank God," she said, then "I waded that little inlet, the water came up to my chin, and then I walked across the open land to this road. It took two hours." When we told her that she had walked through a heavily mined area, she gave me a long, searching look and said, "Let's go home."

That was one ducking trip we almost didn't walk back from. As I was saying, always make sure you have a seasoned guide with you.

Make sure you dress properly for ducking. Always pack along a rain outfit. The separates, jacket with hood, and slip-on pants, take up little space and will keep you dry all day. Get the oilskins as first preference, the green nylon as second. They should be large so they pull on easily over your cold weather outfits. Two pairs of gloves (one pair is sure to get sopping wet), hand warmers, the downlined jacket and pants, hip boots, a thermos full of hot soup, shells protected in a waterproof case, and one of those sponge cushions that subs in as a life preserver are little items that will increase your pleasure while ducking. Wear only dark, somber clothing. Don't show up with your red deer cap. Make certain you have your duck stamp and license and plenty of shells. If you get one duck with ten shots, consider yourself a pretty fair shot.

You only have to sit in a duck blind once for the madness to move upon you. Come November, if you find yourself praying for bad weather, consider yourself in. You're a duck hunter. One of the mad many.

CHAPTER 11

Controlled Shooting*

N ILO, the most famous controlled shooting area in the world, spelled backwards is Olin, and Olin spelled any way you wish is Winchester-Western, one of the largest arms companies in the world, with John Olin guiding genius and now chairman of the board of its newly combined operation, the Olin Mathieson Chemical Corporation.

Tall, sturdy, with eyes the shade of the cold steel that goes into his guns, John Olin not only manufactures arms and ammunition, but uses them adeptly and is considered one of the country's outstanding sportsmen—an avid hunter and fisherman. Narrowing his activities down, bird-shooting over a skilled dog, and wading a cold northern salmon stream, are probably his favorite exercises.

Discontent with merely enjoying the sport of bird shooting himself, early in 1951 John Olin decided that he would investigate the possibility of creating fast and lasting bird shooting for all hunters. Thus project Nilo was born.

And although Nilo, as explained is simply Olin backwards, there is nothing at all backward about the program. It's probably the first successful, full-scale, controlled shooting project ever laid out by an individual. It may well prove the impetus needed to start similar programs country-wide, to the everlasting benefit of all sportsmen.

Fearing the depletion of our natural game birds as the end result of over-shooting in many areas of the country, John Olin, appointed the well-known conservation expert Charles Hopkins director of conservation and administrator of the Nilo operation, with express instructions to set up a game farm that would act as a model to be copied by any farmer, sportsman, or conservationist who might be interested. One of the most successful adapters of Nilo in Illinois is Joseph Davidson, who has his own commercial shooting set-up near Braidwood, Illinois.

*All illustrations in this chapter are copyrighted by the Olin Mathieson Chemical Corporation.

120

In the fall of 1955, Joseph Keeley, editor of the *American Legion Magazine,* and Gordon Carroll, then publisher of *Coronet,* both shooting companions of mine, were invited to accompany me to Nilo as the guests of John Olin to see if we could fault the shooting set-up. Charles Hopkins, conservation director of Olin Mathieson, met us at the plane, took us to Nilo and explained the whole thing to us. He is a game bird man, a conservation expert of the first order, and he pointed out that the whole thing was done by the farm manager E. G. "Bud" Clark and one helper, so that the visiting farmers would quickly realize that this was not a fancy operation, but one that they could easily do themselves.

That first morning we hunted ducks. Note that I didn't say 'shot' ducks. I've always been of the opinion that wild duck shooting couldn't be duplicated, or even closely approached. But at Nilo, they don't approach it, they offer a situation that is much more difficult. That morning I shot in a blind with E. G. Clark, a quiet, soft-spoken man who could handle a shotgun like it was a third arm, and Harry Pershall, brother of Cotton Pershall, famous retriever trainer, and Avery Symington, handled the two black Labrador retrievers, Buck Kin and Statesman, young dogs that were already marking falls, and working like polished oldtimers when we gave them the chance.

We were placed in blinds in a ravine several hundred yards from the pond where the ducks would head. The ducks were released from a tower thousands of yards away and in full flight by the time they crossed over the tall trees and the hill that stood directly before us. We were instructed not to shoot back of the blind—either get the birds coming in or miss. The blinds were so constructed that the angle of swing was less than 45 degrees, and by the time the mallards came walloping in they were traveling at least 60 miles an hour.

Twenty or thirty birds came in at once. The first time in, no one downed a bird. In wild bird shooting you can get them as they buzz in to set their wings over the decoys, swing as they flare, and bang away coming or going. Not at Nilo. Either you were on them when they passed you, or you weren't. Most of the time we weren't. It was a lesson in shooting that I thought didn't exist. If anyone ever tells me that game farm mallard shooting at Nilo, or any other place like it is easy stuff, I'm afraid that I will punch him in the nose.

John Olin came down and stood behind the blinds to watch

the fun. He brought his young lab Solo along, hoping that he could give him a good work out. For quite a while it looked like Solo was going back to the kennel without touching a feather, but then we began to make contact and shoot ducks.

In the afternoon we went after pheasants with Elbert Cummings, Bud Clark, the resident farm manager, Larry St. Cinn, and pointer dogs Doc and Joe. Mr. Olin brought Solo along for the experience. Here, again, Joe Keeley, Gordon Carroll, and I who had shot many preserves throughout the country, were surprised. Due to the terrain, some hilly, some cut with deep ravines, some open meadow, the whole acreage cleverly planted with cover and feed crops that would hide, feed, and hold the birds, the whole thing amazingly planned by Charles Hopkins and executed by Bud Clark, we had no easy shots. It was exactly like shooting the wild birds of China or the Dakotas. They were big busters, healthy, strong flying, and they got under way getting up to sixty miles an hour so fast, that you had to get on them immediately or prepare yourself for a fifty yard shot. We must have walked 10 miles after those pheasants, and never have I seen a better illustration of pen-raised birds released and immediately becoming wild ones. We established no shooting records, believe me.

The next day we shot quail. The same story all over again. They were wild flying, and we walked about 10 miles to get a decent bag. Misses were many and the sport was high. John Olin didn't miss, but after all he was born with a shotgun by his side instead of a rattle. The rest of us finally acquitted ourselves with honor.

But gentle reader, don't ever let anyone kid you about controlled shooting being a lead pipe cinch. It can be as tough as you want it. And at Nilo they want it tough. They like the idea of separating the men from the boys. And the three of us who thought we knew quite a bit about swinging a shotgun, almost went home feeling like we were wearing knickers.

Here's how the whole things ticks. If you are interested in setting up your own Nilo, your personal controlled shooting area, precise know-how follows.

Controlled shooting simply means the release of pen-reared game birds before the gun. Brooding and holding pens which require small space have been substituted for the habitat necessary for the production of game birds in the wild, eliminating nesting, loafing, protective or escape cover. One essential form of cover is readily available on the average farm in draw-heads, odd areas and fence rows. If natural release cover is not sufficient, modern farm practices permit the inclusion of food patches, shrubbery clumps, windbreaks and legume strips in the general farm plan.

Nilo controlled shooting area also provides a permanent home for Nilo kennels, another of John Olin's conservation projects which demonstrates the reduction of "flying cripples" in waterfowl and upland game through the use of retrieving dogs. Some 89 skilled Labrador retrievers are on hand to prove Mr. Olin's point.

The area contains 522 acres and includes three former farmsteads. A farm plan has been prepared by the Soil Conservation Service, and all agricultural activities are based upon this plan. A four-strip system of crop rotation has been devised which lends itself ideally to the use of the area for controlled shooting after agricultural crops have been harvested. Even under drought conditions, more than 3,200 bales of alfalfa hay were produced on the area in 1954, along with an average yield of wheat, oats, corn and soy beans.

The location of Nilo—only nine miles from the city of Alton, Illinois—demonstrates the value of controlled shooting in taking the pressure off native game. Most states containing large metropolitan areas have special regulations governing controlled shooting, these regulations usually providing for the escape into surrounding territory of a fixed percentage of upland game birds released on any acreage covered by a state license. Thus each controlled shooting area serves sportsmen in two different ways—by licensing places to hunt liberated birds, and by building up resident game populations in the immediate vicinity of each licensed area.

A third method of increasing public hunting through controlled shooting is the establishment of state-operated shooting grounds, utilizing the production of state game farms to provide flying targets.

It is in the field of private operation, however, that controlled shooting has made it greatest progress, having demonstrated that one or more farmers can manage a shooting area successfully as a part-time operation, thus greatly increasing the cash income from acreage usually classified as agricultural land. The ideal situation is for two farmers to pool their acreage, and utilize their own labor—and that of their families—to produce the game birds necessary in offering controlled shooting to the public.

The growing popularity of controlled shooting also is largely responsible for a substantial increase in field trials in the United States, with a corresponding increase in dog ownership. By utilizing techniques developed in controlled shooting, "shooting field trials" are being held successfully on club-operated or commercial areas. Some field trial clubs are even establishing their own grounds where members can train their dogs, with the membership competing at appropriate intervals in formal stakes run off under the club's rules.

Whether the average city dweller's interest lies merely in the sport of shooting, or whether he is interested in a place to train or work his own dogs, controlled shooting offers him opportunities. A busy professional man, such as a lawyer, doctor or dentist, can leave his office at noon, pick up his dogs, and within an hour or so be ready to put in a full afternoon on an area where he is sure to find birds. Even if no club facilities are available, he usually can find some commercial establishment within easy driving distance.

American hunting clubs pioneered preserve shooting, and down through the years developed most of the techniques now widely used*. Only recently have gunning pressure and habitat destruction combined to emphasize the necessity of making controlled shooting available to the man of average means. There are now four principal types of operation, which may be roughly classified as follows:

Club Operation: Controlled shooting area to be operated for the benefit of members just as an exclusive golf club is conducted. Employees perform all labor, including rearing and releasing of birds, training and handling of dogs.

Group Operation: All work on the area to be done by members of the group except the actual rearing of the birds. These may be bought as adults, or they may be reared and held by a farmer or a member of his family, to be used as required.

Commercial Operation: Area to be operated by one or more farmers or landowners, usually on a daily fee basis. This form of controlled shooting offers unusual opportunities for increasing the revenue from agricultural land without interfering with normal farm operations.

Field Trial Operation: This is a specialized type of operation

---

*See Chapter 15, Preserves and Pheasants.

in which the training and working of dogs is the primary consideration. Usually the number of birds required is held to a minimum except for "shooting field trials" held on the property.

Experience has shown that controlled shooting enjoys its greatest popularity when purely natural conditions are permitted to prevail. The average hunter dislikes artificiality of any kind, preferring the American type of field shooting to the European system of driving the birds over fixed shooting positions. It follows that the use of a dog is a must in controlled shooting.

Because the ringnecked pheasant retains all of its wild characteristics even when reared in captivity, this species is a heavy favorite for controlled shooting. Pheasants properly conditioned in holding pens can run just as far, fly just as fast and cackle just as loudly as birds reared in the wild. They also adapt themselves exceedingly well to hunting with dogs of the three principal types—pointing, springing or retrieving.

A pheasant's natural instinct is to slink away from a fourfooted animal, such as a fox, a coyote or a dog, if he can do so without being observed. This natural instinct tells him, however, that he is no match in a footrace with such an animal over open ground. When he comes to a strip of bare ground, he will try to hide, with the idea of seeking safety in flight if he is discovered. Alternating patches of cover with "stopping strips" is one of the techniques developed for the improvement of controlled shooting in recent years.

Another species well adapted to controlled shooting is the so-called "game farm mallard." Sufficiently removed from their wild forebears as to fall outside the federal regulations governing the shooting of wild waterfowl, "game farm mallards" can be trained to follow definite courses, and thus offer pass shooting fully comparable to the shooting of wild birds.

In addition to the high quality of the sport itself, controlled shooting at game-farm mallards offers the opportunity to train retrieving dogs. Thus, on an area offering both pheasant and duck shooting, any type of dog can be made ready for work in the field and field trials. The use of a retrieving dog in controlled duck shooting is just as important as the use of a dog on pheasants in adding to the enjoyment of the sport, to say nothing of the "flying cripples" recovered by the shooter.

Because of geographical differences, the regulations of the various states may differ. The regulations of a state in the "pheasant belt" usually are co-ordinated with their own program for increasing wild populations. In the shooting of game-farm mallards, many states rely upon the location of the specific area to avoid conflict with federal law. Other states, however, have a less uniform pattern of duck flights, and therefore restrict the shooting of game-farm mallards to the same seasons and bag limits which apply to wild waterfowl.

It is important to inquire into the controlled shooting regulations of the state in which a controlled shooting area is to be located.* Whatever these regulations may be, they are certain to point the way to better shooting.

PHEASANT SHOOTING

Since the ringnecked pheasant is most widely used in controlled shooting, any development program can safely be based on this species.

Any type of cover that will hold pheasants will suffice for any other game bird whose shooting is permissible under the controlled shooting regulations of any state. The same holds true for those species, both exotic and native, on which a special season is not provided, but which are subject to the same seasons and bag limits applying to wild birds.

Most states provide a special shooting season on pen-reared pheasants of approximately four months. Allowing for climatic differences, these special seasons begin about October 15, and end about February 15. In northern climates, subject to heavy snowfall, the fall and early winter months are the best.

Clubs and experienced commercial operators have their own programs of pheasant production. But in many cases these are of little value to the individual or group in setting up the original plan. A well-established club may shoot up to 10,000 pheasants a year, but this number may not be required for the average operation for several years. This is especially true of a commercial operation. Controlled shooting may be something entirely new in any community, and nothing discourages an inexperienced operator more quickly than having birds left on his hands at the end of a shooting season.

Since controlled shooting of pheasants requires the services of at least two men, the safest method is to plan the production of the average number of pheasants two men can handle in

*Chapter 5, A Sports Surprise in Every State, has the official state listings where you may write and inquire.

a shooting season. For a club or commercial operation, more personnel may be available, and then the number of birds required will be considerably greater.

Club and commercial operations require two men because four hunters is the largest number that should go afield in any hunting party. One man can act as guide and dog-handler for a party of this size. Should the number of shooters exceed four, another guide and dog-handler will be required. Since most shooting is done on Saturdays and Sundays, any establishment should be able to accommodate at least eight hunters at one time.

Assuming a four-months shooting season, with a capacity of eight shooters, there will be 288 hunter-days if shooting is confined to week-ends only. Holidays are not included in the computation, although they may prove useful in making up days lost through bad weather. Due to this cause alone, a shooting area will not operate up to capacity at all times. Experience has shown that the average number of hunter-days on any shooting area operated by two men will be about 250.

If six pheasants are released for each hunter, the number required for an entire shooting season will be exactly 1500. As the shooting of hens as well as cocks usually is permitted under controlled shooting regulations, the number required may be equally divided as to sex. A recovery ratio of more than 66% cannot be expected, and thus no operator should worry about the percentage of escaped birds. At the same time, the take-home of birds by each hunter will be ample reward for a hard day afield.

Where to Get Your Pheasants

There are several ways to obtain pheasants for controlled shooting. Purchase of adult birds from a commercial game farm is the simplest method if production costs are not considered. Game farms are set up to furnish all the facilities, the food and the labor necessary to rear the birds to maturity. They also are entitled to a reasonable profit so they can stay in business.

On the other hand, a club, a group or a commercial operator may decide to produce pheasants on or near the shooting area. Under this system, up to 90% of the scratch feed required by the birds can be produced on the area. Further, carefully regulated feeding will control the weight of the finished birds, insuring the production of strong flyers.

The commercial operator—preferably a farmer—can convert

his own labor into cash by rearing and holding his own birds. He must be prepared to stand his losses from those poultry diseases which also attack pheasants. But shooting fees not only compensate him for his labor, but also provide a wider margin of profit out of which to make necessary additions or improvements.

In the beginning no operator should plan to produce his own eggs and hatch his own chicks. Quantity production enables game farms to sell day-old chicks at from 35 to 40 cents apiece, depending on the number purchased. Because of the comparatively small requirements of the average shooting area, conducting a breeding and hatching program is not practical. If the operator is a farmer, his waking hours during the laying and hatching period will be fully occupied with agricultural pursuits, including the plowing, harrowing and planting of his brooding and holding pens.

Brooding pens capable of holding 750 pheasant chicks can be erected for as little as $120 in material costs. However, two brooder houses will cost approximately $300 each if they must be purchased new in knock-down form. If the operator has had poultry experience and decides to build his own brooder houses out of cheaper materials he can greatly reduce his initial cost.

By putting two hatches of chicks through his brooders each season, an operator can handle 1500 birds a year. The first hatch must be obtained very early in the season, and the second very late, if he hopes to maintain this schedule. Needless to say, his source of supply for pheasant chicks must be arranged in advance, with special attention to delivery dates.

Manufacturers of game bird feed mixtures usually are prepared to furnish all essential information as to the feeding and care of pheasants. Figures compiled from many sources indicate that it costs from 50 to 60 cents to feed each pheasant to the age of 16 weeks. The lower figure prevails only when most scratch feed for the birds is produced on the premises. Considering the first cost of the chicks, as well as subsequent losses, the cost per bird will be slightly in excess of $1, exclusive of labor. The cost per bird is also increased by losses, and by the holding of birds beyond the age of 16 weeks.

A three-section covered holding pen for 1500 pheasants can be built at a cost for materials of as little as $1,000. Round posts and light poultry netting can be used, with construction entirely by unskilled labor.

The use of heavier wire netting, square posts, and other strong materials can increase the materials cost of a covered holding pen, with accessories, to approximately $3,000. This heavier pen is better adapted to snowy climates, and will require a minimum of repairs. Either type of construction may be used in building brooding pens.

Complete diagrams, material lists and description of accessories for both the farm-type and heavy-duty type of pheasant holding and brooding installations are given on following pages.

THREE SECTION PHEASANT HOLDING PEN FOR 1500 PHEASANTS
AND BROODING UNITS FOR 750 CHICKS

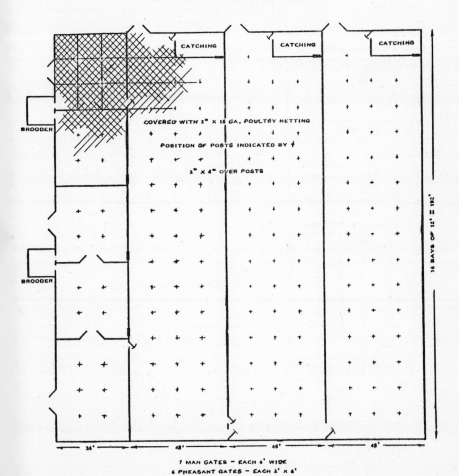

7 MAN GATES - EACH 4' WIDE
6 PHEASANT GATES - EACH 2' X 6'
9 TRACTOR GATES - EACH 16' WIDE

TRACTOR GATE

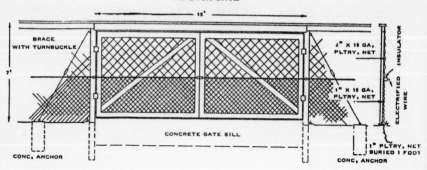

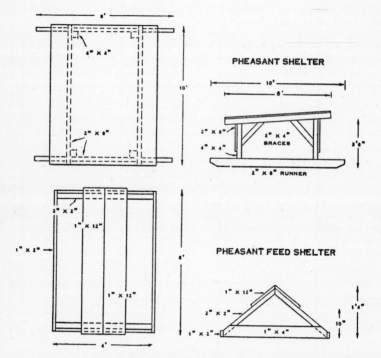

PHEASANT SHELTER

PHEASANT FEED SHELTER

Materials for Heavy-Type Pheasant Holding Pen

4,608 Lin. ft. of 2″ x 18 gauge galvanized poultry netting 6′-0″ wide.
  780 Lin. ft. of 2″ x 18 gauge galvanized poultry netting 4′-0″ wide.
  780 Lin. ft. of 1″ x 18 gauge galvanized poultry netting 4′-0″ wide.
10,277 Hog rings.
   48 ⅜″ Screw-eye bolts.

396 Lin. ft. of ¼" round galvanized wire rope.
48 Turn buckles.
227 4" x 4" cedar posts 10' long.
3,259 Lin. ft. of 2" x 4" structural grade fir.
720 Lin. ft. of 2" x 6" structural grade fir.
20 Extra heavy wrought steel T-hinges.
16 Heavy wrought steel T-hinges.
15 Galvanized safety hasps.
6 Cubic yards of concrete.
2,160 Lin. ft. 9 gauge galvanized wire.
14 Gallons Penta.
Staples.
19 Pull type gate handles.
11 Gate hooks.

Materials for Farm-Type Pheasant Holding Pen

267 Posts, 10' length.
34 Rolls (150 ft/roll) 6' wide 2"-20 Ga. Mesh.
9 Rolls (150 ft/roll) 4' wide 2"-20 Ga. Mesh.
9 Rolls (150 ft/roll) 4' wide 1"-20 Ga. Mesh.
2 Rolls #6 wire.
14 Pairs of hinges.
11 Hasps.
13,622 Hog rings.
4,850 Staples.
316 Lin. ft., 2" x 6".
379 Lin. ft., 2" x 4".
(Note: This type of pen is suitable for farm installations, utilizing materials that can be put together by any farmer. Special bracing may be necessary in case of heavy snowfall.)

Materials for Pheasant Shelters

100 Lin. ft. of 2" x 4" structural grade fir.
14 Lin. ft. of 4" x 4" structural grade fir.
44 Lin. ft. of 2" x 8" structural grade fir.
80 Board ft. of 1" fir sheeting.
40 Lin. ft. of 65 lb. roll roofing.
1 Gallon Penta.
Nails.

Specifications of Brooder Houses

Brooder houses are prefabricated, 12' by 12', with Presdwood sides and wooden floors. Prefabricated brooder houses of this type are sold by several manufacturers of poultry equipment. However, the houses can be constructed of available materials if desired.

Specifications of Feed House

Constructed of Haydite blocks with concrete flooring and wooden roof. Partition across the center so as to provide grain bin and storage space. 3' x 3' bin door provided in the rear.

Width—16'-1½"
Length—20'-1⅜"

Ground level to block top—8'-1½"
Roof peak to block top—4'

Materials for Heavy-Type Pheasant Brooder Pen

943 Lin. ft. 2" x 18 gauge galvanized poultry netting 6'-0" wide.
110 Ft. of 1" x 18 gauge galvanized poultry netting 4'-0" wide.
360 Lin. ft. of 9 gauge galvanized wire.
2,380 Hog rings.
1,282 Lin. ft. 2" x 4" structural grade fir.
332 Lin. ft. 2" x 6" structural grade fir.
870 Lin. ft. 2" x 18 gauge galvanized poultry netting 4'-0" wide.
52 4" x 4" cedar posts 4' long.
24 Heavy wrought steel T-hinges.
7 Galvanized safety hasps.
5 Gallons Penta.
   Staples.
12 Pull type gate handles.
5 Gate hooks.

Materials for Farm-Type Pheasant Brooder Pen

31 Posts, 10' length.
3 Rolls (150 ft/roll) 6' wide 2"-20 Ga. Mesh.
2 Rolls (150 ft/roll) 4' wide 2"-20 Ga. Mesh.
2 Rolls (150 ft/roll) 4' wide 1"-20 Ga. Mesh.
2 Pairs of Hinges.
2 Hasps.
1,752 Hog Rings.
241 Staples.
80 Lin. ft., 2" x 6".
64 Lin ft., 2" x 4".

(Note: Specifications of brooder houses given previously can be used. Otherwise, brooder houses of similar size can be constructed or improvised.)

Pheasant Installation Accessories

2 Brooder Houses.
6 Pheasant Shelters.
   Feed House.
2 Brooder Lamps (4 Bulb Type.)
8 Light Bulbs (GE 250W).
6 Feeders (5' Oakes Floor Type).
10 Feed Pans (Oakes with wire guard).
6 Automatic Waterers (Brower Airdome Automatic Fount No. 200 J.C.)
50 Insulators.
   International Electric Fence Controller.
   Spool Electric Fence Wire.

How to Release Your Pheasants

Purchasing or producing healthy, strong-flying pheasants is the first step toward satisfactory controlled shooting.

Even more depends upon the manner of their release. The

recovery ratio on birds liberated by mass release on unprepared ground can be very low. By contrast, the recovery ratio on birds released singly or in small groups into carefully prepared cover can be high.

The operator is interested in conducting his area in the black at all times. To do this, he must approach as nearly as possible the recovery ratio permitted by law. His members or customers soon will become dissatisfied with conditions when only one or two birds are recovered out of six released—or any other figure indicating a recovery ratio of only 30 or 40%.

A commercial operator, seeing his patronage dwindling, may try to remedy the situation by releasing more birds. He soon finds himself in a position where the cost of birds liberated exceeds his income from shooting fees. No business can long survive when outgo exceeds income. He eventually gives up, not realizing that the time to insure a satisfactory recovery ratio is at least one full agricultural season in advance of the actual liberation of the birds.

His problem may be either too much cover or not enough, depending on the normal agricultural use of his acreage. If he is attempting to set up a controlled shooting area on an abandoned farm or plantation, hunting pheasants will amount to searching for the proverbial needle in a haystack. There will be woody vegetation everywhere into which the birds can escape by running. Repeated mowing of stopping strips, alternating with strips of cover, should precede any attempt to shoot pheasants on the property.

At the other extreme is unusually flat acreage, farmed "on the square" according to clean-farming methods. The operator can inaugurate a modern system of strip farming, alternating legume strips of "green manure" with small grains or other crops. In some cases, fall plowing must be dispensed with if the legume strips are to be used as cover. On the other hand, fall plowing or seeding of grain strips will provide the necessary "stoppers" and increase the productivity of the legume strips.

Between these two extremes is the average American farm— or farms—with the usual percentage of wildlife land, and with any number of natural release points, such as drawheads, odd areas, shrubbery clumps, fencerows and timber edges. Modern farm plans may have been prepared, stressing practices beneficial to wildlife. There even may be multiflora rose fences, field borders and strips or patches of sericea lespedeza to check erosion. Such acreage needs very little in the way of improvement, except to balance the number of release points as between hunting courses.

The mass releasing of pheasants has the decided advantage of requiring only the services of one man, regardless of the length of time in advance of actual shooting that the birds are liberated. Too often, in the case of small areas, the birds take flight immediately, and put the boundaries of the area behind them. They may work back onto the area, if food and cover has been provided. Often, however, they are a total loss.

Most states in the pheasant belt limit the size of controlled shooting areas for just this reason. The more pheasants that escape into the surrounding territory, the more the natural backlog of wild birds will be increased. The shooter, however, is paying his club dues or his area fee for the sole purpose of finding birds. If the birds are not there, obviously he can not find them.

The individual release of pheasants into good cover is the best insurance against loss of birds by "spooking" or running. Usually, the release of each pheasant with its head tucked under one wing will cause the bird to remain quiet until the operator or his assistant has left the scene.

In the case of very small areas, where pheasants easily can fly across the nearest boundary, "rocking" or "dizzying" is widely practiced. This operation, however, must not be carried to extremes. The effects of vertigo or dizziness should last just long enough to prevent the bird from flying or running away. In no case should any physical or artificial means be used which permanently will deprive the bird of the use of any of its faculties.

The greatest objection to the individual release of pheasants is the manpower required. If only two courses are planted, this method of release will require at least two men. At the same time, in the case of a small area, it will pay for itself by increasing the area's recovery ratio.

Preparing The Shooting Area

Cover strips of dense legumes and grasses are helpful in setting up a shooting program on the average farm. This type of cover is normally used on modern farms where crop rotation is practiced and may be utilized without extra cost to the farmer.

A cover strip is usually from 25 yards to 50 yards wide and makes an ideal part of the shooting course. Surrounding the cover strip, the land should be plowed, disced or mowed to provide a stopping strip. This stopping strip will cause the pheasant to either flush or turn back into the cover strip. This will increase the chances of the hunting party recovering the bird.

Lespedeza and sweet clover provide good cover strips. These are usually seeded into the grain crops in the spring. Farmers can provide other cover strips by cutting their cereals high to leave a tall stubble for the birds to hide in. Rows of corn stalks may be left in the field and the farmer can go back and harvest the corn after the hunting season.

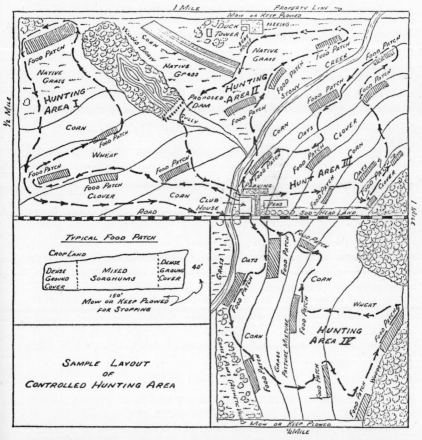

Practically every square foot of the average farm can be utilized for controlled shooting if natural release points are augmented by well-located food patches. In the diagram, provision has been made for four different pheasant courses and a duck-flight installation, all on one 480-acre farm.

Providing cover is not expensive nor does it take much of the farmer's time. In many states, various agencies will help with the cost of planting.

The operator should take advantage of the services offered by the Soil Conservation Service, state agriculture departments, forestry services, game departments and experimental stations. They are eager and willing to assist farmers who show an interest in good land usage and wildlife conservation.

Most farms also have draw-heads which can be developed as release points. If natural plant growth is not adequate in the draw-heads, sericea lespedeza can be seeded to provide an excellent growth.

Draw-heads are not used in producing cash crops, and the farmer is usually willing to develop them as cover or release points. This is in keeping with good land usage as advocated by the Soil Conservation Service because it helps stop erosion.

Seeding sericea lespedeza should follow the normal practice advocated in the area by county farm advisors, county farm planners, the state game department and successful, experienced farmers.

Shrubs are desirable in limited numbers. They should be planted so as to allow open spaces between the plants as they reach maturity. It will also be necessary to see that the shrubs do not grow too tall. The operator must be as careful to not have too much cover as he is in providing enough cover. Some types of shrubs tend to spread and the operator must guard against their over-running the area.

Clumps of shrubbery also can be planted on eroded spots, odd corners, sink holes and other places which are not under cultivation. The plants should be spaced four feet by four feet to leave open spaces for wildlife. These clumps will serve as release points, loafing and protecting cover.

Multiflora rose, shrub honeysuckle and wild plum are recommended for clump planting. Clump planting also aids in stopping erosion.

Cultivated Food Patches

The number, size and shape of the odd areas on any acreage will determine the extent of food patch plantings, if any are needed to augment natural cover. If the topography of the land does not provide sufficient food-patch sites independent of normal farming operations, a few rectangular food patches can be spaced throughout the cover strips.

FOOD PATCH ROTATION

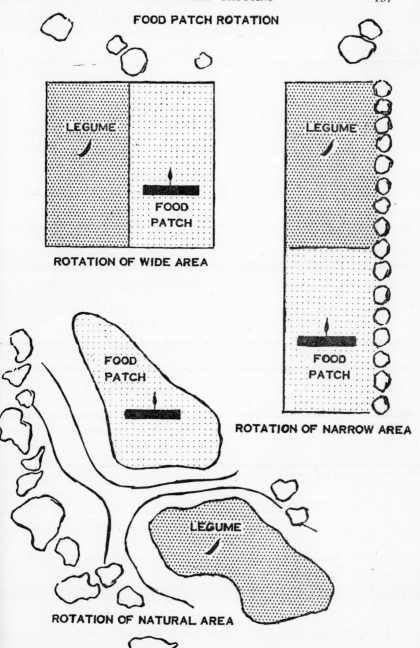

ROTATION OF WIDE AREA

ROTATION OF NARROW AREA

ROTATION OF NATURAL AREA

Since food patches are intended to provide cover as well as food, more plantings will be required than the minimum necessary to sustain a wild population. While the size may range anywhere between ¼-acre and 2 acres, at least one food patch should be provided for each 20 acres of the shooting area.

If sufficient ground is available, food patches should occupy not more than one-half of an odd area, with the other one-half being planted in a legume strip. The two different types of plantings then are alternated each year, as food patches will impoverish the soil in the same proportion as any other grain crop. When available space does not justify this method of alternating food patches and legume strips, double the number of food patch sites can be selected, and plantings alternated in succeeding years.

The soil should be prepared well in advance of planting time, which will be in the first two weeks of June. After the initial plowing, the plot should be worked at intervals. Finally, the seed should be broadcast in soil that has been worked down to a garden-like seed bed, and a final thorough harrowing completes the job.

The following seed mixture has proved highly satisfactory at Nilo, particularly when strains are used that are adapted to a dry climate:

Black amber cane	3 pounds
Orange amber cane	3 pounds
Cowpeas or soybeans	1 pound
Atlas sorghum	2 pounds
Kaffir	3 pounds
Sudan	1 pound

This quantity is ample for planting one acre. Substitutions may be made when necessary, but always with the idea of obtaining a healthy growth of stalk as well as well-filled heads of grain.

Hunting The Cover Strip

A cover strip—otherwise a hunting course—for controlled shooting is from 25 to 50 yards wide. It can be covered safely and efficiently by four guns in line, spaced eight or ten yards apart.

The line of guns contracts or expands as the hunting course narrows or widens, but there need be no doubt or hesitancy about who is to take the shot. The right hand pair of guns works as a team, taking all shots on the right side of the course.

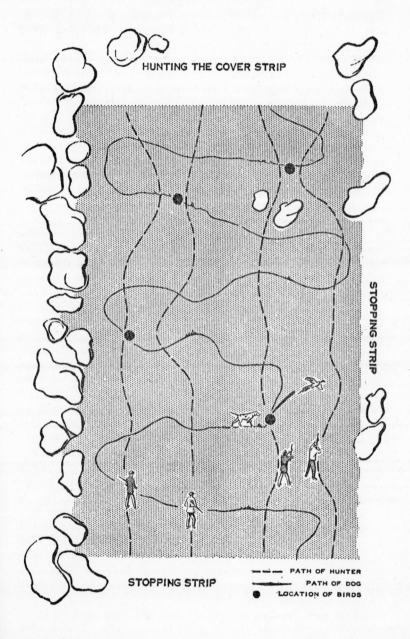

HUNTING THE COVER STRIP

STOPPING STRIP

STOPPING STRIP

PATH OF HUNTER
PATH OF DOG
LOCATION OF BIRDS

The left hand pair of guns covers the left side. Straightaway shots down the middle are taken either by the right hand pair or the left, at the suggestion of the guide.

For efficiency, the guns should never gang up on the same side of an obstruction, such as a fallen tree, a clump of bushes or a stand of evergreens. This maneuver, however, sometimes separates the gunners, and reduces visibility because of natural obstacles. Protective clothing should be worn by all gunners to supplement the practices of safe gun handling.

At Nilo, a "safety jacket" of pure white is worn by all gunners. These slip-on garments are patterned after the ordinary button-type windbreaker, but are sleeveless, and large enough to be worn over regular clothing in cold weather.

A cap of fluorescent material, preferably bright orange in color, also greatly aids visibility while hunting.

No guarantees of any kind are offered to hunters under the Nilo system. If one or two hunters out of a party of four are so unskilled as to cause excessive missing of birds, the guide should quickly re-arrange his party so that poor field shots are backed up by more experienced hunters.

The guide should carry a gun, to be used ordinarily only in the recovery of cripples. If it is demonstrated, however, that a hunting party is composed principally of poor field shots, he should back up a pair of poor shots on one flank—only shooting after his guests have expended the cartridges in their guns. Most of his shooting thus will result in long falls, but with the use of dogs, there should be no great loss of birds.

If a hunt is properly managed, a party of four should experience no difficulty in recovering 50% of the birds released. This will result in a "take-home" for each hunter of three birds. "Par for the course" is 16 birds, or 66%. This gives each hunter four birds. If the bag is between 12 and 16 birds, the extras can be given to party members who obviously have bagged more than their share.

Nilo hunting technique is based on the furnishing of a well-trained dog for each group of four. If the group should be made up entirely of personal friends and hunting companions, members of the group can be permitted to use their own dogs. The guide, in some cases representing a commercial operator, can not be held responsible for poor shooting or inefficient dog work in the field.

Controlled shooting is well adapted to "shooting field trials" now coming into great popularity with sportsmen's organizations, but requiring a different technique in the field.

A member or guest may enter his own dog, and a number of pheasants—usually three for each hunter—are planted on each half-hour course. Entries are divided into braces, and care must be taken to plant the allotted number of birds on each course. The hunters then shoot over their own dogs, and retain the birds killed. First shot goes to the man whose dog points the bird or birds. The others merely back him up.

Each club usually fixes its own standards for a controlled shooting stake, but the hunter whose dog works to the gun, and quarters his ground intelligently entirely upon the course, has an obvious advantage. In addition to birds bagged, trophies are awarded as in ordinary non-shooting field trials.

Most clubs or organizations lay out a continuous circular strip of terrain to be covered. Because all of the dog work occurs in cover strips or food patches, a view of the entire running usually can be obtained from access roads within the hunting circle.

GAME-FARM MALLARDS

The shooting of game-farm mallard ducks along a well-prepared course has been described as the nearest thing ever devised to the pass shooting of wild waterfowl under ideal conditions.

If the line of flight of the ducks happens to coincide with the prevailing wind so that the fowl zip along ahead of a tail wind at about 120 miles an hour, it is just about the sportiest shooting imaginable.

Legal restrictions on this form of controlled shooting vary widely in the different states, but all have one object in view. This is to prevent a flock of game-farm mallards from acting as decoys to attract wild waterfowl, which is illegal under federal law. In Illinois, home state of Nilo, game-farm mallards are classified as farm poultry and may be shot in any quantity at any time. However, licenses are not granted for controlled shooting areas in locations where wild waterfowl might find their way into shooters' bags.

At the other extreme, some other states located on established flyways have not classified game-farm mallards as legal outside the federal regulations governing the taking of wild waterfowl. Under this type of regulation, controlled shooting of game-farm mallards is subject to the same bag limit and the same seasonal restrictions as wild waterfowl. Here again, there is only one way to be sure as to the law. Consult your state game department.

Even under the same restrictions governing the taking of wild waterfowl, controlled shooting at game-farm mallards is proving to be highly attractive to residents of metropolitan areas who would have to drive great distances to get any wild duck shooting at all.

There are three basic requirements for controlled shooting at game-farm mallards:

1—A holding pen, with or without a release tower, where the birds are fed, and where they can be held pending release.

2—A small farm pond or timber pothole where the birds will spend the daylight hours. The pond should be 400 to 500 yards from the holding pen. It should be enclosed by a 6-foot fence.

3—A walkway approximately 20 feet wide, and at the beginning, enclosed by 18-inch fences connecting the holding pen and dabbling pond. These 18-inch fences are removed as soon as the ducks can fly between holding pen and dabbling pond.

The ducks are placed in the holding pen when they are about six to seven weeks old—several weeks before they can fly. They are held in this pen several days, always with feed before them, but with only enough water for drinking purposes. At the end of this period, they should be driven to the dabbling pond every morning, and back again at night. In this way, they learn that food is always available in the holding pen, but that the only opportunity for swimming and dabbling is at the pond.

By the time they can fly the ducks have begun to cover the distance between pen and pond in the shortest time. As their powers of flight develop they will start flying short distances along the walkway. Finally, they will begin flying the entire distance. At that time, the 18-inch side fencing of the walkway should be removed, and a "landing field" near the holding pen should be mowed for their convenience.

At 12 weeks of age, practically all of them will fly from pen to pond in the morning, and from pond to pen in the evening. By this time, their lives have been regimented through training to the point where only two places are important to them—the pen where they are fed and the pond where they swim and play. Often, in returning to the pen at dusk they will exercise by flying about the surrounding countryside. The dabbling pond is kept as free as possible from any aquatic life, and thus the ducks have never learned to forage for themselves.

At Nilo, two large-sized farm ponds are located within 300 yards of the holding pen and the dabbling pond. Yet not a single game-farm mallard has attempted to alight on one of these two ponds. They become creatures of habit.

Some establishments begin shooting as early as September 1, if state laws permit. At this time, however, many of the ducks are still carrying pin feathers. If shooting is not begun until October 1, the birds are more mature, are faster flyers, and have developed normally into a real table delicacy.

This method of setting up for controlled shooting at game-farm mallards is based on the purchase of the birds from a commercial game breeder at the age desired. In many respects, ducks are much easier to raise and hold than pheasants. There is no danger from cannibalism and ducks are immune to many diseases to which other game birds are susceptible.

Depending upon the law of supply and demand, game-farm mallard ducks can be purchased at prices ranging up to $1.50 for six-week-old birds. Feeding costs will be four or five cents per bird per week. Ultimate costs will depend upon the number of birds held and for what length of time.

On the following pages are presented a ground sketch of the Nilo controlled duck shooting establishment, details of construction of a tower and holding pen, and lists of materials. As in the pheasant installation, prices depend largely upon materials used and method of construction.

No details of pond construction are given, since physical characteristics of the terrain largely will govern the type of pond to be constructed. In most cases, ideal specifications for a farm pond need not be followed, since it is not desirable to stock the pond with fish or to induce the growth of food or cover plants. An acre or so of water up to three feet deep is usually sufficient.

Materials for Heavy-Type Duck Holding Pen

912	Lin. ft. of 2″ x 18 gauge galvanized poultry netting 6′-0″ wide.
2,308	Hog rings.
307	Lin. ft. of 9 gauge galvanized wiring.
954	Lin. ft. of 2″ x 4″ structural grade fir.
324	Lin. ft. of 2″ x 18 gauge galvanized poultry netting 4′-0″ wide.
324	Lin. ft. of 1″ x 18 gauge galvanized poultry netting 4′-0″ wide.
1	Cubic yard of concrete.
18	½″ Eye anchor bolts.

GROUND SKETCH . . . DUCK INSTALLATION

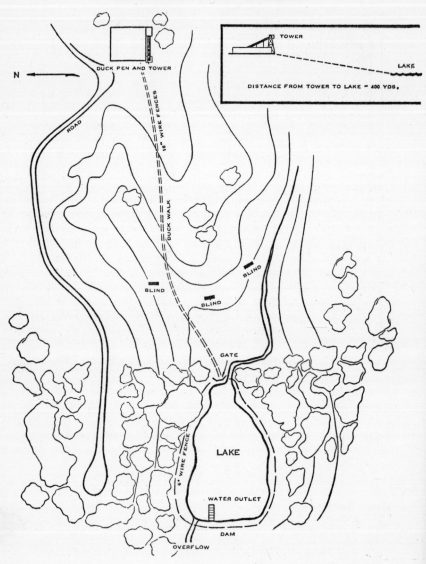

DUCK FLIGHT TOWER & HOLDING PEN

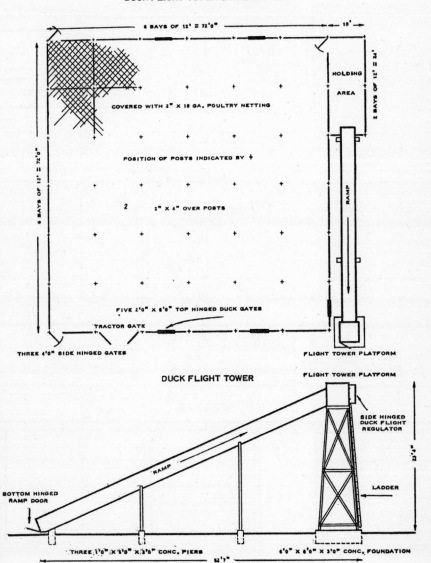

THREE 4'0" SIDE HINGED GATES

FLIGHT TOWER PLATFORM

DUCK FLIGHT TOWER

TRACTOR GATE

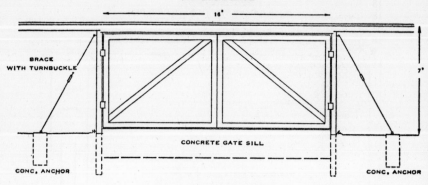

CORNER BRACING & GATE

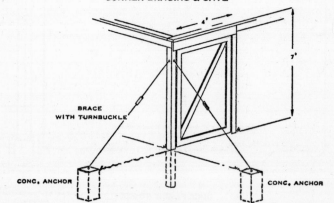

DUCK GATE

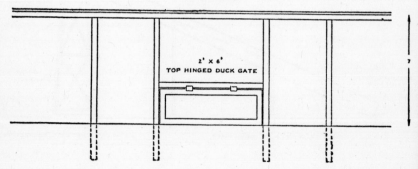

162 Lin. ft. of ¼" wire rope.
18 Screw-eyes ⅜" round galvanized.
18 Turn buckles.
67 4" x 4" Cedar posts 10' long.
18 Heavy wrought steel T-hinges.
9 Galvanized safety hasps.
5 Gallons Penta.
Staples.

Duck Tower

Ground to platform—approximately 22'-5".
Platform to handrail—3'-6".
Platform width—4' x 4'.
Ramp—3' wide, 48'-8" long, with side boards 24" high.

Materials for Farm-Type Duck Holding Pen

91 Posts, 10' length.
8 Rolls (150 ft/roll) 6' wide 2"-20 Ga. Mesh.
4 Rolls (150 ft/roll) 4' wide 2"-20 Ga. Mesh.
4 Rolls (150 ft/roll) 4' wide 1"-20 Ga. Mesh.
½ Roll (850 ft.) #6 wire.
8 Pairs of hinges.
8 Hasps.
4,276 Hog rings.
531 Staples.
169 Lin. ft., 2" x 6".
256 Lin. ft., 2" x 4".

(Note: No materials are listed for Duck Tower, since slope of ground may render tower unnecessary. Waste lumber and other materials at hand can be used provided safety factor is given full consideration.)

List of Required Accessories

*Duck Lake Fencing
(6' one-inch mesh)

*Duck Walk Fencing
(18" one-inch mesh)

Duck Waterer
(100 gal. Oakes Summer Fount Hog Waterer)
Duck Feeders
(Five 5' Oakes Floor Type)

* Depending on length required.

CHAPTER 12

The Shooting Eye

THE curl of smoke lifted as light and innocent looking as a white feather in the breeze. Across the wide swath of valley, exactly one mile, one hundred and eighty seven feet distant, the man in the distinctive field uniform of a general, staggered and fell dead. Aides rushed to his side. Confusion and pandemonium broke and one of the most terrible cannon fusillades of the Civil War was unleashed in the direction the curl of smoke and death had drifted.

Behind that long and fantastic shot that routed the heavy concentration of soldiers and threw them into the state of leaderless bewilderment, stood several impressive factors. The most important of these was a 25 power telescope with so light and so large a field that it even then rivaled some of those made today. It had a scale on its rifle mounting that was adjustable both vertically and horizontally and read in minutes of angle. The rifle that hurled the lead, some thirty pounds in weight, was a muzzle-loading, percussion lock, target rifle, and its maker's name, Abe Williams, was marked cleanly on the barrel.

The man behind the rifle could have been a West Point graduate, Captain John Metcalf, sort of a prototype of a Civil War captain. The entire incident of the general who might have been named Little Georgie Lainhart, was reported by Charles Winthrop Sawyer, author of the Firearms in America series, himself a consulting engineer on firearms and ammunition

Also behind that herculean shot was careful preparation: Bushes had been replanted to form the screen, and a small cellar dug and floored. Sawyer believes that some fifty soldiers were used, bearing planks, scantlings, carpentry tools, surveying instruments and the big rifle. Then a sturdy table was constructed on the flooring of the cellar; a lever operated muzzle raising device was installed. The captain who peered through the telescope and downed the general then had the blind covered with canvas that had been painted a natural green.

So there was much more involved than peering through a telescopic sight and pressing a trigger.

Back in those early days theory and practice in long range firing often failed to agree. Then, when powder was a varying compound, theoretically, ballistics served merely as a broad basis for practical work. So the good Captain Metcalf probably provided a means for testing his own calculations. He may have had a white mansized silhouette erected at exactly the same distance as the enemy general's tent. He sighted in and practiced often before making his long shot.

Thomas Hall, Gun Curator of the Winchester Arms Company, an avid and reliable student of firearms, tells me that Charles Sawyer was remarkably accurate and that the killing of the Civil War general he described in his book was highly possible.

Today, scopes are continuing the remarkable pace they began back in the muzzle-loading rifle days. And don't let the gadget-look of scope-equipped rifles scare you off. The day the genius sat down and decided that the "spy" glass could be used on the rifle as easily and effectively as in your hand, a whole new vista unfolded for the shooting man.

Let's decide how many types of scopes there are, what they are used for and how they might possibly improve your shooting.

On the simple basis of magnification, riflescopes fall into three classes: (1) The target scope with a high magnifying power and a small field of view. These usually run in power from 10X to 25X. (2) The big game or hunting scope, with somewhat low magnification and a wide field. They run from 2X to 3X. (3) Small game scopes. This is the in-between category for the person interested in varmint shooting and high magnification. But the target object, such as the wily woodchuck, sometimes is fast moving, consequently a wide field of view is needed. This scope can run anywhere from 4X to 8X.

Confused? You needn't be. Simply decide what type of shooting you are interested in and have your rifle mounted with the apropos-type scope. If the words magnification and field seem to be loosely used, let's work on them for a minute. It is a clear fact, everything else being equal, the more the object you are shooting at is magnified, the more possible a hit and the more accurately you can draw your bead on it. This sounds easy. Get the strongest telescopic sight available and you are in business. You can't miss. That isn't the case. Unfortunately, the more we magnify or enlarge the object telescopically, the more we tamper with the field of vision and light or illumination. Consequently, if you are a target shooter and can sit down and shoot in proper lighting conditions at an object that is immovable, then you want sharp and high magnification, for the wide field isn't necessary and you can almost choose your illumination. But if you are after mountain sheep or goat, brown bear or antelope, then you know that you may be shooting on dark days at fast moving objects, and it is wise to select the hunting scope that doesn't magnify quite so much, is well illuminated and has a wide, clear field, which is conducive to fast, snap shooting. The varmint shooter sometimes shoots at distant stationary objects, sometimes at moving targets. He needs magnification, plus light and field. A distinct problem. But scopes in the 4X to 8X class turn the trick.

So-called eye relief is another important angle to consider when selecting a scope. A simple test is the ability to slap the scope to your eye anywhere from two to five inches and immediately see the full field of view. If the field narrows when you make this test and a black ring grows around it, beware of the scope. It won't be practical for your needs. You, as a shooter, know that you don't always press your cheek on exactly the same part of the gun comb every shot. Thus, if you have a scope that demands that you place your eye at one fixed spot for every shot, then you are in trouble. Eye relief is necessary and every one of the good scopes has it, running anywhere from 4 to 6 inches.

Another point to consider is the reticule pattern (the sighting member of your scope) in the telescopic sight. Most rifle scopes seem to have wires strung across a metal frame, although there now seems to be a growing tendency to use simple engravings on the glass itself. One thing to remember in selecting the scope and the correct type reticule whether it be a crosshair, a dot, a tapered post, or a post and crosshair combination, is that the reticule line should not be too fine. The fine line type of crosshair is not easily visible except against a bright background. Lean toward the coarse crosshair, the kind that can be instantly seen and lined up even in dim light, yet not so coarse that the reticule itself tends to obscure the target.

Probably the most important single factor to consider in selecting your scope is the adjustment. Unless the scope is zeroed in properly and accurately, the entire function of both rifle and its sighting instrument is lost. Remember the job of the scope is to bring the game or target and the crosshairs of the reticule into the perfect and identical focus, and at the same time to firmly establish a line of sight that is parallel to the bore of the gun, except for trajectory elevation. This elevation is accomplished by internal adjustment which may move the sighting reticule or by external adjustment tilt the entire scope, or by the happy combination of both.

I, personally, as a game shooter and not a target shooter lean toward internal adjustment. One that accident can't alter and curious tinkering can't mess up.

This matter of adjustment also brings another facet into focus: Mountings. The actual mounting of the scope on your rifle is important. It must hold the scope in a fixed position, and also sometimes provide for adjustments for lining up the scope and the rifle. There are a couple of types of mounts which are most commonly used. The kind with the convenient, quick adjustment feature, the other where the adjustment may take as long as ten or fifteen minutes. Again, I lean toward the scope that has the internal adjustment in the tube itself and not in the mount. There was a time a few years back when the mechanism for moving or changing the point of impact of the bullet was exclusively in the mount. But today you have a chance.

A hunting experience that happened to me a few years ago will illustrate better than a string of sentences what the internal adjustment means and how important it can be to a shooter.

I have a friend several years older than I who lost his left leg in World War I. But being an avid sportsman, that didn't slow him down at all. He had an artificial limb fitted and kept right in there with the best of them in the duck blinds, on the deer trails and even walking fields after pheasant. It happened that we were both anxious to get a big brown bear in Alaska. There's a variety of the Grizzly called the Sitka which seems to find life on the Baranof Island, Alaska, particularly satisfying. We decided to try for one of these big fellows. My friend and I both packed .30-06s, with telescopic sights that were adjustable from the mount.

It also was a fact that without a scope on his rifle my friend would not be able to do much big game shooting or varmint shooting either, because the chore of walking would knock the sport out for him. As a matter of fact, the scope is awfully

kind to your feet and even saves shooters with two whole legs
many a weary mile.

One early spring day when the cold wind was stirring around
Alaska, and the sun a weak and vapid fellow, we were slowly
shivering up a trail slope when my friend slipped, fell sharply
against a tree, giving himself and his rifle quite a bang.

Shortly after that our guide pointed out a big brown bear
moving slowly up a slope about 200 yards from us making
for a copse of trees on a distant bluff.

Up went my friend's rifle. He did everything right. Led,
exhaled, pressed the trigger gently. And he missed. By the time
we awoke to the fact that he had made a clean miss the bear
was 500 yards away, too far for me to work on him with my
hunting scope—and he was now traveling fast.

What had happened was that the fall against the tree had
struck the rifle mount and threw the rifle off its zero. There
wasn't time to readjust. So one of those rare shots of a life-
time was muffed.

Most shooters today demand that the vertical and horizontal
adjustments for their telescopes be built right inside the tube
itself. And most of the good present-day scopes do have this
internal adjustment. But there are good scopes that have the
windage and elevation adjustments in the mount. One that I
know is excellent has only two moving parts on the mount.
One-piece steel double cones adjust for both windage and elevation. And the scales are calibrated in the simple scale of one
division to an inch at 100 yards. Lock screws and adjustments
are operated by a coin. The manufacturer, Bausch and Lomb,
claims that there is nothing delicate about this mount-adjusted
sight, that it retains zero and that any blow that would throw
the rifle off zero would have to be severe enough to dent the
barrel of the tough aluminum scope.

So, actually, you can take your choice. But regardless of the
type adjustment, some scopes aren't too accurate in their movements. I suggest that a scope be tried before you buy it,
especially if it's one of the higher priced jobs.

Here's one way you can test its accuracy:

Place the scope in a padded vice, have it facing some blank
object such as the base of a large tree or a stone wall. Pace it
off, so that you know at exactly what distance you are training
the scope. Today, most scope adjustment dials are graduated
in minutes (one minute is equal to one inch at 100 yards), or

they are equipped with the click method, where each click is a fraction of a minute.

With the scope held motionless in its vice, any slight movement of the windage or elevation should bring forth a like movement of point of impact at the target. The movement in the scope must be extremely sensitive to be effective and worthwhile. If the movement has backlash or is jerky in either windage or elevation, then the adjustment is bad. Now try moving the windage and see if it makes a change in elevation, or try the elevation and watch for change in the windage. If this happens, you are really in trouble and you've got a bad scope. For a setup like this is apt to change the gun's zero setting when the gun is fired.

I'd play it safe and get one of the good rigid mounts and the scope with highly sensitive and dependable internal adjustments. These type mounts will last for years and, if properly fitted, can be depended upon for a good many years.

In selecting a scope also try to get one of the kind made of aluminum or aluminum alloy. They are sturdy as steel and bear up under gun recoil much better. Also they're lighter to pack along.

Now let's get a trifle technical again and suggest that you make sure the optics or the lens of your scope is hard coated. Sometimes called "lens coating" it is a process for applying a thin, transparent film of magnesium flouride to the surface of a lens in order to reduce the reflection of light, as well as to increase the transmission of light through the lens. The film of the hard-coated lens is about four one-millionths of an inch in thickness. For example, this page you are reading is about 800 times thicker than the coating on the lens of your scope—a coating that greatly increases the accuracy of your shooting. The Army discovered this during the last war, marked it top secret, coated all military camera, binocular and rifle scope lens and got the top performance from all three.

Walter L. Pierson, Executive Vice President and Treasurer of O. F. Mossberg & Sons, Incorporated, the first company in the United States to manufacture the low priced scope, tells me that his company has run a test in retail sport stores throughout the country and come up with the fact that three shooters to one buy the rifle that is scope-equipped. Once the improved vision is pointed out to the shooter, he does the rest.

It seems that back in 1935, O. F. Mossberg, the founder of

the firm, developed the complex that his company must do anything it could for the convenience of the shooter. He manufactured a medium priced rifle and, during that year, came out with a telescopic sight that could be attached to the rifle. As a matter of fact all Mossberg guns were tapped and drilled for scopes. If a person didn't want the reasonably priced scope with the rifle, dummy screws were inserted in the drilled holes and no harm was done. Since 1946 all Mossberg rifles have come from the assembly line with a simple grooved slot for the scope.

O. F. Mossberg worked his scope line out on a practical basis. Reasoning that a 4 power scope brought the target or hunting object four times nearer the shooter, he pointed out to his customers that his internal, coin-adjusted scope, could be bought for under ten dollars and that the scope would pay for itself in shooting pleasure, accuracy and meat in the pot within the first few days. They found he was right.

The Lyman Gun Sight Corporation, which considers itself dean of scope manufacturers, puts about fifteen different absolutely top scope models on the market, ranging from $2\frac{1}{2}$ power to 30 and has carefully pointed out in a 10 point program why it pays to use a scope. Maybe the answer to why you need a scope is included. Here they are.

Correct Focus—Any object sighted with a scope is clear and distinct as well as being magnified in size.

Brightness—Looking into a good scope reveals a bright image of game or target. A proper scope gathers most of the light coming direct from the target and eliminates reflections and stray light.

Corrects Faulty Vision—Shooters with near or far-sighted vision can adjust the eyepiece of their scope to compensate. Thus they can compete on an equal basis for game or better scores.

Easy Alignment—The sighting member of the scope, the reticule, is easy to place on game, and is in the same focal pane as the image. Positive sighting without blurring.

Less Error—A telescopic sight removes one source of error in sighting—the limitation of the human eye to discern small objects at long range. Thus, it is more accurate than a metallic sight, as is proved in modern competitive shooting.

Matches Best Guns and Ammunition—The only way to get the best from a gun and ammunition is with a sight which is more accurate than either of them—a scope sight.

Corrects Faulty Sighting Habits—Canting a gun or movement

while sighting is quickly noted with the crosshairs of a scope and can be easily corrected.

Judging Point of Aim—Where most long distance shots taken with metallic sights are guessed as to point of aim, a scope "pinpoints" the area being aimed at.

Safety—A man never looks like anything but a man through a scope. Positive identification of game is possible.

Trophy Shooting—Before bringing down game, the conditions of hide and horns can be determined before shooting. Sportsmen who are trophy hunters appreciate this.

And we've got a couple of points. As we stated earlier, a scope is good for your feet. By properly using the scope, you can glass an area and save many steps. The scope also is an aid to conservation. You can quickly see through the eye of your scope whether the animal you are shooting is the illegal female or the legal male, thus preventing the wasteless kill of an animal that you wouldn't be able to claim anyway.

The W. R. Weaver Company of El Paso, Texas, is another manufacturer that realizes that an inexpensive scope is a must for shooters. Their scopes range from less than ten dollars to just under fifty and come in several ranges of power. Their new K4 scope matches with the tops on the market and their K6 and K2.5 also range with the best.

Weaver even has the K1 which is a unique scope for the shotgun. The reticule has a large aiming dot, which is supposed to show the shotgunner the exact point where the center of the shot pattern will strike. The important factors of swinging and leading are also aided with the K1, say Weaver. They also state that the expert shotgunner should shoot with both eyes open. With the K1 shotgun scope the shooting eye looks into the scope and sees both the target and the aiming dot. The other eye remains open and, as it looks down the side of the gun, also picks up the target.

One of the drawbacks that I see is that the shotgun scope would slow down your snap shooting on various types of game birds and that the gun must be cheeked in the same position each time to benefit from the sight. Few gunners cheek the same each time. Weaver believes that the aiming eye acts as a rear sight, and if the eye position varies, aim will vary. This, they say, accounts for many a miss.

There is shooting value in the K1 shotgun scope. It may be a step in the right direction. If scopes aid rifle shooters to the extent that they do, why can't their optical power be brought to shotgun field? It's an interesting experiment.

Hensoldt, known throughout the world for the excellence of their optics, has five scope models on the market, the most powerful of which is their Zeil-Dialyt 8X, running down to the Duralyt 2¾X. These scopes are a product of Western Zone of Germany and the so-called Zeiss Company in the Eastern or Russian Zone is not even recognized by the Zeiss people responsible for Hensoldt.

Texas seems to have a small corner on scopes, with the Stith Scopes and Mounts people in San Antonio giving Weaver a run for their money. They manufacture the Bear Cub series running from the Bear Cub 2¾X Double to the Bear Cub 6X Double. They specialize in hunting scopes and handle only internally adjusted models.

The John Unertl Optical Company of Pittsburgh, Pennsylvania, have two scopes I like, the 2¾X Falcon, and the 4X Hawk, both hunting scopes. They also have a 6X Condor which seems to be working out well.

R. A. Litschert of Winchester, Indiana, brings an innovation to the scope market with their Spot Shot attachment which fits many of the various makes of hunting scopes. It's an install-it-yourself operation. With the Spot Shot device you can change your low power hunting scope to a fine varmint scope up to 8X. This means that with the expenditure of under twenty dollars and a few minutes of your time you can have a scope that will suffice for practically any hunting need. The attachment lines up perfectly on your present scope, due to the new Litschert installation principle. The tubes are not threaded; but the threads that are already in your own tube are utilized.

Bausch & Lomb, well known for their good optics, are featuring the Balvar 2½ to 4X, a variable power scope and the Balfor 4X and Baltur 2½X both fixed power scopes. As with Lyman, the Bausch & Lomb scopes are in the expensive bracket, but seem to be well worth the money if you can afford them.

If you're missing game and plunking when you should be plinking, maybe you need a scope on that rifle. But it's up to you. It's your eye and your ego.

CHAPTER 13

How To Lasso A Lion

THE leap took the boy completely off the horse and sent him
stumbling before the four men. Excitement was so bright
on his face you could even see it in the darkness of the Arizona
night.

"It's happened, Dad," he said. "A big cat just got that heifer
you've been planning on keepin!"

This was almost like an old Western scene, frozen in time.
Night in the Chiricahua mountains of Arizona; night in the
Apache country of Geronimo and Cochise, a rider stumbling
into the light of the fire telling a story of violence. Only this
time the savage killer wasn't an Indian. This time the killer was
a craftier, more indestructible being. The cougar, the American
mountain lion. Scourge of Western ranchers, each of these clever
cats take one calf, one heifer, one colt from a ranch every week.

But this time the cougar's timing and judgment was off. He
had taken a prize heifer from the range of one of the top professional lion men in the country. He had invaded the wrong
acre. The cat had brought Warner Glenn, the son of Marvin
Glenn hurrying to the campfire. Marvin Glenn, a cat hunter
who had one of the choicest packs of lion hounds in the United
States, a man who had caught 80 lions, 220 wildcats and 10
bears was deeply insulted.

He just invited an old friend, Alfred Paul Jr. of Paul Spur,
Arizona, lion hunting. Paul had brought along Tommy Lark
of Santa Barbara, California, James Blakely, an old classmate,
and Blakely's friend Felber Maasdam. For two days Glenn and
his friends had arisen at dawn and rode through scrub oak,
yuccas and catclaw without catching sight of a cougar.

Now in cold defiance, a cat had crawled into Glenn's own
ranch and broken the neck of his best heifer.

His lean face tight as wet leather, Marvin Glenn turned to
face his guests. "Fellas," he said in a soft drawl, "we're in for
some fun. We're goin' catch this cat alive. We'll take the hounds,

a piece of rope and go out and lasso this fella. He's killed his last piece of beef."

"Now wait a minute, Mr. Glenn," Tommy Lark said. "Let's not go off half-cocked! I know you're burned up, but let's not take any chances we'll be sorry for."

"I'm with Lark," said Maasdam. "We ought to at least take a gun."

Alfred Paul smiled. "It's all right, guys. It's quite a stunt, but Marv's done it before. Whenever he has a special peeve for a lion he'll catch him alive and sell him to a zoo. He kinda thinks that's worse than shooting the cat."

A few minutes before, Glenn had been giving them a fill-in on cougars. He had told them that the cougar was the fourth largest in the cat family, second largest on this continent. A male cougar sometimes reaches 200 pounds and has a complete length of from eight to nine feet. Every week throughout the year a cougar will kill at least a deer and three or four smaller animals besides. If near a ranch the cougar will take one or two colts a week and sometimes as many as three young head of cattle. Under that sleek tawny hide is tremendous strength and it is not unusual for a cougar to kill and make off with a Braham steer.

It is unusual for a cougar to attack a human but there is a recorded case of the big cat killing an old woman and a young boy in the Arizona mountains. Marvin Glenn himself was badly bitten in the thigh by a big male cougar. The cat had been wounded and was cutting up some of his good hounds when Glenn rushed in. He still has a slight limp. So the plan of Glenn's to go out and lasso one of the snarlers wasn't received with too much enthusiasm.

Glenn layed it out for the next morning. It was absolutely necessary that they get to bed immediately as they had to climb out long before dawn, have the horses saddled up and be on the trail at five a.m. The hounds had to be able to pick up the track of the cat before the sun burned the dew off. Moisture had to be on the ground or the hounds would not be able to scent-run the cat to a tree or a ledge. Very few humans have ever seen a cougar. They are crafty, nocturnal felines and it is almost an impossibility to tree one or even see one unless you are sitting on a strong and steady horse and have a top pack of hounds to nose the cat out. Glenn made this all very clear.

The next morning before the sun began to rim the Chiricahuas, Glenn stirred his guests into action. He was already in the saddle when he called them and his pack of hounds, black and tans, red bones, walkers, blue ticks, red ticks and a bloodhound were whining and making eager noises deep in their throats.

Not one of the party carried a gun. Glenn asked them not to. He wanted to lasso the lion and said if someone got panicky and shot the cat and didn't kill it there could be trouble. A hound could be killed if the wounded cat dropped in their midst or one of the hunters could be mauled to death.

Young Warner Glenn took them to the place of the kill. Glenn climbed down from his horse and pointed out cat sign. There were a few deep scratches in the earth and a V-shaped heap of dirt. Cats can always be trailed by this sign. To them it is some sort of language. They invariably leave little V-shaped mounds on passing or meeting places.

About ten feet north of the sign Marvin Glenn pointed out a round padded track with two high ridges and three indentations in the heel pad. "It's a big tom and he's traveling fast," Glenn said.

The trailing was slow. The sun seemed to move up from behind the blue-gray mountains with the speed of an elevator, and the moisture was fast disappearing from the ground. In making the kill and in scratching up the ground, the lion left plenty of confusing scent. It took Glenn awhile to get the dogs on the right trail. He led his horse and many times pointed up the visible trail to the hounds; trail, which although hot, circled and slowed down the hounds.

Then the hounds really swung into it. The various breeds reached every octave, every note in the musical scale. The excited music they made sent tingles up the backs of the hunters. The hunters out after a lion with a piece of rope and a young green stick.

Glenn explained as they rode after the hounds that the cat was a smart one. He was hitting as much rock as he could to delay the hounds and was making for some high bluffs and caves to the north.

They rode silently for two hours. Then suddenly and without warning the hounds went crazy and the hunters galloped their horses after the fast-moving Glenn, through scrub oak and cutting manzanita trying to keep up with the dogs.

The dogs seemed to be running with their heads in the air, winding, not ground trailing.

"The cat's close," Glenn shouted.

Then the voices of ten maniacs tore at them. The hounds had treed the lion. Once heard, it is a sound never forgotten.

It was a black-jack oak tree. High in its branches was a flash of cream, then the black muzzle and masklike face and insane eyes peering down at them. It was a large male, snarling and spitting at them in crazy rage.

One of the hounds, a little mad with excitement tried to climb into the tree, succeeded in getting up aways, and then wham! Fast as a flick of light one of the large creamy arms came down and slapped the hound in the face. Glenn clucked in sympathy and dismounted to examine the hound. Her nose was bloody and broken and her front teeth were shaken loose, but luckily the cat had his claws retracted when he slapped and the hound would recover.

Glenn started to spin the lasso from the ground. It was a long throw. The lion was too high. Every time the rope sailed near him he flexed his paws and sent them out at the rope with the inch and half claws unsheathed.

Then according to his friends, Alfred Paul did a foolish thing. He asked for the rope and started up the tree. He got close enough to count the black hairs on the lion's belly and see the froth bubbling in the spit of the snarl and gently tossed the rope. It settled about the cat's neck. Quickly he drew it tight, looped it over a branch pulley-fashion, and made his way back to the ground.

The sudden weight of the lion on the rope sent it slipping to the ground, belly-up. Glenn quickly grabbed it by its long tail and Maasdam got around in front and grasped the rope well up from the lion's neck and the long white teeth. Together they stretched 200 pounds of murder out on the ground, each pulling in the opposite direction.

Before they started out Glenn had given full instructions on the exact procedure. The other two men each got a rope on the forefeet, and pulled the feet apart. Glenn took the green stick out of his pocket and with amazing speed and dexterity stuck it in the lion's mouth and the big white teeth clamped down. He bound the jaws around the stick, locking it firmly behind the long front teeth and clamping the mouth shut. The front feet were then tied together. Then the rear feet were secured and all four feet tied together.

The four men picked up the fearsome, nightmarish creature

to load on a horse. He butted at them with his huge head, unable to understand why he couldn't tear at them with his teeth and his stiletto claws. He blew froth in their faces and snarled his hate. But his cattle-killing days were over. Marvin Glenn had his revenge. He still was the big lion man.

Someday you might see this lion in a zoo somewhere in the United States, and when he looks at you with those enormous, insane-green eyes, contemplate for a moment on the hobby some men have of catching creatures like him with a piece of rope and a young green stick.

There really isn't much to it. You only need a few ingredients: A man like Marvin Glenn, a pack of good hounds, some sturdy horses, a rope and a stick—and a gutful of courage. That's all you need. You might try it sometime. Think of the pictures you could get for your album.

CHAPTER 14

Shooting For Pennies

I F you are the type who can trot out and buy a $12,000 sports car without taking out a second mortgage on your house, or the sort who counts out big-numbered folding money for a Belgian over-and-under or a British fly-rod, this isn't for you.

This chapter is for the man who has to count his dimes and quarters, if not his pennies, when it comes to recreation. In short, for most of us.

Last year approximately 14,000,000 Americans bought hunting licenses and went out with shotguns and rifles in hope of getting meat for the pot. Millions more burned up a lot of ammunition shooting at targets, trap and skeet, or just plain plinking.

It stands to reason that only a small percentage of these people are wealthy sportsmen, and by the same token it is obvious that shooting is an inexpensive pastime. More accurately, it *can be,* and in this chapter I plan to tell of the ways and means being employed by millions of Americans to shoot to their heart's content without going broke in the process.

As a matter of cold, statistical fact, most people can readily afford an occasional day's shooting, even when they are firing 12-gauge shells or large caliber cartridges. The outlay is likely to be closer to five dollars than ten, and what other sport comes so cheap? Even a few hours of driving, or a quick trip around a golf course will cost more, in some cases considerably more.

However, thanks to the ingenuity of various unsung inventors and the ability of American manufacturers to make good things at low cost, it is possible to shoot every day in the week without having to hock the family jewels. And that makes a set-up that is good for everybody.

The manufacturers are assured of a large and steady demand for their products. This means that the cost of production is kept at an absolute minimum. The cost being low, shooters can afford to do more shooting. As their shooting skill develops, their enthusiasm for the sport grows and they become prospects

162

for more and better arms, ammunition and accessories. In short, everybody is happy.

The key to low-cost shooting today is the .22 caliber rifle cartridge. Costing only a cent and a fraction, despite the fact that it contains several rather costly components and represents an involved and precise manufacturing process, the .22 is the shooter's big-bargain buy. Because of this cartridge, highly accurate rifles and pistols of reasonable cost are available for all but a tiny percentage of the shooting done by rifle and pistol users. And, because of closely matched weapons, it is a simple matter to develop one's shooting skill with a weapon shooting the .22 and go from that weapon to one just like it that uses a heavy caliber cartridge.

Many of the major arms companies long ago came to the realization that inexpensive shooting is the wide-open door for the beginner, the extra push he needs to get started. With this in mind they developed autoloaders that shoot .22 short, long and long rifle cartridges, interchangeably and automatically without adjustment. When you realize that a box of fifty .22 short cartridges costs 44 cents against the 67-cent price of the long rifle, it's evident that the arms companies had penny saving for the shooters in mind when they designed these guns.

Manufacturers have also kept the big game hunter and the big bore target man in mind. For those shooters, who have to develop supreme shooting skill, Winchester developed the 52 and Remington designed the Model 37. These are top-grade target rifles. Each weighs about 12 pounds, each is chambered for the .22 long rifle cartridge. The theory here produced rifles the .22 devotee could shoot to his heart's content in matches and target practice. Unlike the usual light-weight .22 rifle they have a substantial feel. The big bore man can use them at practice and then, when the chips are down, switch to his bolt action, .30-06 smoothly without losing any skill. When you compare the 67-cents price of a box of fifty .22 long rifles against the steep tag of $3.70 for a box of twenty .30-06's you'll grasp what we're talking about.

Other manufacturers have rifles with special features to appeal to the economy minded. Mossberg recently came up with a new .22 caliber tubular deluxe repeater. They claim that this rifle has the largest magazine capacity of any made, holding either thirty .22 shorts or twenty long-rifle cartridges. These new and versatile .22 rifles are a boon for shooters. It means the shooter can make the choice himself of how much he wants to pay every time he pulls a trigger.

Marlin, which has always featured lever-action hunting rifles, makes it possible for the hunter to keep his hand in economically by means of its famous 39A, a .22 lever-action rifle which permits an easy transition to a corresponding big-bore Marlin.

Savage stresses economy in a highly practical way in its Model 24, an over-and-under which gives the shooter the choice of a .22 caliber cartridge or a .410 shotgun shell. This versatile, light-weight gun further qualifies in the economy league by its low price, $36.95.

But shooting isn't just rifles. Makers of pistols and revolvers also know that financial short cuts are necessary if they want to keep their shooting public interested in pulling triggers.

Smith & Wesson have made an important contribution to economical handgun shooting with their Masterpiece Target Revolvers. The guns are all made on the same frame but in three calibers, .22 long rifle, .32 Smith & Wesson long and .38 Smith & Wesson Special. Known as the K-.22 Masterpiece K-.32 Masterpiece and K-.38 Masterpiece, they all weigh 36 to 38 ounces loaded. Thus it's a simple matter to go from one to the other.

Another member of the family, popular with law enforcement agencies, is the 34-ounce Combat Masterpiece made for either .22 long rifle or .38 Smith & Wesson Special ammunition.

The K guns come with six-inch barrels, while the Combat Masterpiece is a holster gun with four-inch barrel. Law enforcement agencies frequently order the .38 Special caliber Combat Masterpiece guns for actual duty, while at the same time ordering counterparts in the .22 long rifle caliber for practice shooting.

A. A. Pate, Sheriff of Calhoun County, Alabama, explains the procedure:

"For six years," he says, "we in Calhoun County have been using Smith & Wesson guns. The Combat Masterpiece in the .22 caliber which is identical in every other respect to the gun in .38 caliber is being used by our department for target practice and in the training of new officers. This gun is accurate and gives us the feel of the heavier caliber guns. For our men who carry the .38 Special Combat Masterpiece on duty, the .22 caliber in this model offers the nearest equivalent to the heavier gun. In addition, the great saving in ammunition in actual practice and target use of the .22 cartridge against that of the .38 is tremendous."

When Walter W. Sanborn, service manager of Smith & Wesson, attended the meeting of the International Association of Chiefs of Police in Miami in 1951, several of the chiefs told him that "the saving to the taxpayer involved in the use of the .22 caliber Combat Masterpiece in training new officers and on the target range was enough to take a significant position on Annual Reports."

And what is the saving to the sportsman? Pick up your pencil and work it out. Do you shoot a .32 or .38? If you do, you probably like the heavy and dependable feel of that gun in your hand. But you also know that every time you press the trigger of the .32 it costs about six cents; on the .38 it's eight cents. But with the K-22 or the .22 caliber Combat Masterpiece you have the same weight gun, and it costs a little over a penny a shot. That's a real saving, isn't it? With the money saved in actual firing you can buy a .32 or a .38 and use that gun on those occasions when you feel that the heavier caliber is absolutely necessary. All this can be done without any loss of skill, for you have been using the same weight gun in the lesser caliber.

Colt's Manufacturing Company, too, have several items that were engineered with more economical shooting in mind.

Colt's manufactures the Official Police Revolver which is popular with law enforcement agencies. It is built on a heavy .41 caliber frame and chambered for either the .38 caliber special cartridge or the .22 long rifle. The latter is purchased for training rookie police and for target practice. In addition, Colt's manufactures the world famous government model .45 caliber automatic, the standard side arm of United States armed forces for years. A similar weapon is also made in super .38 automatic caliber.

One of the most ingenious money-savers in the entire arms field is a conversion unit, made by Colt's, which will convert either of these heavy calibers to .22 caliber long rifle in thirty seconds. Selling for $40.00, it has a floating chamber which multiplies the recoil of the .22 caliber long rifle bullet four times for perfect ejection. Here's a simpler picture of what Colt has done with this device. A box of .22 long rifles costs about 67 cents for fifty. Fifty .45 cartridges cost $5.00. A saving of $4.33 on a single box. A good return on a $40.00 investment!

The automatic target pistols in .22 caliber made by Colt's

are also well known. Among these is the "stripped down" Challenger at comparatively low cost for the economy-minded.

Parenthetically, the sort of thing done by Colt's in bringing out the Challenger is similar to the procedure of several other companies. Knowing that not every shooter can afford a lot of money for a good gun, these concerns are laying stress on giving customers "the mostest for the leastest." A case in point is the Harrington & Richardson Model 922, a 9-shot solid frame revolver that shoots .22 shorts, longs and long rifles. This versatility is found in a good-looking weapon that sells for only $29.95.

In automatics, Ruger has an efficient pistol which is giving a good account of itself, at $37.50, with a target model at $57.50. And if you're looking for a really low-cost pistol, a new one called the S-M Sporter is available at only $19.95. Resembling a Luger, it is a single shot .22 which does everything automatically but load a new cartridge into the chamber. Highly accurate, it makes an excellent trainer for the fellow who eventually wants to shoot with an automatic.

The High Standard Manufacturing Corporation has gone right to the core of the handgun shooting problem. Knowing that cost is so important, they have recently perfected and added to their line what they claim is the only .22 autoloading pistol made in the United States specifically designed for the .22 short cartridge. They call this model the Hi-Standard Olympic. It was originally intended for the 1948 Olympic Matches, but constant use and study of the weapon has brought ou' the fact that not only is the Olympic a top target pistol, it's also a versatile plinking gun; one that will pay for itself in short order. Figure it like this: A box of .22 long rifles costs 67 cents and the shorts are only 44 cents. Every time the shooter fires 50 shots with the Hi-Standard Olympic model he is saving 23 cents. So four boxes save you almost a dollar.

From a practical viewpoint, perhaps the best picture of economy to the shooter using the .22 caliber is painted by Joseph A. Curry, Assistant Chief Inspector at the New York Police Academy in New York City. With more than 19,000 graduates of this academy serving as New York's Finest, Inspector Curry's words take on added significance.

"For the past number of years," Inspector Curry says, "the New York City Police Department has employed the .22 caliber revolver in its recruit-training program.

"In addition to the financial saving, the use of the .22 makes the teaching of good shooting fundamentals much easier, due to the lack of recoil and muzzle blast which greatly affect beginners . . ."

During the last war the Royal Canadian Air Force built up a solid and respectable record in the air over England, France and Germany. This reputation was constructed on a solid foundation of good marksmanship. Realizing that the more its air cadets shot, the better marksmen they would become, the R. C. A. F. decided to try something novel. Hundreds of Mo-Skeet-O sets, consisting of scaled down traps, rifles and small clay birds, were purchased and the fledgling fly boys got their original aerial gunnery know-how by walking the rounds of a skeet field shooting a light smooth bore .22 caliber rifle and .22 long rifle shot cartridges. This did two things. It gave the young cadet confidence in a firearm without the weapon jolting him every time he pulled the trigger, and the inexpensive method of shooting made it possible for the R. C. A. F. boys to shoot thousands of rounds daily in practice rather than just a few hundred.

Tracking a clay target in the air with a shotgun and blasting it from the sky at the proper moment is good practice for aerial gunners. The lead, the follow-through and the actual pulling of the trigger approximate the action of firing a machine gun at a moving target. Mo-Skeet-O uses the shotgun technique with the .22 smooth bore rifle and the versatile shot cartridge.

This lesson learned by Canada during the war is currently being put to use by thousands of Boy Scouts in America and by sportsmen in many parts of the country. More than 300 Boy Scout camps used the Mo-Skeet-O Trap, .22 smooth bore rifle, shotshell system, in their summer programs last year.

One of the finest trap shots I know does most of his practicing with the .22 smooth bore and the shot cartridge. He claims that it closely approximates the shotgun, and that if you get good at knocking down the clay birds, sold with the Mo-Skeet-O trap and gun, you'll have no trouble on the skeet or trap range or in the field after ducks and geese.

The Model 80 Mo-Skeet-O trap costs $16.00 and the single-shot, bolt-action rifle about $22.00. Larger trap and repeating type Mo-Skeet-O shotguns are also available. As for the economics—a box of 25 12-gauge shotgun shells retails at $2.50, and a carton of 100 of the normal size clay targets goes for $2.20. The Mo-Skeet-O trap uses midget clay birds which cost $4.07 for 450; the .22 long rifle shot cartridges are 94 cents for a box of fifty. The Mo-Skeet-O trap and targets can give good practice to the average wing shot with his regular field gun, especially for quartering shots or cross overs. The targets travel up to 75 feet. The shot pattern of the .22 shot cartridges is about 15 inches.

Among serious shooters, the big bore crack shots who know that bullseyes don't just happen but come from constant practice, the most important aid to shooting is a set of hand loading tools. In fact, without such equipment few expert shooters could afford the hundreds of rounds they have to fire to develop the skill to win matches.

Milton E. Hicks, ex-sales manager of Colt's Manufacturing Company, credits hand loading with even more:

"Reloading," he says, "helps to hold together almost every pistol club in the country. Most clubs have a hard core of expert shooters who want to understand just what happens when the firing pin falls, the bullet streaks out the barrel of their guns and arrives at the target. They take up hand loading and get the answer through putting together their own cartridges."

Hicks tells the story of an old friend of his named Jack Stiles who moved to Coral Gables, Florida. Stiles decided he wanted to do some shooting so he reloaded some empty pistol cases, cut a path through some underbrush on a vacant lot near his home, pasted a paper target on a palm tree and fired about a hundred handloads at it with his pistol. His neighbor, attracted by the sound of shooting, came out and watched. He told another neighbor; in a few months Jack Stiles and his early spectators became a shooting club. Now, because of the fact that one man was interested in hand loading and shooting, Coral Gables has one of the best pistol clubs in the country. Many of these men are kept on the range through the economical medium of hand loading.

Another example of what one man interested in hand loading can do was pointed out to me right in my own backyard. I live in Roxbury, Connecticut, not far from Danbury, a city of about 30,000 people. It seems that one Burton Humphrey, who lived on the outskirts of Danbury, interested Captain J. Howard McGoldrick of the Danbury police force in hand loading several years ago. It was at a time when war restrictions were on, ammunition was difficult to get and the police departments of the country were growing stagnant so far as shooting practice was concerned. Humphrey had all the equipment

necessary to hand load. He found an avid audience in the
Danbury police. He taught Captain McGoldrick, the good captain passed his knowledge around, and before long eight patrolmen were gathering at Humphrey's house regularly to try their
hand at loading ammunition.

I visited the red-bricked police department in Danbury,
where I met Chief of Police Faverino Mazzia, who took me to
Sergeant Willis E. Woodin, the man now in charge of hand
loading in the department. There, in a neat room dominated
by a long wooden table containing a set of reloading tools, I
talked to Sergeant Woodin about hand loading. The necessity
of operating on a slim budget and the desire of the Danbury
police force to become and stay expert shots, made the hand
loading endeavor a popular one.

In less than a year, he said, he and helpers had hand loaded
over 25,000 rounds. The hand loading is done every Monday
night from October to May 1st by patrolmen who are off duty.
Chief Mazzia estimates that they are able to save about five
cents a round when his men hand load the .38 wadcutters they
use. With a force of 39 regulars, 45 specials and 130 auxiliary
police, there's a lot of hand loading around Danbury. The
hand loading operation, instigated by a sportsman and brought
to perfection by the police of that city, is a project of importance. In dollars and cents, Sergeant Woodin estimates that they
save about $60 every evening on an average night's production
of 1,200 reloads.

The Danbury Police Department paid for their hand loading equipment in two nights (in ammunition money saved),
and, according to Captain McGoldrick, the natural rotation of
policemen who assist in the hand loading operation has in-
jected a new respect for shooting into the entire department.
He believes that when a man has hand loaded a cartridge he
has a new respect for it. It is his own handiwork and he isn't
going to do any foolish shooting.

"Hand loading," adds Captain McGoldrick, "brings the
shooter right down to basics. Teaches him about powder,
primers and bullets, and if the man has a real interest in shooting, hand loading is bound to make a better shot out of him."

The Lyman Gun Sight Company of Middlefield, Conn., sell
a high percentage of the handloaders their equipment, including the bible of the activity called the "Ideal Hand Book on
Reloading Ammunition," now in its 39th edition. With inexpensive items such as their Ideal Economy Set and the Quick

Reloading Set, which include the Ideal Hand Book, Lyman
has placed more hand loading equipment in American homes
than any other manufacturer.

Lyman insists that there is little danger attendant in hand
loading and offers the following suggestion to help the hand
loader:

(1) Read and understand the entire hand loading procedure
before starting.

(2) Contact an experienced reloader and watch him work.

(3) Buy the tools suited to your needs—according to the
amount of reloading you plan to do.

(4) Line up the sources for your components in advance.
(Components are empty cases, primers, powder, and bullets.)
The important ammunition manufacturers offer component
parts of cartridges for hand loaders. Your sporting goods dealer
carries them or can get them for you.

(5) Use good judgment and ordinary care in every operation.

In addition, the Lyman experts advise shooters to use only
guns that are in good condition, and not to experiment in hand
loading beyond the limits of safety.

The last point is something that the enthusiast should keep
in mind in case he is ever tempted to try to break through the
sound barrier, ballistically speaking. He is likely to learn what
happens when an irresistible force, a heavy charge of powder,
meets an almost immovable body—a gun chamber.

Serious accidents can also result from careless measuring or
use of the wrong kind of powder. For example, the fellow who
thinks that the same kind of powder that goes into a pistol
cartridge will do for a rifle cartridge stands a good chance of
turning up in a surgery ward. Gun manufacturers, incidentally,
report a growing number of damaged guns resulting from careless hand loading—so watch your step. Still, *your* chances of
avoiding trouble are probably close to 100 percent. The fact
that you are reading this chapter indicates that. The fellows
who get themselves fouled up are invariably those who attempt
to do something without learning anything about what they
are trying to do. Assimilate knowledge from responsible sources
first before you begin loading your own.

By the same token you ought to be able to save some money
from here on out, and do more shooting than ever. Thanks to
the people who turn out our guns and ammunition, shooting
is one sport that everyone can afford.

CHAPTER 15

Preserves and Pheasants

THE barroom voices of the crows grew into one loud coarse scream bringing us outdoors on the run, guns in hand. Living in the country at our place, *Bluff's End* in northwestern Connecticut, surrounded by over 150 acres of wild forest, facing a huge open meadow across which there were two daily flights of crows and many other kinds of birdlife, my wife and I had become conditioned to the wild noises that were a blessed relief after the even wilder sounds of the mad island of Manhattan.

Although neither Mary Lou nor I decked ourselves out in any Ernest Thompson Seton cap of wildlife knowledge, we did understand crow talk, and this particular melding of sound meant that there was a hawk in the vicinity—a big one and a dangerous one.

She saw him first making his climb to get above the black bandits who were wise to his murderous ways and detested him above all else save possibly that deadly killer of anything that moved, the Great Horned Owl. But this was *Accipiter gentilis* himself, the great goshawk with his transversely barred plumage, his short wings, his orange eyes, and great curved killer's beak. He brushed off the crows easily by the simple expedient of gaining altitude so fast that they couldn't reach up to him.

This was the same clever goshawk we had seen standing like a tall hangman one quiet evening on one of the small shooting platforms just large enough to accommodate a box of shotgun shells that comprised one station in our six-station homemade skeet range. We stopped the car and he watched us intently from one hundred yards. We could see the wild blaze of his eyes and he gently got into the air as I attempted to walk closer.

Later this same goshawk polished off all my squab-producing White King pigeons, leaving our freezer bare and my enmity against his killing ways full-blown. But try as I might, I never could stalk close enough to take a shot at him. He is still one of my small frustations. A bird with a brain.

The convolutions of the human mind are strange and I

never see or hear of a goshawk anymore that I don't remember some of the pleasantest shooting days I've ever had.

I recall the day at George Boehm's 800-acre pheasant preserve at Huntington, Connecticut. When the shooting day ended he invited us into his home for a hot drink and the feel of glowing logs throwing their warmth into his pleasant, pine-paneled study where the late afternoon shadows were beginning to gather. He turned on a desk lamp and as light flashed on it brought into bold view a shape on the desk. A mounted goshawk, his eyes still blazing, long talons clutching a cock pheasant. I think I flinched a little when I saw it and George Boehm said, "I bet none of you fellows can identify that dirty buzzard. Anyone that does gets extra cream in his coffee."

I did, but quickly to prove that it wasn't from a sense of great wildlife knowledge, told about my own goshawk. But the thing that made that evening a pleasant memory wasn't the talk about the hawk, but the vivid reliving of the hours we had just spent shooting.

Gordon Carroll, a tall, blond Anglo Saxon had made an especially impressive double shot and the guide Tony and George Boehm were still talking about that, and my Weimaraner male, Mark, had made one point, broken when the bird took wing, pointed another, then one at a time, retrieved to me both birds Carroll had shot. About an hour earlier he had gone on point at the top of a hill about a half mile away. We started for him, but the bird was nervous, didn't hold and got into the air, Mark hard after him. I took my time. The cock pheasant was high, the wind was behind him and he was moving at about fifty miles an hour, the sun gleaming on his iridescent ruff. I drew on him, moved ahead about eight bird lengths, then pulled the trigger without stopping the motion of the gun. He plopped, Mark on the ground under him, waiting. I can still hear George and Tony shouting as Mark came to me with the big bird in his mouth. That was a high moment when my Weimaraner was in for some loud praise.

All that day the shooting had been fast. Most of the shots had been long. Every bird but three were killed over Mark's marblelike points. And that day made Gordon Carroll and I think of another on a preserve just outside of Gettysburg, Pennsylvania. Gordon is one of those relaxing, entertaining shooting companions. He has an educated tongue and a dry wit and is probably, next to Eltinge Warner, my ex-boss on

Field and Stream Magazine, one of the most accomplished bird shots I have ever met. I have never seen him miss a bird; never seen him flutter or flub a field shot. His field manners, his knowledge of wildlife, his young enthusiasm for bird shooting make him a top hunting sidekick.

When talking about pheasant shooting his favorite cliche is, "No one ever misses a bird by over shooting. They're always behind." And he is right. His advice and mine on everything from ducks to the dodging dove is: "Swing your gun ahead of the bird. Never shoot directly at it. If you put your gun on the bird then pull ahead several bird lengths, dependent upon the distance, always moving the gun in a follow through of the flight, and never stopping it to pull the trigger, you place a path of shot for the bird to fly directly in, and it's almost certain to be a direct hit."

It's decidedly a knack to steel yourself into keeping the gun moving and not stopping it when you pull the trigger. But if you want pheasants in the bag, you better practice this in dry runs, without shells for at least a half hour every day before you take to the field. Like golf, tennis or baseball, shooting is a sport for the skilled. You don't pick your gun out of the rack three or four times a year and expect to just naturally become a hot shot. It takes some doing—and by doing, you've got to actually *do* it. Don't just talk about it, shoot as often as possible.

The place in Pennsylvania we recalled was the Harris and Stipe Game Farm just outside of Gettysburg in Adams County. Gordon and I were there as the guests of Wallace Bracken. And because he was such a great guy, good friend and enthusiastic sport, we went despite the cold December weather and the two feet of snow on the ground. The three of us, hunting without a dog, making all tough, long shots at birds who spooked easily on the crusted snow, brought to bag 60 pheasants. It was the kind of pheasant shooting you dream of but never expect to experience.

Another good one was with Mary Lou, my wife and constant hunting and fishing companion, at the John Ballantine preserve in Southbury, Connecticut (now out of business). We worked with two dogs, our Weimaraner pair, Mark and Sis, and were the subjects of the pheasant shooting sequences for the Paramount picture THE DOGGONEDEST DOG, a story of Weimaraners and their abilities. We hunted in tall corn and Mary Lou, shooting a Winchester 20 gauge pump, outshot me four to one. I had a Browning over-and-under 12 (she has too), but she has remarkably keen ears and could tell by the rustle of the corn shocks when the birds were ready to take to the air.

All of her shots were long, at least thirty yards, and she brought down six without a miss. The funny thing is that the dogs who usually retrieve to me, brought all the birds to her, as if to say, "She shot 'em. She gets 'em." This little twist brought quite a bit of laughter from audiences after the picture was released.

I have many warm memories of days afield gunning pheasants and I'm sure that they wouldn't exist, wouldn't be possible without preserves.

Another experience I think of often began in lower New York State on Don Spencer's well-known preserve where I shot as the guest of Antoine Gilly. Antoine physically is just the opposite of Gordon Carroll. Short, dark and Gallic, he is known as one of the finest chefs in America. He owns the famous La Cremaillere in Banksville, New York, just four miles from exit 31 on the Merritt Parkway, and is accustomed to a stream of the famous pouring through his doors. He has that relaxed knack of treating all people as if they were of equal royal blood. To him this is not a crazy, confused world, but one of constant enjoyment.

I think he gets more actual fun out of pheasant and duck shooting than any person I have ever met. This morning we met at the guest lodge where Antoine was waiting with three of his friends. They were all French and were speaking it softly and excitedly when I entered. Antoine poured me a glass of dry white wine and spread a cracker thickly with a delicious wild duck pate that he had made and served at his restaurant. It was 7:00 a. m. and that was the French sportsman's idea of breakfast. It is now mine. On this cold late November morning the white wine went down easily, smooth and warming all the way.

It had been decided that we would shoot pheasants in the morning and mallard duck in the afternoon. The birds had been released the day before and were roving the 300 acres as cocky and self-assured as any wild bird, and with the added bonus of a full belly, strong wings and blooming good health— assets that the wild pheasant sometimes doesn't have, land cultivation and natural enemies being what they are. Most preserves furnish good guides and skillful gun dogs, and Spencer's was no exception. We went out with an old leathery-faced farmer who knew bird hunting better than plowing and a lean black-and-white pointer dog who illustrated how well he knew his business by slamming to a point one hundred yards from the lodge house. As his guest, Antoine insisted that I take the first shot, so I moved up to the rock-steady pointer slowly, gun at the ready, and then like a burst of flame a big cock pheasant went into the air. I swung at his big shape, pulled the trigger and missed! I had been overconfident when I saw his big body and had not led enough. A pheasant's air-speed is deceptive and they get more distance and speed out of their powerful wings than the vaunted grouse, a fact most hunters argue.

After some good natured chiding, we moved along and got three more points with two direct hits, and one winged bird that took an hour to hunt down. Antoine, and I agreed with him, refused to move on for more birds until the crippled one had been retrieved. We had a brief argument with the pointer but he finally saw it our way and did a magnificent job of trailing the running bird and brought him back.

Finally we came to a big meadow and Antoine suggested that I work the other side and he would walk along the near perimeter. We didn't have to tell the pointer what to do, he started through the middle, neatly quartering as instinct and training had taught him. I moved along at a fairly fast clip then suddenly a hen whipped up in front of me. I had almost stepped on her where she crouched in the brown rye. She circled and flew in the opposite direction. The guide was standing in my line of fire so I couldn't shoot. Antoine quickly sensed what had happened, raised his gun and then with a perfect follow-through shot brought the bird down. I went over to where it had fallen and paced the distance off. Antoine Gilly had made a dead center fifty yard shot. A rare thing in shotgunning. And there wasn't any luck connected with it. He just did everything right.

When I told him what the distance was his face glowed and he danced. "Wait'll I tell them this! I am so happy you paced it, no one would believe it otherwise!" he chortled. I don't think I've ever seen a happier man—not in the sense of personal achievement, but in that of being alive and able to walk and shoot on this particular crisp morning in November.

We finished off the morning and returned to the lodge for lunch with four fat pheasants apiece, the smell of gunsmoke around us like perfume, and a whopping big appetite.

Lunch, as was to be expected with Antoine Gilly as host, was superb. Roast breast of guinea hen, wild rice with a wine gravy, pureed peas, and a magnificent white burgundy. After coffee and a chat we went out to shoot ducks. The sun was shining. It was great to be alive.

There is more technical information about this particular kind of duck shooting in Chapter 11 on controlled shooting. The ducks were released on a high hill about a mile away from their home pond. We were placed in strategic positions around the pond. Several ducks came in at a time traveling at about fifty miles an hour. We called our shots and did not shoot at random or more than once at one bird. No more ducks were released until the liberated ones had been bagged or had flown away. We were using the then new Winchester magnum shells that had been perfected to avoid crippling ducks. They really worked. We walked away from an afternoon of fast duck shooting without leaving one cripple. We quit at dusk. By that time we each had five ducks, the retriever was tired, and we had had as fine a shooting day as you can possibly get in the United States in our century. The ducks were high flyers, healthy, and tough to knock down. The pheasants had been jittery, quick to fly and fast when aloft. None of it was the shooting-in-a-barrel business that many shooters believe preserve hunting is.

It had been a rare pleasure to shoot with sportsmen like Antoine Gilly, and his friends Henry Guiguet, and E. J. "Gene" Armelin, men who called all shots, never left a cripple, knew how to use their guns and their manners. Those were the sunny days afield. The glorious mornings.

Most preserves raise their pheasants under high wire where the birds can exercise and develop wing muscle. Large areas are wired so they also can run and build up the leg power so necessary for survival. You rest assured that no preserve bird is diseased, that it comes of good sound stock, that it has been vaccinated, that it has been fed corn and other foods that will not only keep it healthy, but make the flesh tender, juicy and tasty. Wild birds sometimes have a bitter flavor, picked up from the berries and seeds from wild plants that they eat.

Many preserves release your pheasants several days before you arrive, believing in permitting the birds to get the lay of the land, its convenient rabbit holes, its hedgerows, and brushiest areas. These birds are fed at regularly established feeding stations so that they will stay in the territory, and sometimes the preserve owner will go out with a couple of his good dogs and flush the birds so that they begin to know what men, dogs and guns are all about. But this isn't necessary. The instinct of the gaudy ringnecked pheasant brought to this country from China by Judge O. N. Denny in 1880 is strong, and his will and wile to survive have placed him at the top of the list of all game birds. He can run like Nashua, hide in a few blades of grass, lay as silently as a snake, and fly faster than any of the other birds with the exception of the duck and the dove.

I know a preserve in Connecticut that thinks so much of his sagacity that it releases all but a few of the pen-raised pheasants at the beginning of the hunting season, knowing that their brains and the available feed will keep them around for the paying customers.

But best of all, on preserves you can shoot as many birds as you want, either sex, and you shoot in safety. Preserves have a strict limit on the number of hunters allowed on their acreage at one time. Usually the rule on a 300 to 1,000-acre preserve is no more than two parties of hunters with no more than four in each party, and each group with a guide.

License fees vary. In Connecticut and New York, it is possible to purchase a one-day hunting license for $1.00. Pennsylvania demands the regular full resident or non-resident license. Here, again, it is wise to write to the preserve you are interested in visiting and ask about license regulations.

Many of the preserves open their season on September 15 and run straight through until March 15. Pheasant shooting on public lands, as most of you know, varies in each state but is never over three weeks. And it can be dangerous. When more than eight hunters are beating the birds (if they are there at all) out of even a 100-acre plot, there is the constant risk of everyone there, including the dogs, being at the mercy of a careless shot. And preserves furnish dogs and guides, some even hunting clothing, guns and ammunition. Work out on your fingers how much it costs to bring a good gun dog to the peak of perfection, keep him trained up, kenneled and fed. Then throw in a dollop of extra shooting months, a pinch or two of safety for seasoning, and maybe you'll come to the conclusion that preserve shooting is your dish.

Of course prices vary in different preserves and from state to state, but the norm is from four to six dollars per bird. Some preserves expect you to pay the guide five dollars for his work; some that you pay per bird released, some per bird actually shot and in your game bag. It is intelligent to query the one you are interested in as to these points. Another thing I like about them: They have farmers nearby who will pluck the birds you bag for a small fee. And that's one heck of a job as any weary hunter knows. And just try passing the buck to your wife! In this case, coming home with a day's bag all neatly cleaned and plucked, the wife you save may be your own.

For the convenience of you intelligent people who have bought this book, I have canvassed all the states to discover which of them allow preserve shooting. They are listed below. Write them for prices, as they fluctuate somewhat year to year. This complete list of shooting preserves exists in no other book. You'll find that the popular and hardy pheasant is the main attraction of the majority of shooting preserves with some also stocking quail, ducks and the interesting chukar, a fast game bird slightly similar to our grouse, imported from the mountains of India for your sport.

You'll probably be somewhat surprised that states like California don't list preserves. In that state so-called membership clubs dominate the shooting scene with special arrangements also possible for duck shooting. Flip to chapter five, *A Sports Surprise In Every State,* where all the state conservation officials are listed, and write to any state not listed below for their reasons.

SHOOTING PRESERVES IN THE UNITED STATES

Owner or Operator	Address
ARKANSAS	
M. D. Brownstein	Hotel Shirley, Newport, Arkansas
Max Crawley	Route 2, Gravette, Arkansas
CALIFORNIA	
(See page 189)	
CONNECTICUT	
George G. Boehm	Mohegan Game Farm, R. F. D. #2, Trumbull, Connecticut

Owner or Operator	Address
Henry Bernard	Bernard's Game Farm, R. F. D., East Haddam, Connecticut
Samuel L. Benedict	Bethlehem, Connecticut
James F. Smith	Cedar Ridge Hunting Preserve, 897 Congress Street, Fairfield, Connecticut

ILLINOIS

Carroll Berry Taylorville,	Midstate Pheasant Area, Christian County, Illinois
John Calhoun Bath,	Loganberry Lodge, Mason County, Illinois
Joe B. Davidson Monticello,	Hunting Enterprises, Inc., Will County, Illinois
Carl Koch Breese,	Beaver Prairie Game Preserve, Clinton County, Illinois
Oscar Linn Canton,	Linn Farms, Inc., Fulton County, Illinois
E. E. Schmidt, Pres. Box 349, Rock Island	Gopher Gulch Gun Club, Rock Island County, Illinois
Sam Shamhart R. F. D. #2 Wheeler, Illinois	Crab Apple Gun Club, Jasper County, Illinois
Ralph Smith Oswego, Illinois	Ringneck Acres, Kendall County, Illinois
Leo Whalen Hanover, Illinois	Whistling Wings Club, Joe Daviess County, Illinois
Edward R. Wild Route #2, Long Grove, Prairie View, Illinois	Gander Mt. Gun Club, Lake and McHenry Counties, Illinois

INDIANA

Marvin Maier	Bremen, Indiana

KANSAS

Ray Crail Wichita, Kansas	Yates Center, Kansas
George Haum Wichita, Kansas	Aetna, Kansas

Owner or Operator	Address
Payne Retner Wichita, Kansas	ElDorado, Kansas
John Costello Topeko, Kansas	Hoyt, Kansas

KENTUCKY

Miller Welch	1028 Cooper Drive, Lexington, Kentucky
Charles R. Jones, Jr.	West Paducah, Kentucky
M. B. Williams	414 E. Tenth Street, Bowling Green, Kentucky

MARYLAND

Tommy Adkins	Tri-State Sportsmens' Club, Box 748, Salisbury, Maryland
Pierce H. Bates	Harford County Pheasant, Shooting Club, Darlington, Maryland
Mitchell Digges or Joe Tucker	Port Tobacco Valley, Pheasant Farm, La Plata, Maryland
J. Dorman Hall	Hunting Creek Pheasant, Shooting Grounds, R. D. 1, Prince Frederick, Maryland
John Hammond	Hammond's Long Acres, Woodmont Road, Hancock, Maryland
C. C. Stephens	Triggaland Kennels and Game Farm, Brookerville, Maryland

MISSISSIPPI

Kaywood Plantation	Kaywood Plantation, R. F. D., Hazelhurst, Mississippi
French Camp Academy	French Camp Academy, French Camp, Mississippi

MISSOURI

The names and addresses of the various pheasant and chukar shooting farms are as follows:

Roy L. Farms, 7 N. Brentwood Avenue, Clayton 5, Missouri.

Missouri Quail Hunters', Inc., B. A. Zerschey, Treas., 6904 Parkdale Drive, Normandy, Missouri.

Baier's Den Kennels & Game Farm, Peculiar, Missouri.

Aressar Ranch, Inc., Burlington Junction, Missouri.

Clifford W. Kahler, Dalton, Missouri.

Bernard McMenamy, Jr., 1914 Clay Street, St. Charles, Missouri.

R. H. Blum, 2429 Independence, Kansas City, Missouri.

Milton Duenke, 1045 Jennings Road, St. Louis 21, Missouri.

John N. Marshall, Willow Farms, Inc., Granite City Steele Company, Granite City, Missouri.

Owner or Operator	Address
NEVADA	
Gene S. Minor	Dayton, Nevada
Roland Wiley	Pahrump, Nevada
NEW JERSEY	
Serge Chiarotto	Panorama Pheasantry, R. D. 1, Milford, New Jersey
William Cowie	Cowie's Game Preserve, South Road, Chester, N. J.
Duncan Dunn	Amwell Shooting Preserve, Star Route, Ringoes, N. J.
Claude Eby	Big Spring Game Farm, Sussex, New Jersey
John Esposito	Esposito's Pheasant Farm, 180 Hollywood Avenue, Caldwell, New Jersey
Paul Kundra	Three Grand Shooting Preserve, Star Route, Freehold, New Jersey
Frank Kymer	Kymer's Game Farm, R. D. 2, Branchville, New Jersey
L. R. MacQueen	Ramorie Kennels, Pottersville, New Jersey
James L. Munson	Valley Brook Farm, P. O. Box 36, Bevans, New Jersey
Thelma Nielson	Hidden Hollow Game Farm, R. D. 1, Hackettstown, New Jersey
Olive Oberman	Homestead Game Farm, Deans, New Jersey

Owner or Operator	Address
John Titman	Ringneck Manor Game Farm, R. D. 2 Sussex, New Jersey
M. R. Woodruff	Hermit's Hollow Shooting Preserve, R. D. 1, Milford, N. J.

NEW YORK

F. H. Bontecou, Jr.	Tower Hill Pheasant Farm, Tower Hill Rd., Millbrook, New York
Jim Boyd	Pine Tree Shooting Preserve, Thompson Ridge, New York
Jasper Briggs	Brae—Burn Kennels, Harriman, New York
Joe Cox	Joe Cox Game Preserve, Pawling, New York
Chet Crevelling	Pheasant Fields, R. D. 1, Freeville, New York
A. J. Curry	Rock View Game Farm, Clinton Corners, New York
Anthony Da Biere	Breezy Knoll Pheasant Farm, 10 Main St., Fonda, New York
Guy De Stafano	Orange County Gun Club, R. D. 1, Chester, New York
Phil Doremus	Bershire Shooting Preserve R. D. 1, Craryville, N. Y.
J. C. Georg	Lucky Star Ranch, R. D. 1, Chaumont, N. Y.
Harold Gray	Deep Spring Shooting Club, Oakfield, New York
J. A. Hammerle	Quaphegro Game Farm, P. O. Box 91, Schuyler Lake, New York
Kenneth Hard	Suffolk Lodge Game Preserve, Brookhaven, Long Island
Clarence Henninger	Findley Lake Preserve, Findley Lake, New York
Theodore Kurrus	Dutchess Valley Rod & Gun Club, Pawling, New York

Owner or Operator	Address
Frank Klein	Laurel Hill Farm, Stormville, New York
Victor Larson	Vic's Kennels and Game Farm, R. D. 2, Ashville, New York
Herbert S. Lein	Niagara Game Farm, U. S. Highway 20, Ripley, New York
Herbert S. Lein	Niagara Game Farms, R. D. 1, Lockport, New York
Colin Livingstone	Livingstone Pheasant Farm, R. D. 2, Middletown, N. Y.
Alex MacGregor	Rath Mohr Pheasant Farm, Hopewell Junction, N. Y.
Thomas Mackin	Bar T-M-T Hunting Preserve, Box 204 B, Staatsburg, New York
Frank McEachern	Partridge Land Lodge, R. D. 1, Redfield, N. Y.
Fred H. Popans	Wilfred Farms, Chatham, New York
Mrs. Kenneth Reiss	Reiss Game Preserve, R. D. 2, Cuba, New York
George Schellinger, Jr.	Spring Farm, Sag Harbor, Long Island
A. G. Scott	Iron Kettle Game Preserve, Box 86, Schenevus, New York
Don Steger	Cold Brook Game Farm, R. D. 1, Homer, N. Y.
Harry Thatcher	Thunder-Ten-Bronckh, Tilley Foster Rd., Carmel, New York
R. E. Underhill	Robert E. Underhill, R. D. 1, Poughkeepsie, New York
Harry L. Washburn	Washburn's Game Farm, R. D. 1, Lake Luzerne, New York
Pete Wassilieff	Pete's Game Preserve, R. D. 2, Pine Bush, New York

Owner or Operator	Address
OHIO	
Brad Granfield	Gill & Quill Sports Club, Box 895, Sandusky
L. E. Downey	Saybrook Pheasant Shooting Preserve, 211 Center St., Ashtabula
Bob Fenn	Fennwood Shooting Park, R. D. 1, Bellevue
Edward Douglas	Arrowhead Club, 6665 Barton Rd., North Olmstead
Windsor Ford	Whitford Woods, R. D. 2, Middlefield
James N. Brown	Sunnyslope Farms, 328 East Liberty St., Medina
John Moxley	Hill 'n Dale, Medina
R. B. Ridenour	Pheasant Shooting Preserve Inc., 90 N. Diamond St., Mansfield
Dutch Martin	Prairie Lane Game Farm, R. D. 4, Wooster
H. H. Hollister	Cherry Bend Pheasant Farm, R. D. 4, Wilmington

PENNSYLVANIA

Mrs. B. F. Barnhart	Barnhart's Pheasantry, Rt. 1, Elizabethville, Penna.
Harry F. Beegle	Bedford Hunting Lodge, R. D. 2, Bedford, Penna.
Warren E. Berger	Blue Mountain Pheasantry, Rt. 1, Linglestown, Penna.
Alexis L. Clark	Maple Farm, R. D. 1, Wysox, Penna.
A. E. Daniell	Daniell Farm, R. D. 3, Claysville, Penna.

Owner or Operator	Address
Arthur R. Eakin	Gaybird Farms, Box 1, Carversville, Penna.
R. L. Harter	Harter Game Farm R. D. 1, Northumberland, Penna.
Anthony Imbesi	Briardale Game Farm, Bedminster, Penna.
Jake Hayes	Jake Hayes Pheasant and Mallard Hunt Area, Rockton R. D. 1, Penna.
Carl K. Jones	Kings Lake Shooting Preserve, R. D. 1, Oakdale, Penna.
Curtis F. Kreiser	Palmyra Pheasant Farm, R. D. 1, Palmyra, Penna.
J. R. Logan	Logan Kennels, R. D. 4, Gettysburg, Penna.
Salvatore Marone	Marone's Regulated Shooting Grounds, R. D. 1, Oxford, Penna.
Frank Marsh	Rolling Hills, P. O. Box 225, R. D. 3, Blairsville, Penna.
Roy C. Martin	Broad Acres, R. D., East Waterford, Penna.
J. L. McDowell, Jr.	Madison Twp. Hunt Club, Light Street Post Office, Columbia County, Pa.
J. W. Morrision	Brunswick Shooting Preserve, Orwigsburg, Penna.
John J. Murphy	Murphy Game Farm, Star Route, Pottstown, Penna.
Richard M. Roberts	Roberts Pheasant and Turkey Farm, R. D., Tamaqua, Penna.
George H. Ryman	Ryman's Gun Dog Kennels, Shohola Falls, Penna.
Joseph G. Segulla	Segulla Hunting Grounds, R. D. 7, Jackson Center, Penna.

Owner or Operator	Address
Frank O. Simmons	Maple Farm Shooting Preserve, R. D. 4, Meadville, Penna.
Larry E. Stipe	Harris & Stipe Pheasant Farm, R. D. 4, Gettysburg, **Penna.**
Charles H. Swartz	Scrubgrass Farm, R. D., Titusville, Penna.
Allen J. Tate	R. D. 1, Wattsburg, **Penna.**
Richard J. Troy	Seley Farms, R. D. 1, Atlantic, Penna.
Maurice D. Waters	Waters Game Farm, R. D. 1, New Providence, Penna.
Daniell L. Yingling	Twin Hemlock Pheasant Farm, R. D. 1, Gettysburg, Penna.

RHODE ISLAND

B & K Wild Game Bird Farm, Inc,	Old Hartford Pike North Scituate, Rhode Island
Hianloland Farms, Inc.,	West Greenwich, Rhode Island (Coventry, RFD)
Newport Country Club,	6 Catherine Street, Newport, Rhode Island
Peace Dale Shooting Preserve,	Rose Hill Road, Peace Dale, Rhode Island

TEXAS

J. C. Benedum	Fairway Farm, San Augustine, Texas
Frank G. Hill	Quail Hill Farm, Tyler, Texas
Frederick T. Houghton	Cock Walk Farm, La Grange Texas
Richard R. Shipp	Tarkinton, Clevelland, Texas

VIRGINIA

Roy Campbell	Louisa, Virginia
David E. Laird, Jr.	R. F. D. 2, Richmond, Virginia

Owner or Operator	Address
Helene and Francis Omlor	R. F. D. 1, Oakton, Virginia
Walter Rice	R. F. D. 1, Lynchburg, Virginia
Walter G. Smith	Trevilian's, Virginia
Clarence D. Truxell	Middlebrooke Star Route, Staunton, Virginia
W. N. Wilbur	Box 206, Warrenton, Virginia

WISCONSIN

W. W. Evans	Fall River, Wisconsin
Leeds Preserve (J. N. Williams, Sec.)	c/o General Casualty Co., 117 E. Wilson St., Madison 3, Wisconsin
Martin E. Griepentrog	Route 1, Pardeeville, Wisconsin
Florence S. Chapman	Route 2, Waunakee, Wisconsin
John S. Dreher	105 State St., Madison, Wisconsin
Dr. James A. Jackson	Route 1, Waunakee, Wisconsin
R. H. Jackson, Jr.	415 N. Carroll St., Madison, Wisconsin
H. S. Johnson	17 Cambridge Rd., Madison 4, Wisconsin
Robert Pfister	1937 Regent St., Madison, Wisconsin
Dr. E. F. Schneiders	113 N. Carroll St., Madison, Wisconsin
A. W. Schorger	424 University Farm Place, Madison 5, Wisconsin
Dr. James M. Wilkie	110 E. Main St., Madison, Wisconsin
Beaver Dam Hunting Club (Walter Schweitzer, Pres.)	812 De Clark St., Beaver Dam, Wisconsin
Ben W. Place	218 Highland Ave., Hartford, Wisconsin
Alvin H. Pluckhan	107 North St., Juneau, Wisconsin
Rubicon River Game Assn. (Harry U. Amidon, Mgr.)	32 N. Main St., Hartford, Wisconsin

Owner or Operator	Address
Russell A. Wilcox	326 E. Lake St., Horicon, Wisconsin
A. T. Brenner	108 S. Main St., Fond du Lac, Wisconsin
H. F. & D. Club, Inc. (F. E. Rueping, Treas)	c/o Rueping Leather Co., Fond du Lac.
Ralph E. Petersen	159 Oak St., Berlin, Wisconsin
W. H. Arnold	731 Park Ave., Beloit, Wisconsin
Bark River Game Pres., Inc. (Malcolm F. Rogers, Pres.)	Route 1, Sullivan, Wisconsin
Black Hawk Club (Allen P. Jones, Sec.)	Ft. Atkinson, Wisconsin
R. L. Deckert	Route 1, Nashotah, Wisconsin
Deer Creek Hunt Club, Inc. (Arthur J. Gruennert, Sec.)	Jefferson, Wisconsin
French Road Hunting Club (Ed. Hinterberg, Sec.)	811 Tenth St., Watertown, Wisconsin
Hugh Highsmith	Route 2, Ft. Atkinson, Wisconsin
Jones Dairy Farm (Ed. C. Jones, Sec.)	Ft. Atkinson, Wisconsin
Kieckhefer Box & Lumber Co. (Wm. H. Kieckhefer, Pres.)	1711 W. Canal St., Milwaukee 3, Wisconsin
Mrs. E. Z. Menhall	Route 1, Milton Junction, Wisconsin
Leo W. Roethe	1216 W. Sherman, Ft. Atkinson, Wisconsin
Dr. F. E. Shearer	Edgerton, Wisconsin
P. O. Krumm	5314 Lakewood Ave., Chicago, Illinois
Mosquito Valley Shooting Preserve (Dr. C. I. Perschbacher, Pres.)	520 Zuelke Bldg., Appleton, Wisconsin
Rock Creek Farm (Horace D. Klein, Pres.)	St. Croix Falls, Wisconsin
Caldwell Shooting Club (Andrew Clark, Sec.)	East Troy, Wisconsin
Eagle Lake Shooting Pres. (R. B. Voelker, Sec.)	402 William St., Racine, Wisconsin

Owner or Operator	Address
Harry H. Rarich, Jr.	1237 Cleveland Ave., Racine, Wisconsin
Arthur J. Usher	7339 Chappel, Chicago 49, Illinois
James T. Atwood	1400 Eddy Avenue, Rockford, Illinois
George W. Hevey	115 Elm St., Milton Junction, Wisconsin
John Roe	c/o H. A. Roe Co., 105 E. Second Ave., Dixon, Illinois
Tracy Hunting Club (Renile E. Bowles, Sec.)	525 Monroe St., Janesville, Wisconsin
Elmer Billing	Williams Bay, Wisconsin
George W. Borg	190 E. Pearson St., Chicago, Illionis
George E. Brennan	Route 1, Lake Geneva, Wisconsin
Crane Farms Preserve (F. F. Elliott)	836 S. Michigan Ave., Chicago 5, Illinois
Elkhorn Game Club (A. C. Olseon, Pres.)	411 N. Wisconsin Ave., Elkhorn, Wisconsin
C. B. Habecker	Lake Geneva, Wisconsin
T. H. O'Brien	Killerney Acres Ranch, Delavan, Wisconsin
Edward M. Olson	843 Lakeshore Drive, Lake Geneva, Wisconsin
Daniel Peterkin, Jr.	Stenning Farms, Lake Shore Drive, Lake Geneva, Wisconsin
Rainbow Springs Farm Club (Allen Shoup, Treas.)	Route 1, Mukwonago, Wisconsin
James D. Swan, Jr.	Delavan, Wisconsin
A. T. Westmas	126 South 6th St., Delavan, Wisconsin
Russell A. Zimmermann	33 North LaSalle St., Chicago, Illinois
Edmund J. Copps	Route 1, Nashotan, Wisconsin
Dr. Ward Evenson	1208 Grant, Waukesha, Wisconsin

Owner or Operator	Address
Edwin A. Gallun	1818 N. Water St., Milwaukee, Wisconsin
Harold Hodgson	Route 4, Box 401, Oconomowoc, Wisconsin
Holiday Farms Inc. (George H. Magaw, Pres.)	Route, Box 238, Waukesha, Wisconsin
L. L. O'Bryan	Lakewood Farm, Mukwonaga, Wisconsin
Oconomowoc Game Fields (I. J. Perkins, Prop.)	Route 4, Box 376, Oconomowoc, Wisconsin
Edwin Wohlt	Fremont, Wisconsin
H. H. Clark	P. O. Box 945, Oshkosh, Wisconsin
R. E. Gruenhagen	361 Algoma Blvd., Oshkosh, Wisconsin
E. C. Leach	755 Algoma Blvd., Oshkosh, Wisconsin
Elliott A. Parker	Route 5, Eau Claire, Wisconsin
Mrs. Angeline Clark	Blonhaven Game Farm, Route 1, Janesville, Wisconsin
I. J. Perkins	Oconomowoc Game Farm, Route 4, Oconomowoc, Wisconsin
T. H. O'Brien	Killarney Acres, Delavan, Wisconsin
Glenn E. Hughes & William J. Smith	Box 253, Janesville, Wisconsin
Van Zeeland Brothers	Fox River Valley Game Farms, Inc., Route 2, Kaukauna, Wisconsin

CALIFORNIA

These are not shooting preserves, but fee hunting clubs that welcome public inquiry.

CASTLE ROCK LODGE—Lake County. Club located on West Gibson Road, 8 miles west of Middletown. 320 acres. $4.50 per day—opening week and $2.50 per day for every day after. Ted Stevens, 426-25th Street, Oakland, Calif.

MB HUNTING CLUB—Yolo County. Club located on State highway 16 Road, 2 miles NW of Rumsey. 160 acres. $25.00 per season. N. Fred Bruhm, Rte. 1 Box 33A, Dixon.

RANCHO NAN-Q—Kern County. Club located on Adobe Road 15½ miles south of Bakersfield. 70 acres. 6 blinds. $350 per hunter for the season. Stockton Quincy, Rte #2, Box 574, Bakersfield.

PERATI CLUB—Glenn County. Club located on 3 miles east, 1 mile north of Norman, SW corner Culver Ranch, 140 acres. $10.00 per day. Jack Perati, 160 East 14th Street, Oakland.

PACIFIC FLYWAY HUNTING CLUB—Inyo County. Club located on Highway 6 Road, ½ mile east of Highway 6. 280 acres. 18 blinds. $20.00 opening day, $15.00 thereafter. John Grant, 200 N. Catalina St., Los Angeles.

THE APACHE CLUB—Merced County. Club located on Duck Club Road, 3 miles Southeast of Gustine. 528 acres. 20 blinds. $200.00 per blind in advance. Frederick E. Harrison, P. O. Box 436, Aptos.

DOUBLE D HUNTING CLUB—Colusa County. Club located on Hiway #20, 18 miles west of Williams. 20,000 acres. Season $50.00, daily $10.00. Ronald E. Williams, P. O. Box 565, Williams. (Deer, dove, duck)

V. V. COLEMAN HUNTING CAMP—Lake County. Club located 1 mile from County Road, 3 miles west of Cobb P. O. 350 acres, $3.00 per day or $5.50 for 2 days. V. V. Coleman, Lower Lake.

LITTLE LAKE HUNTING CLUB—Inyo County. Club located on Hiway 395 & 6, ¼ mile North of Little Lake. 1200 acres. 10 blinds. Fees $15.00 per day per person. T. J. Bramlett, Little Lake.

BUCK HORN HUNTING CLUB—Lake County. Club located 2 miles west of Witter Springs near Hiway 20. 400 acres. Fees, $10.00 per man per day. Guy E. Pyle, Witter Springs.

SUTTER BASIN GUN CLUB—Sutter County. Club located on O'Banion Road 16 miles SW of Yuba City. 1000 acres. 42 double blinds. Fees $10.00 per day, $125 per season. Nick G. Martin, Rte 1, Box 731, Tree Breeze Motel, Chico.

THE OAKLAND ROD & GUN CLUB INC.—Colusa County. Club located on Highway #20, 2 miles east of Williams. 20,000 acres. 87 blinds. Fees various. J. R. Young, Supt., P. O. Box #391, Williams.

STANDARD GUN CLUB—Merced County. Club located on North Mercy Springs, 5 miles north of Los Banos. 700.79 acres. 45 blinds. Fees $175 per blind per season. Dwight G. Vedder, Manager, 811 West 7 Street, Los Angeles.

CHAPMAN GOOSE AND DUCK CLUB—Imperial County. Club located on Estelle Road, 6½ miles NW of Calipatria. 80 acres. 9 double blinds. Fees, $10 daily. R. M. Chapman, 110 W. Bonita St., Calipatria.

GILBREATH BROS.—Kern County. Club located on Corcoran, 5 miles north of 466 Highway. 1200 acres. 75 blinds. Fees $10 per day. Vernon and Elmer Gilbreath, 1019-3rd Street, Wasco.

PLEASANT GROVE DUCK CLUB—Sutter County. Club located Jackson Road, 18 miles north of Sacramento. 180 acres. 20 blinds. Fees, daily shoots $15.00. Season, $400 a blind, guests $10 per day. Antonio Fiori, Rte 1, Box 42, Pleasant Grove.

MALLARD PONDS DUCK CLUB—Butte County. Club located on Butte Co., Chico. 12 miles SW of Chico. 9000 acres. 60 blinds. Fees, season pond rental $150. Day shooters, $7.50 and $10.00 per day. E. O. Wraith, P. O. Box 582, Chico.

J. H. CAVE RANCH—Colusa County. Club located on Colusa Junction

4½ miles West of Colusa. 640 acres. 5 blinds. Fees, $10.00 per day per man; doubles only. J. H. Cave, Box 297, Williams.

WILLIAM MOSESIAN—Kern County. Club located on Adobe 15 miles South of Bakersfield. 50 acres. 10 blinds. Fees $357 per blind per season. William Mosesian, 1772 Locust Ravine, Bakersfield.

SPORT HAVEN—Fresno County. Club located on Highway 180 23 miles west of Fresno. 320 acres. 35 blinds. Fees $10.00 per day. Private Blind $400 per season. J. H. Kerr, 13812 So. Budlong Ave., Gardena.

LANES VALLEY HUNTING CLUB—Tehama County. Club located on Highway 36—1 mile NE of Paynes Creek. 2200 acres. Fees $10.00 per person, 1955 buck season only. Charles H. Moulton, Paynes Creek.

LOS BANOS LAND & CATTLE CO.—Santa Cruz County. Club located on Santa Fe 5 miles south of Los Banos. 1380 acres. 50 blinds. Fees $150.00 for season. L. C. Matiasevich, P. O. Box 958, Watsonville.

BASS LAKE DUCK HUNTING CLUB—Eldorado County. Club located off Highway 50, 27 miles from Sacramento. 162 acres. 16 blinds. Fees $3.50 morning—$2.00 evening or $5.00 per day. M. W. Jannke. Rt. 1, Box 82, Shingle Springs.

SPRIG GUN CLUB—Colusa County. Club located on Colusa Gridley road 13 miles NE of Colusa. 3500 acres. 25 blinds. Fees membership $120 per season. Harold Pentico, Rt. 3, Box 378, Chico.

BAR B-W ROD & GUN CLUB—Imperial County. Club located on American Legion road 2 miles from Brawley. 240 acres. 15 blinds. Fees $10 per day per person. Jack McMillan, Rt. 1, Box 69, Brawley.

NORTHERN CALIFORNIA DUCK CLUB—Colusa County. Club located on San Jose road 6 miles northwest of Colusa. 175 acres. 20 blinds. Fees $10.00 per day—10 shoots $75.00. $150.00 per season. Leo A. Yates, Box 182, Colusa.

S AND R RANCH—Kern County. Club located on Ave. "A"—1¼ miles west of Sierra Hiway. 80 acres. 9 double blinds. Fees $10.00 per person per day. U. S. Sorensen, 345 No. Keystone, Burbank.

CHAPTER 16

New Horizons for the Sportsman

THE clouds hung above the hills like soft smoke and as a hawk cut through one of the cumulous puffs, floating as effortlessly as a piece of wind-blown paper, my father stopped his uphill climb.

"That's quite a fellow," he said, pointing at the hawk. 'There're a lot of old wives' tales about how they carry off chickens and do harm to song birds. And maybe they do take a few but mostly they get mice and rats and snakes. Never shoot one, son." He smiled and his fine teeth showed white against the tan of his face. He nodded his head again as the hawk swooped. "That's a red-shouldered hawk, one of the most majestic birds that lives in God's big acre."

That conversation occurred on East Hill north of Elmira, New York when I was fourteen years old. And the portion of it that has lodged in my memory, shining like a piece of gold all these years is the phrase, "God's big acre." My father often referred to the world of the outdoors that way: the streams teeming with fish, the green-hatted hills alive with soft-eyed deer, wary foxes and gentle, mincing animal folk like rabbits, squirrels, raccoons and the misunderstood skunk.

Since those days when I wandered the hills with my father, shotgun under my arm or fishing rod over my shoulder, much has happened. The march of civilization has trod down many of the outdoors places. Great farms and cattle ranges have sprung up, new highways have pushed through, the course of rivers has been changed, whole forests have been felled to make room for power dams. A great metamorphosis has occurred.

But not as great as many of the gripers say. Today wondrous things are being done for the American sportsman that would amaze and delight your father and mine. God's big acre is being zealously protected for your benefit.

How would you like a map, giving in precise detail all the rivers, brooks, trails, cliffs and other physical features of any area you may be interested in hunting? Or how about a booklet

193

naming the good highways in any state you may mention,
where the best hunting and fishing is, where top guides are
listed, convenient and reasonable motels and hotels itemized?
Maybe you'd like to have a wild boar hunting trip in Tennessee
planned, a quail shooting date fixed up in Georgia, go where
the rabbit hunting is best in Pennsylvania, take out after an
antelope in Wyoming? Would you care to have a chart showing
exactly how many and what species of fish were planted in
streams and lakes for your benefit?

In most cases, all you have to spend is three cents to get
hunting and fishing information that will change your sporting
horizon and bring within easy reach species of fish and game
that are unavailable in your own state.

For example, do you know of the National Parks Service?
With the assistance of both state and federal agencies last year
this service released over 6,358,418 fish that are yours for the
catching in waters of 14 of the big parks. In addition, the
National Parks Service prints a booklet: *Let's Talk About Fishing* which they will send you for the asking. The booklet contains the rules and regulations of the Parks, gives creel limits
and has information slanted to help you, like the following:

"You may wonder why fishing rules differ between parks and
sometimes between parks and adjacent states. The National
Park System stretches from tropical swamps to arctic tundra and
includes rich and poor waters. In some places, the growing season is short and in others it is long. All of which adds up to
the fact that there are a lot more fish to be had in some waters
than in others. Consequently, seasons must vary in length and
catch limitations must be greater or smaller. Where several hundred pounds of fish are available from each acre of rich water,
catches can be much more liberal than where only from 10 to
15 pounds of fish per acre are present.

"In addition to a wide variety of waters, national park areas
contain most of the common game fishes found in the United
States. We all know that fast growing bass and sun fish in warm
waters require less protection than Eastern brook or cutthroat
trout which live in cold mountain lakes or streams. Even in the
individual stream, the size and makeup of the fish population
does not remain constant. When fish are abundant, the fisherman may take more; when they are scarce, he must take less.
These natural fluctuations mean changes in the rules—sometimes
from year to year . . ."

In all of the parks there are rangers to answer your questions, guide you to cabins, show you the picnic spots, and pass out various kinds of printed information that will be of help. Many of the parks have boats available and, if you tire of fishing, there are guided tours that will bring you back to the sport of dunking a line refreshed and full of the vitality that only a change in scenery can give.

After reading the free booklet that you've sent for and getting into the spirit of the thing, you may have a particular park you'd like to visit. If so, just drop the National Parks Service, Department of the Interior, Washington 25, D. C. a line and ask them to send you a chart of the fish released. On this chart, neatly graphed, are the exact number and kind of fish released in certain parks. Take Glacier National Park. Last record of fish released in that area was 1,514,643. Of this number 39,308 were brook trout; 1,462,885 were blackspotted trout; 12,450 were lake trout. Olympic National Park got 163,837 fish. Rainbow trout amounted to 79,400; Bearslee trout, 9,812; and 74,625 blackspotted trout. Yellowstone Park benefited to the extent of 1,840,-300 fish—of these 20,000 were brook trout; rainbow trout, 50,250; grayling, 500,000; brown trout, 109,600; blackspotted trout were dumped in the amount of 1,160,450.

And so it goes. You can't exactly call each fish by name, but the chart gives you a precise idea of which parks have the most fish, what varieties were stocked and where they came from.

State parks also offer excellent service and the majority of states have an organization called State Parks Commission, or Parks and Forest Commission. Almost without exception they are headquartered in the various state capitals. For example, in Connecticut, the Parks and Forest Commission is in Hartford, and all you need do to find out about the facilities of the parks in that state is drop a line. In Pennsylvania, it's Harrisburg; in New York, Albany; in Georgia, Atlanta.

Although hunting isn't allowed in either state or national parks, both do a lot to help the hunter. In Longfellow-Evangeline and Marksville Prehistoric Indian Parks, Louisiana, deer have been furnished from the park deer pens to many of the larger areas, and from the roaming of deer on these acres to open hunting ground have come many a prize head.

Antelope, moose, elk, many species of deer, rabbits, squirrels, game birds of all kinds, have become so abundant in some state and national park areas that for their own good, they are weeded out and shipped to other territories where they are used to help restock depleted areas and improve the hunting. This rebalancing is all done for the benefit of the sportsman.

Did you ever hear of the U. S. Geological Survey? Neither did I until a few months ago. It sounds stuffy and uninteresting, bringing forth visions of dusty rooms and the dull picture of men who make a study of rock masses. Actually this organization offers the sportsman one of the most unusual and helpful services of any of the many agencies.

Ask yourself as a hunter or a fisherman what is the most important asset you can have. In addition to a right and left foot, your answer might be to know where you are while afield. Or to have the ability to scout out new hunting highways. I had heard that for twenty cents or so you could get a map of any area from the Geological survey, so I stuck fifty cents in an envelope and asked for a map of Roxbury, Connecticut where I live. Roxbury is a rural area, some 100 miles from New York City, with its total population somewhere about 300. I wasn't hopeful.

Back came two maps, one a large, minutely scaled, excellent map of Massachusetts, Rhode Island and Connecticut. A map that gave a clear, overall picture of the entire state of Connecticut. The other map was also a large one of Roxbury and territory. On the back of this map was a list of symbols showing how to properly read it. For example, a church was marked with a small cross, a trail with a series of dots or a broken line, a mine or quarry with a small crossed pick and shovel.

I spent one hour reading the Roxbury map and discovered three new fishing streams and a series of open meadows near a heavy woods that looked like good pheasant cover. Every bridge, no matter how small, road junction or lane; cliff, small and large hills, old mines, all the physical aspects of Roxbury were spread before me as clear as if I was suspended over the area and had the ability to look down and spot the countryside. Better than a compass or as good as a guide, these maps are available to everyone.

I understand that index maps of every state, Alaska, Hawaii, may be obtained free. Copies of the standard topographic maps such as I just described are yours for 20 cents each; river survey maps are 10 cents per sheet and special maps are available at different prices.

Orders for all maps should be addressed to the United States Geological Survey, Washington 25, D. C. (Or to Denver 15,

Colorado, for maps of areas west of the Mississippi.) Prepayment is required and may be made by cash, money order or check, payable to the Director of the Geological Survey.

The Fish and Wildlife Service, a federal unit attached to the United States Department of the Interior, is another agency working full time for the person interested in the outdoors. Since May the Fish and Wildlife Service has conducted a wildfowl survey of the entire United States and Canada. From this study which is made at the breeding grounds, and is compiled from both ground and aerial observation, will come information about breeding pairs, water conditions and the new generation of birds. By means of the latest sampling methods, representative data will be gathered from all corners of the North American continent where waterfowl are known to breed.

Out of these studies comes information which increases your duck-hunting pleasure, tells when the big duck flights are due, approximately how many birds there are, and helps set the bag limits.

In addition, the Fish and Wildlife Service fishery biologists participate with the states in developing unexploited fishing potentialities of various waters for your benefit. They strive continually to improve fishing conditions, even to the extent of supplying individual fishermen with fish for their own private ponds and lakes. They get about 50,000 requests a year for these fish for stocking purposes and, working with the states, cheerfully supply the requested fish.

Also, the Fish and Wildlife Service coordinates effort among states to increase and distribute supplies of game animals of all kinds. It's a gigantic and effective service, dedicated to help the sportsman that few have heard about.

The Fish and Wildlife Service gets its help directly to you through your own state. It might be interesting for you as a sportsman to know that in administering the national wildlife refuges which, as of July 1952, numbered 272, with a total of 17,409,968 acres, the Fish and Wildlife Service cooperates with the states in a number of ways, a few of which are listed below:

(1) The management of parts of national wildlife refuges for the public hunting of migratory waterfowl, upland game, and big game by state conservation departments or jointly by the state conservation departments and the Fish and Wildlife Service. This program has enabled thousands of hunters to assist in the harvest of surplus wildlife and to participate in waterfowl

hunting where these activities do not interfere with the primary purpose of the national wildlife refuge program. State cooperation also enables the utilization of a resource through public hunting activities for which the Fish and Wildlife Service has no direct authorization or funds.

(2) Management of designated parts of national wildlife refuges for public fishing by state conservation departments. These programs have enabled the public to enjoy better public fishing at nominal cost through state management.

(3) The joint development of wildlife management areas by state game departments and the Fish and Wildlife Service. These projects consist of Federal and state-owned lands for which the plans of acquisition, development, and management are coordinated, enabling major projects for wildlife management to be accomplished which would be impossible through individual efforts on the part of either the state or the Federal Government. These projects are such that the purposes of both the national migratory bird management program and the state wildlife management program are benefited.

(4) Lease agreements with state conservation departments for the management of lands under the custody of the Fish and Wildlife Service. In the main, these are areas acquired under the Bankhead-Jones Farm Tenancy Act. The custody of these lands was transferred to the Fish and Wildlife Service by the Soil Conservation Service or its predecessor agencies. The transfer of control of these lands to the states for administration relieves the Federal Government of responsibility for the management of lands for wildlife purposes where such lands do not have significance in the national program.

(5) Cooperative agreements for the management of national wildlife refuge lands by state conservation departments. In general, these lands are of significance for waterfowl management, but are of such small size as not to warrant major expenditures by the Federal Government. Benefits are secured by the state through the management of such lands as a supplement to adjacent lands owned by the conservation departments of the respective states.

(6) Joint management of upland-game animals on national wildlife refuges. This program provides for a coordination of the management of upland game on Federal lands with the management of such game outside the Federal area. Since the management of upland game is a state responsibility, the joint

endeavor relieves the Federal Government of responsibility for a species which is primarily controlled by the state conservation department and gives the state conservation department a voice in the management of species on the Federal area.

You probably didn't know it, but you as a hunter, a sportsman who buys guns and ammunition, play a large part in helping yourself to better sport. An organization called the Pittman-Robertson Wildlife Restoration program operates on the 11-cent tax from the gun and ammunition dollar. It helps maintain and increase game flocks and herds, through land purchases, habitat improvement and research. By a formula based on paid hunting licenses and area of the state, each one of the states receives its share of the annual tax receipts. The various state game and fish departments select, plan and direct their programs after approval by the U. S. Fish and Wildlife Service.

The states own all lands purchased and the improvements made on their lands. Project costs are paid on the basis of ¼ by the state and ¾ by Pittman-Robertson funds. These funds are made possible because of you, the individual sportsman and your purchases of guns and ammunition in the enjoyment of the sport of hunting.

Your eleven pennies in action work something like this: Five pennies are spent for improving game ranges. Food and cover plantings on private and public lands, with a present planting of 75,000 coverts for pheasants and rabbits, 8,000 miles of multiflora roses hedges as a natural protection for animals, and the growing of enough lespedeza plots to feed 100,000 quail coveys.

Duck marsh constructions of all sizes from the small ones of one acre and up in New York State to the giant Roseau marsh of 51,000 acres in Minnesota, and game restocking in 30 states of wild turkey, antelope, deer and others, meaning the restoration of hunting seasons on some species of game birds and animals that had been on the closed list for many years. In 7 states, the creation of new watering places have extended the game range.

Two of these eleven pennies go for buying wildlife lands. For example, 45 states have bought new wildlife areas—more land than in the state of Delaware. This land has marshes for ducks, homes for upland game, winter range for big game and places where you can hunt.

Another penny is spent for maintenance such as plowing fire breaks and making improvements that keeps wildlife areas at top production. The other coppers go for administration, in selecting, planning and supervising to get the most out of each penny and for fact finding or research. This research has pointed the way to game abundance and maximum bag limits for hunters. Out of the Pittman-Robertson program has come modern game management that provides game for twice as many hunters as in 1938.

But the states themselves do much to directly aid the sportsman. If you're interested in finding out what the various states have to offer you in the way of hunting, the first step to take is to turn to chapter 5, A Sports Surprise In Every State, and check the state's addresses. Drop a note to the one you are interested in.

On the back of some of the state hunting and fishing regulation booklets, you'll find lists of conservation officers with their home addresses and phone numbers. These men are interested in helping you to better your local hunting and fishing. Call or write your local officer and ask him about new fishing streams, or areas where public shooting may be good. In some cases, they can also tell you of private lands where top shooting is yours for the asking. If the conservation officers are not listed on the regulation booklet, ask the person you bought your license from (town clerk, etc.) who he is and how you can get in touch with him. It'll be worth your while.

Inquiring about the broader scope, I made a test case of Maine and, checking the state guide in Chapter 5, found that the Department of Inland Fisheries and Game had Roland H. Cobb as commissioner and was headquartered at the State House, Augusta, Maine. Directing my letter to his attention, I simply said that I resided in Connecticut, knew nothing whatsoever about Maine and wanted to know what I could find out about that state's hunting and fishing possibilities. Promptly I got back a letter from Guy P. Butler, Executive Manager of the State of Maine Publicity Bureau, the official to whom Mr. Cobb had directed my letter. Mr. Butler told me that he would be glad to answer any specific questions I wanted to ask. In addition, he sent 12 booklets of varying size and subject. They were: a beautifully illustrated booklet, entitled Maine Hunting, containing pertinent information about types of game to be found in Maine, length of seasons, territories where various kinds of game were plentiful; a book of gamelaws, one on Maine's inland ice fishing laws, another on open water fishing laws. One of 120-pages titled, Motoring Through Maine, giving routes, descriptions of every city and village, exactly what they had to offer, lists of cabins, motels, restaurants, hotels, guides —the whole thing completely and effectively indexed. Attached to this was the official Maine highway map, illustrated and keyed to especially help the sportsman. Another 32-page book called Fishing In Maine, telling what species you will find, when and where to fish and how much it will cost, plus its twin, called Hunting In Maine, with the same type information on game animals, where to go, places to stay, etc. Then two small booklets, Maine Canoeing, Maine Fishing, giving in brief, almost capsule form all there is to know about these two sports, plus maps to illustrate points made in the text. A small folder, Maine Camp Sites, with the material bearing out the title, telling just about everything there is to know about camping in that state. Then the *piece de resistance* in the form of a large 120-page book, Maine Invites You. This breaks down every county in Maine, not only by location, but gives a brief history, tells what is available, not only for the sportsman but for the sightseer. It has a profusion of places to stay, to eat at and to see, plus several pages of postcards that say, "Your advertisement in *Maine Invites You,* interests me. Please send information concerning . . ." All we had to do was fill the cards in with places that interested us and mail.

After reading the lot, I felt that I knew enough about Maine to tackle either a full scale hunting or fishing trip without further reference. My three-cent stamp had brought about $20.00 worth of books, leaflets, folders, maps, and booklets and new sporting knowledge about an important state.

Next, checking Chapter 5, I wrote Louis Clapper, administrative assistant of the Game and Fish Commission of Tennessee and told him that I was interested in joining a wild boar hunt. Back came a letter advising that I must make application for a place in the public drawings which will determine which parties will be permitted to participate. Along with the application was a letter telling all about boars and boar hunting in Tennessee, a map of the Tellico wildlife management area, a list of places to write for accommodations and guides, and the current hunting regulations. Realizing that I was interested in hunting, Mr. Clapper also sent a list of conservation officers, broken down by territory, that I might contact and told of the excellent duck shooting at Reelfoot Lake and the West Tennessee River bottoms, advising of guides and places to stay while there.

Besides this, I got a packet of 14 booklets, similar to those I had received from Maine, telling of how to make your way around Tennessee, giving complete fishing and camping information on the TVA impoundments, the great lakes of the south, and many other fishing and hunting points in that state.

So if you've had an idea that the American sportsman is the forgotten man, forget it. Not only is all this vast outdoor information yours for free from the state and federal agencies, but new plans and endeavors are underway to improve and keep your natural heritage of hunting and fishing better than it ever was.

CHAPTER 17

Dog Data

L ATELY all kinds of statistics have been popping up proving
that mental ills and disturbances of dogs are on the increase. Veterinarians in the United States and England are on
record as establishing that the dog is susceptible to as many
diseases as man. Arthritis, diabetes, rheumatism, brain disorders,
neurosis, in fact all the diverse diseases and sicknesses that civilization produces are now being discovered in our canines.

Many old-time dog men shake their heads in disgust at the
array of facts proving that the dog is as weak as his master.
"All a lotta darn fool nonsense," one of the veteran dog men
told me recently. "My dogs is out year 'round. Rain or shine,
snow or sleet, and they're healthy as a milk-fed calf. Got two
hounds that clean up the bones of our Christmas turkey every
year. Never hear a bad word out of 'em."

The old fellow wasn't exaggerating. My grandfather had a
pack of hounds that actually lived on the results of the chase,
whether it be fox, bear or cat. The old gentleman would let the
mob of dogs go after the game was downed and they'd usually
eat everything except the hide.

Maybe the old fellows had something. I don't say they're
wrong. But all of their stories can't alter the present situation.
In the old days our dog population was comparatively small.
Today, we have over 22,000,000. Yesterday, dogs were treated
like dogs—today we're doing everything possible to treat them
as anything but animals. In fact, a certain university has established a research organization to study behavior in dogs and
prove that "dogs are people," as one magazine article on the
project stated.

Dogs have become sophisticated apartment-dwellers. They
have their nails manicured and their hair "done" regularly.
But we aren't too concerned with that type of animal here.
These pages are used as a medium of conveying material of
interest and information to gun dog owners. Gun dogs are those
canines (you remember) that hunt, point and retrieve game of

203

all kinds. They are the rugged dogs who receive exercise regularly and are often called the "aristocracy of dogdom."

Unfortunately, the mental ills and the diseases of man are plaguing the "outdoor" type of dog as well as the city slicker.

"Veterinarians in the United States and England who have studied the problem of canine mental upsets are convinced that overbearing owners who insist on having their dogs live almost like people are doing inestimable harm to the mental and physical health of the entire species," the American Veterinary Medical Association reports.

This association containing some of the best veterinary brains in the country says: "Forced into a supervised routine where it cannot escape human domination, the dog will adapt itself to the moods and peculiarities of its owner. If the 'boss' is mean or jittery, the chances are better than average that the animal will develop some of these traits.

"Likewise the dog which practically lives in its owner's lap is liable to get a health-wrecking diet, especially if it acquires a fondness for pastries and candy. Too much of that kind of food replacing part of the required meat protein intake is blamed for an apparent increase in the number of canine diabetes cases. This disease, comparable with the diabetes occurring in man, strikes at the age of 6 years or over. The animal tires easily, becomes weak, and develops an abnormal appetite for food and water, yet loses weight steadily."

Sobering words from an organization of this caliber. The Association sums up the whole observation in this manner: "That pooch who has to dig or beg for its daily bone may not be so bad off after all."

I personally don't think that the problem is this bad in the gun dog world. There is plenty of cause for alarm, but still time to take sensible steps.

Too many gun dog people are making darn fools of their dogs. They keep them indoors, fail to give the family any proper instruction on how to handle the dog, and the inevitable happens. The children mollycoddle the dog, women bill and coo baby words over it, neighbors drop in and invite the dog up on their lap. Remnants of the birthday cake, leftover ice cream, the extra doughnut or creampuff are often slipped to "the cute rascal."

There is no time balance for the gun dog. Hunting seasons are short, lazing periods long. In time, working on and accustomed to the above house routine, the promising gun dog (even though previously trained) soon becomes spoiled, a creature of whim. Made the darling of the house and even the neighborhood, he comes to expect the little favors, considers the caressing and petting as a matter of everyday course. Many entire breeds have been ruined in this manner. Both the Irish Setter and the Cocker Spaniel, originally excellent gun dogs, have become mollycoddles. Certain thinking groups are taking steps to rescue these breeds and return them to the field where they belong, but it would take very little research for any interested person to dig out and absorb their sad story.

Fortunately there is a way to enjoy your gun dog as a pet and companion and still have him operate effectively in the field.

I have always advocated that a good gun dog can also be a good pet. There is perhaps no better companion or friend than your gun dog—but there are conditions. Your gun dog (above all other breeds) must respect you.

In order to build that respect, there are several things you can and must do:

First, that good old sense that so many of us seem to be without, Common Sense, is a definite requisite. If you have a kennel, by all means keep your dog there. Whether you think so or not, the dog appreciates his privacy—a place where he can take a sprawl or snooze without some person coming up and gathering him in their arms and cooing. You can use a little psychology in connection with a kennel. Bring your dog in the house for a certain number of hours every day if you wish. This is a good idea. Let him know you're friends. But also let him know that you are the master and he is the dog. When you open the door, you go out first, the dog follows. When you call him, he responds, you don't go chasing. If he jumps on you, stick out your knee and knock him off, or step on his toes and he'll soon realize that it isn't the proper thing to do.

If the dog sulks and disobeys, back to the kennel with him. Make him realize that good conduct is rewarded, not by food tidbits but by the privilege of spending his usual allotted time in the house of his master.

For those of you who don't have a kennel, and must keep the dog inside, the problem is somewhat tougher but not impossible.

Admonish your family not to shower the dog with love and kisses. If the dog obeys a command and conducts himself properly in the house, then he should know it. Pet him, call him a good fellow. But for heaven's sake don't take the dog in your lap and drool over him.

See that he gets regular exercise and (this is most important) put him on a definite diet. Feed him at the same time everyday. And dole out his food according to his age and his body wants. If he's a big dog, naturally he needs a larger caloric intake. A puppy should be fed three times a day, a dog six months of age twice, a year of age once, or perhaps one light meal in the morning and a heavy one at night. But once you have determined the feeding time, adhere to that schedule. Make the dog realize that he gets fed during those hours—and at no other time. Don't give him table scraps and tidbits whenever you feel the urge. If you do, it will be to his detriment.

The various vitamins are good for your dog. Mix them with his food. See that he gets calcium, cod liver oil, wheat germ oil. Most of the reputable dog food companies publish the facts on feeding. Ask for them, read them and benefit.

The type of food is up to you. But the diet should be balanced, and the food should contain the meat-protein ingredients the dog's health demands.

Your dog should have a certain corner (most ideally in the kitchen) that he can consider his own. His own mat or bed should be there. If you start your dog this way, you'll find that he'll stay off the furniture and will return to his corner with the words, "Go to your bed."

Some among you will read this and say, "This is not for me. I keep my dog in a kennel the year around." If this is true, by all means this is written with you also in mind.

If you own say, a pointer, or setter, a labrador, or spaniel, and keep him in the kennel most of the time, except those rare hours when the dog goes hunting with you, then you are as guilty as the lover-dover who spoils his animal. Your dog is not a hunting machine to be cranked out of his kennel a few hunting hours a year and ignored the remainder of the time. The hunting dog needs love. He should be taught to realize that he is not only hunting for himself and the fun of it, but he is out there working for his master—a swell guy whom he has plenty of respect for.

In order to accomplish this you must do more than have your dog trained to hunt. You must make him your companion. During the long summer months pick up your walking stick and go out into the hills with your friend, your gun dog. He'll enjoy it whether you have a gun or not and you will too. Bring him in the house once in awhile—let him know that he's one of the family. Don't overdo it, but get acquainted with him. You'll find if you show a little consideration for that kennel dog of yours he'll hunt better for you come next season. Know why? Mainly because he'll begin to get the idea that the two of you are a team—that you're both out there doing the same thing, and having fun doing it. The dog will soon slip into the pleas-ing pattern—the habit of pleasing you. And you'll get twice as much—ten times as much—fun out of your days afield.

Most people don't understand how easily a dog can lose respect for a human being. One of the quickest ways to bring this about is by overpetting, too much fondling of your dog. If you practice this slobber-and-drooling-over-dog technique, then you may as well make up your mind that the dog already has dragged you down to his level mentally. When he does do something good and you reward him for it by a pat on the head, it no longer means anything. By that time he's looking for a slightly rare filet mignon as the payoff. But, if you pet him seldom, then only when he deserves it, he comes to respect that action and looks for it—even strives to please so that he will get it.

Sure dogs are lovable, cute, adorable, throw any adjective you wish—but keep this fact under your bonnet: they are dogs. Try to treat them as such. They will appreciate it. If some of these many-degreed brain guys could look into the mind of a dog these days, they'd probably find a great big wish there: Undoubtedly most dogs are wishing for, "The old carefree life of a dog."

If you aren't a dog owner, but want to be, I'd suggest that you start off the right way by buying a puppy. Never buy a grown, so-called trained dog. If you do, you'll probably get another person's mistakes all rolled up in a ball of fur. It is true that some people do purchase adult, trained gun dogs. But these are the men who have little thought for the love or even the companionship of a dog. They want hunting machines. If it could be done with four wheels and a motor, so much the better.

It will help if you will try to select a puppy that has good field forbears. The trite phrase "like begets like," isn't exactly true where animals are concerned but you will find that you will have much better luck in training a dog that has field dogs and hunting blood in his background. The way to ascertain this is by a study of pedigree. Find out if the pup's sire and dam are hunters. Not just hunters by "say so," but dogs who are presently hunting for their owners. One of the smartest dog men I ever met would never buy a dog until he had seen that dog's parents hunt. So if you possibly can, investigate the parents of the puppy you are interested in buying. Of course, there is always the possibility of getting a lemon even with thorough checking. But if you give yourself that extra break, it might pay big dividends come hunting season.

Always deal with reputable breeders. Don't look for a bargain. In the long run the cheap dog is the costly dog. Pay the reputable breeder's price and start off the right way.

Study your puppy carefully before you buy him. Go back and see him several times. Select the bold, aggressive dog, never the timid animal, no matter how much he plays on your sympathy. Look for a shiny coat, a bright eye.

I, personally, don't believe in training the young dog in obedience as a preface to actual field training. There are two schools of thought on this subject, but it has been my experience to discover that the dog that has been the bright youngster in obedience is lost in the field, even with training. He is inclined to hang around his owner's heels and, because in obedience he awaits an order before making an action, he feels lost in the field where he is more or less on his own. Obedience is a destroyer of initiative, making the dog completely dependent upon his master for the command to action.

I am against seriously field training a puppy. Your dog should have his growing up period just as any child. He can be yard-trained, taught the simple rules of good behavior earlier but he should be given time to develop. One year of age is the best time to start to work on your dog. This doesn't mean that he isn't to be exposed to birds and permitted to whet his instinct before that time. Percocious puppies, those smart little fellows who point and hunt beautifully at three months of age, can be destroyed as field dogs if the unwise owner starts to bear down on them at that age.

One of the most promising young dogs I ever saw was ruined by a hard-headed owner who swore that he was going to have his dog steady to wing and shot and accomplished as a retriever by the time he was five months of age. This dog had everything but literally had the fun of hunting, trained and knocked out of him by a thoughtless owner.

There aren't many commands connected with yard training. Your dog should be broken to the leash, taught to sit, heel, come when called, learn the meaning of the words *yes* and *no,* and it is always helpful to instill the meanings of the words *sit* and *whoa* when the dog is still young. If you field train the dog yourself then you'll probably want to use the word "whoa" to slow him down and stop him. All the remainder of the yard training is more or less to establish proper behavior pattern.

The first thing to teach your dog is his name. Everytime you feed him call him by name. Before you place his pan of food on the floor, say "Here, Joe, Joe." This may seem silly at first, but before long you'll note that the pup is responding to this procedure. After several days of this, try calling him by name *before* you feed. Call him from a distance, for example from another room and when he appears make much over him, pet him and then immediately feed him, calling him by name as you do so. When you take him for walks, always precede the walk by calling his name several times. In brief, try to make him associate his name with everything pleasant. A week or so of this practice and your pup will know his name and respond with alacrity when called.

While we're on the subject of training in connection with feeding we might as well mention two other procedures that can be used. While feeding, or just before, is a good time to teach the pup to sit and to be steady to the pan.

The simple method of teaching a dog to sit is done by pressing down on his hindquarters with the left hand. Then with your right hand, hold his paws as firmly to the floor as you can —make these motions simultaneous and command "sit" while doing this. In the beginning he'll be a little balky and you'll find that you'll have to make the pressure on his rump a strong and firm one. Here's where the food comes in. Place his pan with his dinner on the floor while you're teaching him to sit. When you've finished several of the sit exercises, permit him to eat, calling him by name at the same time and praising him. Make the sit lessons short. All training should be confined to brief periods. Remember the puppy is immature and tires of things of serious nature quickly. And there's a psychological problem involved. If you do persist in the training, even after the pup is tired, you may lose patience and do things that you wouldn't when thinking clearly. Also, the dog will understand this and may fear the training period the next time. So for the sake of your dog and your own patience, make your training periods short and effective.

After you've taught the young dog to sit, you might try making him steady to pan. Teaching him restraint. This is done again by placing the tempting pan of food on the floor, commanding the dog to sit, and then admonishing "no, no," and making him sit until you call him by name and say "yes, all right you can eat." At first you'll have to restrain him, probably with leash until he understands that he is to sit quietly and not touch his food until you say his name and the word "yes." This lesson won't take long. It's surprising how fast the pup will learn when he has his tasty pan of food sitting there as a reward for learning.

It's important to teach the pup the meaning of the word "whoa" as early as possible. This also can be done at mealtime. Place his food on the floor and tell him *whoa* holding him back on leash until he seems to understand, then snap the leash off, tell him *whoa,* when he starts for the food. Enforce this command until he knows the meaning of the sharp word. One reason I use the food cycle as the best for practical training is because to a pup, or a grown dog for that matter, eating is probably the most important function in life. If you can teach him the commands and the restraint you later want to bring into play in the field while he is sitting there watching and wanting his food, it makes complete sense that the lessons will be learned thoroughly. He wants that food. And he knows that if he behaves properly, he'll get it. But there's also another facet. The food is a great temptation to him and he's inclined to feel that the food is more important than any training lesson. Consequently, if he learns his lessons well while waiting for food you can rest assured that he'll do all right under less morally tempting circumstances.

The word "no" also should be used at all times when the pup is doing something wrong. Use it when he does the wrong thing on your living room floor, when he starts clawing and biting your best chair or shoe; in fact at any and all times when his manners are incorrect. He'll come to know and respect that short, snappy word. And it's up to you to see that he does.

In reviewing the preceding I note that breaking to collar and lead isn't mentioned. That is a simple lesson but one that should be done at an early age. You'll probably find that the breeder has already put a little chrome chain-link collar on your pup. If the pup comes without collar, get him one immediately and put it on. Make certain that you get the kind that he can't slip off and one that he can't choke himself on. Let him wear it for several days to get used to the feel before you try snapping on a lead. You'll probably find when you first snap the lead on and try to take a walk with the pup that he'll go completely crazy. This may take a little patience on your part, but you'll discover that he will soon tire of the wild jerking and yanking and will stand to the lead. When that happens, snap the lead off, let him walk around without it, then snap it back on again. It's also a good idea to tie the lead to a tree or some stationary object so that he will learn that the lead really means restraint and will come to respect it. Don't, under any circumstances, tie the lead to a tree then go away and leave the puppy. Stay close, watch what happens.

When he has properly learned what the lead means, then it's time to take him for a walk and teach him to heel. This is about the only time you should really try to keep the young dog under actual restraint by command. I can't stress too strongly the need to let the young fellow have his head while in the field. He should be able to roam and romp to his heart's content and nose-discover everything from a gaudy, elusive butterfly to the fascinating scent of the field mouse. In other words, he's got to learn what it's all about—the meaning of the birds and bees. And he can't if every time he starts a nose investigation you call him back and begin giving him some command and lesson which he isn't too interested in and is too young to properly absorb anyway.

There's been controversy as to the correct side to teach the dog to heel—left or right. The simple truth is the dog should heel on the side that is most convenient for you. If you use your right hand to carry your gun, and people do seem to use the right hand more often than the left, then it is proper to have the dog heel close to you on the left where he won't in any way constrict or hamper your movement.

Don't attempt to teach heeling until you and your dog know what the lead is all about. In other words, take walks with your dog and try to keep as much slack in the lead as possible. When he starts straining and taking you for a walk, rather than you taking him, then you should yank him back, talk to him, occupy his attention and then continue walking. The point is that you must make him realize what the lead is and to understand that you are the master of it. You'll know when you're ready to begin teaching heel. One day you'll be walking with your dog and you'll realize that he's stopped walking you and, for a change, the dog walking has become a pleasure. The pup will permit the leash to remain slack of his own accord. That's the time to begin the heeling routine. By now he responds to your commands and tugs on the leash and will look at you when you speak to him. Call him by name and say "heel!" At the same time pat your left side sharply and in short little jerks bring the dog to your left side. Praise has much to do with the successful teaching of heeling. After you've tried the heel routine several times as mentioned above, then swing into the practice of merely calling the dog by name and saying the word "heel" this time leaving the leash slack and praising the dog if he comes to your side. If he loiters, make sharp masterful jerks with the leash and bring him into the correct position. Keep this up at a standstill until he begins responding perfectly, then start the walk routine. Walk and circle, first to the right, then to the left, keeping a slack line and the dog at the heel position at your left side all the time. If he falls behind, either pull him forward with the leash, uttering the word "heel," or give a sharp kick as he falls behind. Every step must mean business and you must convey to your dog that you are not playing, that this heeling routine is serious and you will accept nothing short of perfection.

On the right angle turn, it's a good idea to make this turn when your dog is not looking at you. After you've made the right turn, give the leash a firm pull in the same direction. When he catches up pat him and tell him what a wonderful dog he is. Next time you make the turn he'll be ready for you and make it at the same time.

On the left angle turn move firmly to the left, placing your right knee across in front of your left so that the knee serves as a wall against which the dog can't move. Hold the leash with your left hand and keep the dog in place as you move, meanwhile utter the command "heel!"

You can vary this routine. But you need practice as much as the dog does until you can make the turns easily, holding the leash slack and depending upon the dog to follow your training and commands. Remember that you can't be half-hearted about it. Make your commands short, snappy and loud enough for the dog to hear. And say "heel" every time you want the dog to heel. He can't read your mind.

You can make a game of it by walking, then trotting, then running fast and keeping the dog at heel with you. Also try to pick out obstacles like trees, bushes, and move closely to them, keeping your dog at heel all the time. If your pup passed on the wrong side, hang on to that leash as tightly as possible, keeping him in the incorrect position until he realizes he is wrong and corrects himself.

Heeling will come in handy walking your dog in crowds or keeping him beside you while moving to new hunting territory.

The final test, of course, is keeping the dog at heel without leash. Don't attempt this free heeling until he is letter-perfect on leash. It won't be long before a mere tap on your leg will signify to your dog that you want him to heel. As you know, the dog's intelligence is at the top of the animal class and he learns quickly. And I've found once they learn they don't forget.

There are two other matters I want to take up in the yard training of the pup: teaching to *whoa* and to *come when called*. These are important and could be the means of saving your dog's life. From an everyday viewpoint they are both important because it is often necessary to stop a dog in his tracks upon command, and it's always an irritating thing to call your dog and have him completely ignore you.

Whoa is undoubtedly the word that the trainer will use, should you decide to have your dog field trained by a professional. And even if you feel that you have the time and the patience to train him yourself, the word is the best in the dog dictionary for its purpose. You've already made progress in this direction when you taught your dog to *whoa* at his food pan. Remember to use that word in connection with that particular training phase.

Some trainers and books go into great and somewhat confusing detail on this phase of the dog's training, working out cross stake arrangements, tying one end of a check cord to the stake and using a force collar on the dog. I don't believe in it.

Some of the best pros in the country simply tie a long check cord to the end of a substantial collar on the dog. They take him afield after he has had the original *whoa* lessons herein described and teach the dog that he either whoas when ordered or he is pulled to a whoa by the omniscient check cord, long leash or rope.

By now your dog knows his name, is broken to collar and leash and is an old walking companion. He also knows when you say whoa that you don't want him to advance or make any motion. But the chances are once you take him out where it is quiet and Nature herself has spread plenty of tempting items around for your dog to investigate, that he will barely notice you when you order whoa. So when you go for your walk have a long rope perhaps 15 or 20 feet in length attached to your dog's collar (and make certain that it isn't the self-tightening choke collar, or else you can do your dog injury) and proceed to walk with him. When he is out to about the end of the rope command "Whoa!" It's possible that he may stop, but likely that he will not. If he doesn't and moves ahead, place your full weight on the rope. He'll actually make a parabola in the air if he is moving ahead fast enough when you command whoa, and land on his back, a surprised and perhaps disgusted dog. Continue this, even to the point where you leave the end of the rope trail on the ground out of your hands, but moving easily along so that you can grab it instantly when you command whoa. Make certain in this lesson that you instill in the dog the thought that, simultaneous with the command whoa, is the halting motion of the rope. Don't overdo the lesson, but be firm once you've made the command to whoa. When he does start whoaing on command, walk up to him and gentle him, congratulating him on his perception and ability to take orders. Make him realize that you are very pleased that he has learned to whoa when you order it. That's about all there is to it. Don't make the lesson overlong; don't be half-hearted about snapping the dog to a stop with the rope once you've given the command and he has ignored it.

Probably the most irritating of all is the dog who completely ignores you when you call him by name and ask him to come. The method of teaching him to come instantly when called is not unlike that of the lesson of whoa. Just substitute "Come, Bozo, come," for the word whoa, and pull him in by the rope, until he knows he should come when you call his name.

You'll also want to know when your dog is sick, and what to do about it. It'll pay to make the acquaintance of a veterinarian. Make him your dog's doctor and when the animal is ailing, waste no time in getting him to his doctor.

Worms are a constant threat to a dog's health. Some dog owners worm monthly trying to destroy the almost ever-present eggs and larvae. This should not be done until a veterinarian makes a microscopic examination of the feces and actually determines that worms are present. Even then don't give worm medicine without the doctor's approval. Round, Hook and Whip worms are the unholy trio that annoy dogs. Remember dogs that are ill, thin and out of condition should not be wormed. Worm medicine should be administered after a fast of 12 or more hours. No food should be given for 4 hours after worm treatment has been made.

Ear canker is usually caused by dirt accumulating and blocking the canal to the eardrum, gradually producing inflammation and ulcer. Eczema or mange, laceration of ear flap, freezing, or bruising can also induce canker. The retriever breeds can pick up a nice dose of ear canker doing their job in cold winter water.

The symptoms are obvious: Sometimes the dog will carry his head cocked in such a fashion that the affected ear is lowered; a constant shaking of the head and scratching the ear; whining when the ear is touched. Inspect the ear by stretching the flap upward and looking into the channel. Yellowish liquid, discharged and sticking to the hair, and sores may cover the inside ear flap. The dog may be partially deaf, irritable, inclined to bite. Using a solution of equal portions of ether and alcohol, take cotton swab and gently clean wax, dirt and foreign material away. Ear canker can become serious, so naturally when you have administered this simple and relatively safe remedy, try to get to a veterinarian.

Fits or convulsions probably scare more dog owners than any other symptom. Sometimes they are caused by digestive upsets, chilling, severe ear canker, teething, fright or over-excitement, worms or constipation. Symptoms are pretty general: blank staring, running in circles, acute trembling, and rigidity. Usually the mouth muscles are affected, frothy saliva, teeth clamping, sometimes biting the tongue. If it's possible, try to secure the dog so he won't harm himself. Get a veterinarian as soon as possible and remove cause of the attack. This is a matter that demands coolness. Don't get excited. The important thing is not to start shouting "mad dog."

Conjunctivitis or inflammation of the mucous membrane lining the eyelids is caused when the blood vessels in the eye distend converting the membrane into a flaming red. Often pus will flow, virtually forcing the dog's eyes closed. Unless you do a little work and clean the eyes out, the dog may rub his aggravated eye and cause corneal ulcers. Act immediately. Eyelids and area should be gently rinsed and bathed three times daily. Use cotton swabs and any of the good eye washes recommended by your druggist. In addition, see your veterinarian.

General paralysis can be caused by many things: distemper, chorea, constipation if it's a chronic condition and nothing has been done to alleviate it, aftermath of convulsions brought on by intestinal worms. The infra-red lamp does help. Keep the dog's elimination good, feed plenty of light, easily digested food to which liberal amounts of calcium have been added. Often it helps to massage the dog's muscles two or three times daily.

If your puppy is backward, runted, prefers lying in a corner to frisking about, seems to consider walking and mobility a pain rather than a pleasure, it may be possible that he has rickets. Feel the end of each rib. If there's a little swelling or lump there, call your doctor, for there's a good chance that the pup is really sick. Plenty of good strong sunlight, cod liver oil, preferably raw, lime water added to the puppy's milk, all will help bring him out of the doldrums. A good diet, with ground raw bone, lean meat added to the regular dog food will also help. But nothing will be as effective as a visit to a good veterinarian.

The most important single step you can take in protecting your dog from distemper is to get him right down to your veterinarian and have him inoculated against distemper before he has the opportunity of contracting it. Medical records prove that the majority of dogs who contract distemper do so because their owners didn't have enough foresight to have them inoculated. While you're at the doctor's you might as well have the dog inoculated for rabies. Distemper takes on so many forms and its ramifications are so enormous that it is impossible to discuss it intelligently here. Inoculate! When in doubt pick up the phone and call the veterinarian.

It's a good idea to keep a rectal thermometer around the house. The normal temperature is about 101.2 degrees. Remember to lubricate the thermometer with vaseline before using, and clean it carefully by using cotton dipped into a good antiseptic solution. Then shake the mercury down before storing. In taking the dog's pulse, feel the femoral artery inside the thigh. The normal pulse is from 70 to 90 beats per minute.

Get yourself a good stiff brush and give your dog a daily

workout. Keeping his coat clean is a health guard and shouldn't take too much of your time. Keep the wax and dirt cleaned out of his ears. Dip a piece of cotton in a strong salt solution and wipe his teeth after his meal. This will reduce odor and keep his teeth in good shape.

Then there is that plague, the eternal puzzler, the skin disease. The majority of skin diseases in dogs is due to external infection. There are the two principal types of mange, sarcoptic and follicular, caused by a mite not visible to the naked eye. There is external hookworm infection. There are bacteria and other organisms that cause skin troubles. Certain eczemas and allergic skin conditions are sometimes attributed to dietary deficiencies or sensitization.

In all cases of abnormal conditions of the skin, it is important to seek veterinary diagnosis and advice as to treatment without delay. Early and correct treatment can prevent serious complications and hasten recovery. When skin infections become well established or chronic, they are difficult to cure, sometimes requiring painstaking and persistant attention for a long period.

Of great importance in control of skin diseases of all kinds is absolute cleanliness of the dog's living quarters. Fresh air, sunshine, exercise and nourishing food also aid greatly in building the dog's resistance to disease. Regular elimination is important. There must be constant vigilance against intestinal parasites (for worm infestation can cause skin trouble) as well as external parasites. The lesions produced by fleas, lice and ticks, both in puppies and older dogs, are, often, not distinguishable from the dermatitis of eczema or even mange.

Careful examination of the dog's coat will reveal the presence of vermin. In searching be sure to inspect the base of the tail, head and ridge of the back. Flea powders containing rotenone are effective in controlling vermin.

All dogs should be free of the following:

FLEAS—Adult fleas ride around on the dog, with the females laying eggs. Flea eggs can be left anywhere—on the ground or in the house. A bitch in whelp should be kept free of fleas as they will crawl off on the puppies and chew on them, making small raw spots where skin infection can set in.

LICE—A louse attaches its eggs to the hair of the dog. These nits, and the lice, are very small and more difficult to detect than fleas. Large numbers of puppies die every year because of lice that have passed from the mother to the puppies. If numerous enough, lice cause the puppy to become anemic and die. In older dogs, lice tend to concentrate on the ears. An old-fashioned remedy for lice is saturating the coat with a 50 per cent mixture of kerosene and cotton-seed oil for a few days and then bathing with tincture of green soap.

TICKS—The two most common ticks are wood tick and dog tick. They attach themselves to the dog outdoors, or even indoors, where they may have been carried in by other means. When a tick is found on the dog, it should be removed with tweezers, or a gloved hand, never with bare fingers. Make sure to get the head out and paint the spot with alcohol or tincture of metaphen. Ticks are tough and have to be crushed against a hard surface or dropped into kerosene or turpentine to be killed.

In areas where ticks are numerous control is best maintained by immersing dogs in a derris dip about twice a week. Care must be given to prevent the dip from getting into the dog's eyes.

Inflammation of the skin of the ears can be caused by the constant attacks of flies during hot weather. This condition is relievable by the application of ointments. A standard one is comprised of 5 per cent oil of tar in a lanolin base.

Although a diagnosis can sometimes be made from the characteristic features in some types of skin disease, in most cases only microscopic examination will determine the true parasitic or nonparasitic nature of the disease. This is particularly true of mange mites which are detected only by deep skin scraping.

Sarcoptic Mange—Sometimes called Scabies. This is highly contagious, and rigid sanitary measures must be employed in cure and control. The mite is a roundish parasite that bores or tunnels through the skin. This makes it easier to spread, not only all over the body of the dog but to other animals by contact. Sometimes humans spread it from one animal to another.

It starts in small points of infection, little raised red spots that may appear anywhere on the body, although it is generally first seen where the hair is thin, as on the face or legs. The little pimples rapidly increase in number and later rupture, leaving a yellowish gray crust on the skin.

The itching in sarcoptic is always intense, is usually aggravated at night and by an increase in body temperature induced by warm quarters or exercise. Constant scratching further inflames the skin, and in severe cases there is often moisture. As the disease progresses the denuded skin becomes thickened and wrinkled. There is always a characteristic mousy odor.

Young dogs and those debilitated are especially prone to sarcoptic, although any dog can harbor the mite and develop the disease. Frequently a bitch suffering from the disease will give birth to a litter of puppies and in about four weeks they begin to scratch and chew at themselves—and so the disease moves on from one generation to the next.

Microscopic examination for the sarcoptic mite is more difficult than for the follicular mite, and several skin scrapings may prove negative although the dog clinically has symptoms of the disease. Fortunately, even severe cases yield to veterinary treatment. The coat is usually cut short and the entire body is treated rather than local areas. Care must be taken to keep the dog from getting chilled.

Follicular or Demodectic Mange—Often called "red mange." This used to be considered practically incurable but the new rotenone medicants have changed that. However, it is a very insidious infection, and while one area may appear cured, incubation is going on in other areas. It is important, therefore, to start treatment early and be continually on the watch for new spots. The mite, longish and rounded, is so small, and the time it takes to reproduce is so long that sometimes it is weeks before the disease becomes apparent. Due to the fact that the mite burrows down deep in the hair follicles where it reproduces, it is not as contagious as sarcoptic mange but it is spread from dog to dog directly and indirectly from infected kennels, brushes, combs, blankets, etc.

It is more frequently found in dogs under one year of age, although older dogs are susceptible. It usually appears as a thin-haired (almost bald) spot around the eyes or on the front legs but sometimes shows up in other places.

Thorough disinfection of the premises, grooming tools, etc., is essential to control the spread of this disease, for unless proper sanitary measures are taken the condition will continue to crop up even after the owner thinks the dog is cured. Constant watch is necessary for weeks afterwards to spot new cases in the early stages.

Ear Mange—This is caused by a mite similar to the sarcoptic mite. It is discoverable by microscopic examination of the discharge from the ear which will reveal eggs and mites of all sizes.

Many times ear mange is confused with canker but ear mites cause a grayish, dry-type of wax different from the sticky, black wax of canker.

This disease is a slow starter. The dog will scratch at his ears and shake his head, thus spreading the wax and the mites. Very weak solutions of rotenone are effective as a cure and must be put around the outside as well as inside the ear. Various ointments—one consisting of 1 part derris powder (containing 5% rotenone) in 10 parts olive oil—have been found effective against ear mites. Any veterinarian will show you how to apply the remedy he prescribes. Ear treatment should not be undertaken by the amateur as unskilled probing can injure the delicate parts of the ear.

A very smooth, well-mixed emulsion of oil, tar and sulphur is still a popular remedy for sarcoptic mange. Another old standard remedy is a wash made up of 4 ounces of derris powder (containing 5% rotenone), one ounce of neutral soap, and one gallon of warm water. Some veterinarians recommend the use of a benzyl benzoate solution in the treatment of demodectic mange. There are many new and improved remedies for mange, fungi and bacterial infections put out by leading drug firms which have reportedly given excellent results. One of these is an antibiotic scabicide called Tryoscabe. Another is an insecticide-fungicide mixture of finely powdered cube root 25%, Spurgon 5%, and inert carrier 70%.

Premises used by mangy dogs hold the infection for a long period. Therefore, all litter and bedding used by diseased dogs should be burned and the kennels disinfected with a hot, strong coal-tar-creolin solution. This will prevent reinfection of treated dogs or spread of disease to healthy ones.

Eczema—Unlike mange, eczema is neither parasitic nor contagious. Most eczema makes its appearance suddenly, even within a few hours. It produces glistening angry red patches that are very painful. Ordinarily, a cure is effected in a short time. However, some cases of dry eczema may take a chronic course and require several weeks to eradicate, or recur so that the dog seems to be under continous attack. Although there is no hard and fast rule, eczema usually appears along the back and outside of the thighs and at the base of the tail.

For dry eczema, daily applications of calamine and zinc ointment or zinc oleate ointment is beneficial. In moist eczema, ointment will not stick and it is best to use a lotion. Patting baby talcum or surgical dressing powder on the moist red patches will bring relief but alone will not work a cure.

This chapter would be cheating if it didn't come to an end with pertinent information on how to show your dog. Dog shows can be fun, and if you have a purebred registered animal and feel that he has the blue blood of a champion, it could be worth your time and his to take a whack at it. As this is an outdoor book, we suggest that you engage in only the outdoor affairs. They're more fun and your dog stands less chance of picking up disease.

A dog show is the place where dogs compete for prizes, championship points and top awards. It's a place where dog fanciers, breeders, and dog lovers congregate for the purpose of "improving the breed" and for the sport of watching the different breeds of dogs in competition.

The immediate sponsor of a show is a local kennel club or an association of fanciers of some single breed. (The latter frequently sponsor "Specialty Shows," which are shows restricted to a single breed.) The active management of most shows is turned over to a dog show superintendent who supplies the necessary equipment and takes charge of all arrangements.

All dog shows which give points toward a championship are held under the rules of the American Kennel Club, which has the responsibility of licensing superintendents and judges, of registering purebred dogs and of keeping records of the awards and points given every dog at every A. K. C. Show.

Sometimes a club holds a show which is not as extensive or formal as the shows described earlier. At these "Sanctioned Shows" (or "Match Shows") no championship points are awarded, and one of several plans provided by the American Kennel Club is followed. One of the more popular types of informal shows is for puppies only.

If you want to be posted on future dog shows in your locality or would like to enter your dog in a show, write to the Gaines Dog Research Center, 250 Park Avenue, New York 17, New York, for a list of licensed dog shows scheduled in your locality.

The judge is guided by the Standard of Perfection for each breed in making his selection. This Standard describes in detail what would be considered a perfect specimen of the breed. As a further aid to judges and breeders, the Standard sometimes lists definite faults which are to be discouraged or penalized in the breed.

The judge must study each dog very carefully—with his hands as well as his eyes, in motion as well as standing. To check on the texture of the coat, the firmness of muscle and bone, and the soundness of the teeth, a judge has to actually handle each dog. The way a dog moves is considered important—not only as a thing of beauty in itself, but as a crucial test of structure. The handlers of the dogs have to walk, trot and run them while the judge watches from side, front and back.

There are a number of things which the handler can and will do to show off his dog to best advantage, and the dog with a lively intelligent personality and sense of showmanship often has a definite advantage. But the basis of judging in the show rings is the physical beauty and structural soundness which the dog has been given by careful breeding.

To win the top award of "Best in Show" at an all-breed show, a dog must first be placed over all the other entries in his own breed, then defeat all the other breed winners in his particular group, and finally top the first-place winners in the other five groups.

Besides the classes and awards outlined below, many shows have one or more non-regular classes, such as for local dogs only, dogs handled by children, braces (pairs), and teams (four dogs). Wins in these classes do not, by themselves, count toward championships, and the judging often emphasizes quite different matters from the regular classes. The ribbon colors in these non-regular classes are: first, rose; second, brown; third, light green; and fourth, gray.

To be eligible for point-show competition, a dog must meet requirements:

(a) It must be a purebred specimen of one of the breeds recognized by the American Kennel Club.

(b) It must be registered or listed as such with the A. K. C.

(c) It must meet the minimum standards set up for its particular breed.

(d) It must be at least 6 months old.

At the start of a show, most entries are divided into two groups—one for dogs (males) and the other for bitches (females). These two groups are then subdivided into five regular classes according to the entrant's age and previous show experience.

Puppy Class: For dogs over 6 months and under one year of age.

Novice Class: For dogs who have never won a first prize (except in the Puppy Class).

American Bred Class: For dogs (except champions) born in the U. S. A. by reasons of mating which occurred in the U. S. A. or its possessions.

Bred by Exhibitor Class: For all dogs (except champions) owned and handled by their breeders or handled by their breeder's immediate family.

Open Class: For all dogs, including champions.

The judges award colored ribbons—blue for first, red for second, yellow for third and white for fourth—to the first four placings in each class for both male and female groups.

After the five regular classes for males have been judged, the first prize winners of the classes compete for Winners Dog. Only undefeated dogs of the same sex which have won a first prize are eligible. If a dog has been entered in more than one class and beaten in any one entered, he is not eligible to compete for Winners. Top dog receives a purple ribbon and is eligible for points.

The second-prize winner in the class in which the Winners Dog was entered competes with the first-prize in the other four classes for Reserve Winners Dog. No points awarded.

The same procedure is repeated in judging the females to select the Winners Bitch and Reserve Winners Bitch.

The Winners Dog and the Winners Bitch are judged next and one is chosen Best of Winners. This dog receives a blue and white ribbon.

At this point, Dogs entered for Specials Only enter show competition. These dogs must be champions and therefore receive no point awards.

From the Best of Winners and the entrants in the Specials Class, one dog is judged Best of Breed or Best of Variety of Breed (some breeds have two varieties, as in Beagles, and some three, as in Cocker Spaniels). This dog receives a purple and gold ribbon. The victor in this competition has now beaten out all the other competitors in his particular breed.

The dogs that are of the opposite sex to the Best of Breed and that have competed in the judging for Best of Winners and Best of Breed vie for the final award in the breed—Best of Opposite Sex. If there are no Specials of the opposite sex, the other dog which competed for Best of Winners automatically becomes Best of Opposite Sex. The winner of this award receives a red and white ribbon.

The 114 recognized breeds are divided into six Variety Groups —Sporting Dogs, Hounds, Working Dogs, Terriers, Toys, and Non-Sporting Dog. The blue rosette or ribbon designating Best of Group is given to the top dog among all the Best of Breeds in that particular group. This dog is now "Best Sporting Dog," or "Best Working Dog," etc., in the show. Red, yellow and white rosettes or ribbons are presented to the second, third, and fourth place winners in each Variety Group.

The six Best of Group Winners are judged for the top award, Best in Show. If the title is won for a Foreign-Bred dog, there is sometimes further judging for the Best American Bred in Show. Otherwise this honor is automatically given to the Best in Show. A rosette of either red, white and blue, or the sponsoring club colors, designates this honor.

A popular feature of dog shows today are Obedience Trials. In these trials dogs of all breeds are judged on how well they carry out a prescribed set of exercises. Complete rules and regulations for Obedience Trials can be obtained from the American Kennel Club, 221 Fourth Avenue, New York 3, New York and for information on Obedience Training Clubs or Classes in your vicinity contact the Gaines Dog Research Center, 250 Park Avenue, New York 17, New York.*

At all shows licensed by the American Kennel Club, dogs may win points as well as ribbons, cash prizes and trophies. Points count toward a dog's championship and are valuable only to dogs that have not yet won that title. The number of points given to each Winners Dog and Winners Bitch is determined by the number of competitors these dogs topped in the regular classes. Best of Winners is given at least as many points as the Winner of the opposite sex. Similarly, First in Group and Best in Show are awarded the maximum number of points given any breed they have defeated. A dog may win no more than 5 points in one show.

To become a champion, a dog or bitch must win a total of 15 points under at least three judges. The dog must win a minimum of three points in each of two shows not judged by the same person. A champion must have beaten better than average competition at least twice.

---
* The author thanks Gaines Dog Research Center for some of the dog show data and explanatory material in this chapter.

CHAPTER 18

Culinary Compass

(How to find your way around the kitchen)

THERE is the now classic story of the hunter who returned from a long and expensive deer hunting trip in the Canadian wilderness. He was tired; he had spent too much money; his deer was a small one. After the usual domestic small war, his wife decided that she would salvage something pleasant from the whole business and invited several of their friends in for a venison dinner the following evening. The great hunter, now a saddened and somewhat deflated character, brightened considerably and said that was a good idea and by golly they'd go all out and have venison saddle, no less.

He even suggested that he do the roast but his wife vetoed that and said that he would be in charge of the cocktail department and nothing else, that she was going to take no chances. The next afternoon she popped the saddle of venison in the roasting pan at 2:00 o'clock. The guests were to arrive at 6:00 and she wanted to give the meat plenty of time to get nice and tender before she took it out of the oven and served it at 7:00. She had a cute little trick that she had used in the past on a leg of mutton and she decided to try it on the game. She melted a cup of currant jelly in a small frying pan, and used that to baste the venison. She cooked the meat at 350 degrees, basted it religiously every twenty minutes, and gave that roast all the attention and care that she thought it deserved.

While the hunter who was now proud of his accomplishment talked about how he bagged his buck in spite of environmental and distance difficulties, his wife took the huge roast, now a beautiful crusty brown, from the oven, placed it on a heated platter, whipped up a nice brown gravy to go with it and ten minutes later served it to the applause of all seated.

There was only one difficulty. There wasn't a knife in the place sharp enough nor an arm strong enough to cut the venison. Quips about "saddle" of venison were tossed around, and the cook and guests ended up going to the nearest diner for scrambled eggs.

A common mistake had been made and the story just told has become classic because it happens so often. Most people believe that game should be cooked a great deal longer than domestic meat or fowl. In some cases this is true. But venison should be treated exactly like prime beef. The only exception is the tougher portions of the carcass that may be cut up and used as stew. But *all* other cuts should be served pink (not red) and juicy. Venison should *always* be served medium rare. If the meat is overcooked, it becomes so tough and chewy that even the most ardent deer hunter will leave the table in disgust and go out and buy a hamburger.

Speaking of hamburgers, deerburgers are much tastier and well worth the small effort it takes to make them. I grind up about three pounds of lean deer meat with a half pound of lean veal or pork, add three small onions, two small carrots, two celery stalks, all chopped finely, season this with salt and pepper to taste, add one tablespoon of paprika, mix in a heaping tablespoon homemade chili sauce, then mix the whole together and form in patties. Fry the deerburgers in plenty of butter, medium well, and you'll never eat another hamburger.

Before we go into additional recipes, we should point out the second mistake our disappointed cook made. She roasted the saddle of venison no more than three days after the deer had been shot. It would have been unpalatable even if cooked correctly. The only portions of the deer that can be eaten within hours after shooting are the heart, kidneys and liver. The liver is delicious broiled for camp supper even a few hours after the deer has been downed.

The deer should have been properly bled, the carcass wiped off, wrapped in cheesecloth and hung in cold storage for at least two weeks. Aging for a full month is even better. Even waterfowl, pheasant, grouse, rabbits and hares are improved if you let them hang for a few days in a cool, dry place before cooking them.

However, if you want to take the time to really sharpen up a knife, you can slice fresh-killed venison paper-thin (really as thin as $1/4$ of an inch), then saute quickly in butter, not more than twenty seconds on each side, take off and serve on buttered toast. Here, again, if you overcook, the result will sole a shoe. You can also cook the breast of duck and pheasant, or any game bird that has just been killed. Fillet the breast and rub it with butter and salt and pepper, and broil it no more than five minutes on each side. This or sauteing quickly in butter is also the way to serve coot. Just use the filleted breast. I had them a few years ago at John H. Ballantine's, enjoyed them immensely, didn't know what the tender, succulent meat was and when John convinced me that he wasn't kidding, I never have missed a coot since. I like them as well as mallard if they are prepared the quick way. Otherwise they get strong and fishy.

Before we get too deeply into how to find your way around the kitchen, it might be helpful to give a few hints on what to do with your big game animal after you've bagged him. After making certain that the animal is dead, by approaching carefully, gun at the ready, the first thing to do is bleed and draw it.

If you want to save the head for mounting, bleed the animal by sticking the point of your knife to the left and slightly back of the brisket. Get the animal to camp as soon as possible after it is killed. Using a sharp knife open it from brisket to vent and take out, without breaking or cutting, all of the insides. Don't use water on the meat. Using a clean damp cloth, wipe out the cavity and try to get rid of all the blood, then prop the stomach portion open with a stick so that it permits air to enter. Try to avoid letting direct sunlight hit the carcass. If you do this right, get rid of the excess blood and wipe the animal clean, the air will get to the meat, give it sort of a glaze that will protect it from spoilage for a while. It is imperative that you skin the animal immediately when you get back to camp.

It's best to hang it up head-first while you do the eviscerating and cleaning, but if you can't manage this, place the animal on its back and prop it in such a way that the front portion is elevated. When you get it back to camp, hang it by its hind legs and skin it. This can be done by splitting the skin on the inside of the legs in a straight line from the stomach incision to the tarsus joint of the hind legs and to the knee joint of the front legs. Peel the skin by inserting your knife and rolling downward and out, all in one motion. Secure the loosened skin from underneath on the hair side, and then pull down and out on the skin that comes free.

(Hardly a deer season goes by that you don't see literally hundreds of cars rolling along with a deer strapped to the hood, bumper or top. Unless these hunters get their game home in a hurry, they're certain to lose some of it. Leaving the skin on hastens spoilage, and the carrying of the body on the hood or bumper brings it in contact with heat from the car and with insects that also rush spoilage.)

After you've skinned the animal take a sharp knife and cut away all the torn, bruised or bloody flesh that surrounds the wound. Then if you really are interested in doing a thorough job, quarter it (carry an ax and small saw with you) and wrap each portion in cheesecloth. Flies will be the greatest problem now until you can get the meat home into cold storage and cheesecloth permits the necessary air to get at the meat and yet keeps the flies off. Before transporting the meat, make sure it is hung high at night and that you try to get on the road early in the morning. It should be carried inside the car. Smart hunters build a special carrier in their auto trunk, then if the weather is warm they stop at the first general store and get a few blocks of ice to surround the meat and keep it cool until they can get it into proper refrigeration. Then, remember, whether it's deer, elk, moose, caribou, bear, sheep or mountain goat, hang it in cold storage for at least two weeks before you bring it to the table.

With game birds it's wise to bleed them, remove the craw and entrails, and if you care to take the time, dry-pick them soon after shooting. At that time the feathers come off quite easily and you'll find if you wait until you get home to pluck them that the feathers will come off with difficulty and you'll probably have to plunge the bird into boiling water to loosen them. Then when you remove the feathers sometimes the skin comes too, making a messy job. All game birds are improved if they age one week. They should be hung where it is cool and dry.

Remember to remove the scent glands from small game. Look for the small white kernels under the forelegs, and on either side of the spine. If you cook the rabbit, woodchuck, or whatever it is without first removing these glands, the meat will be strong and unpalatable. Age small animals for at least three days in a cool, dry place—if there is no cold storage plant available, use your own refrigerator.

I've found one of the handiest gadgets available for the person interested in cooking game is the relatively new electric frying pan (and although I've avoided commercials, I've discovered that the Sunbeam is the best), mainly because it makes cooking with precisely controlled heat so easy. For pots and pans I'm partial to copper or enameled heavy iron. They are even conductors of heat and cook food to perfection. I use standard measuring cups and devices so that there isn't any guess work. If you're a camp cook, there are clever aluminum nests of pots and pans, complete spice and seasonings packages, foil pans that can be used and discarded, and small charcoal grills and grids that take the haphazard out of woods cooking. But we're concerned with civilized kitchen work on wild game here.

An old chef's rule of thumb is to broil, roast or pan broil tender cuts of game meat such as the loin, saddle, chops, the cuts along the back behind the shoulder. The portions where there is muscle that has been used and therefore may be tough, such as the legs and neck, and the wings of fowl should be cooked with moist heat, that is pot-roasted, boiled, stewed or fricasseed. When in doubt use a pressure cooker, or follow directions given with your electric frying pan, and simmer tough meat in wine and butter at low heat until it is tender to the touch of a fork.

That's enough for method and manner, now for a few recipes that I have tested and used over the years. Some are original; some I have borrowed from friends. They are all designed to make game cookery fun and do justice to your taste buds.

Pheasant in spices. Place a carrot sprinkled with one teaspoon of thyme, one-third teaspoon of salt in the cavity of the bird, then insert one-and-a-half tablespoons of butter. Tie the wings against the body and the legs so that they won't spread and break the flesh when cooked, and place in roasting pan. Cover the bird with three or four slices of butter-dotted bacon and dust with a half teaspoon of paprika, half of salt and one teaspoon of thyme which has been mixed. Put the bird in the oven preheated to 450 degrees F and brown. Then turn the oven to 350 and continue cooking until tender, just under two hours. Baste every twenty minutes with rich stock—chicken or beef bouillon will do. When the pheasant is finished use the basting juice in the roasting pan mixed with the juice of one-and-a-half lemons as your sauce. Slice the bird into serving portions, pour the lemon sauce over, and serve with current jelly.

Pheasant with winekraut. Take two young pheasants, dust with salt and pepper, place in roasting pan and surround with a pound and a half of drained sauerkraut that has been mixed with a cup of dry white wine. Place two thin slices of fat pork over the breasts of the birds, cover and cook at 350 degrees F for one hour. Test the young birds by pinching the legs—if tender and do not resist the slight pressure you apply, they are done. Then remove the pheasants from the pan, slowly stir one tablespoon of flour into the sauerkraut and cook for five minutes. Serve them whole on a warm platter with a ring of winekraut around them. Remember to always tie or skewer legs and wings of fowl to body when roasting. Makes for a nicer looking bird.

Pheasant in jelly. Split a big cock pheasant in half; flatten with a cleaver so that it will lie flat in an electric frying pan, rub both sides with soft butter, sprinkle with celery salt and black pepper and place in frying pan. Turn the dial to 360 until the bird is brown on both sides. Turn dial back to 200. In the meantime melt a small jar of grape jelly and one of current jelly in a separate frying pan until it becomes a smooth liquid. Baste the bird with this every 15 minutes, cook covered for about 2½ hours until tender. Remove bird to warm platter. Stir one teaspoon of cornstarch into pan gravy, adding a little water if necessary, and strain the gravy over pheasant and serve, preferable with wild rice.

Pheasant and champagne. Flatten split young pheasant so that it will fit into frying pan. Rub bird with salt and pepper and soft butter, melt two tablespoons of butter in frying pan, cover and cook over medium-high flame for fifteen minutes; turn pheasant and cook in the covered pan fifteen minutes more. Now lower the flame and cook covered for twenty minutes. Remove cover, add a cup-and-a-half of champagne and cook again over a medium-high flame until the champagne has evaporated.

Pheasant in sour cream. This one came from Sam Ashida, talented chef of Ed Dyer's excellent Young's Hotel in New Milford, Connecticut. Rub two pheasants with salt, pepper and butter. Place in roasting pan with a half cup of water, put in 450 degree oven for ten minutes uncovered. Reduce heat to 350, place in one full cup of white wine and cook covered for one hour until birds are tender. Meanwhile, warm one pint of sour cream in pan and spoon over the birds, coating them completely. Replace in 450 degree oven uncovered until sour cream has turned golden. Remove birds to warm serving platter and serve with mounds of long-grained white rice that has been mixed with the gravy and sour cream remaining in the roasting pan.

Pheasant breast and anchovy sauce. (This is especially good for badly shot birds). Fillet the whole breast, making certain to cut off bruise and wound spots and shaking out any of the shot that may be in the flesh, then fillet again to about ¼ inch thickness, but leaving the fillet as long as possible. Dip these fillets (you should get at least four out of each breast) in one beaten egg that has been whipped with an egg-beater and has had a half teaspoon of pepper and one of celery salt added, then roll in bread crumbs. Fry in sweet butter until they are golden, then place in a buttered baking pan or dish and pour the sauce of four melted anchovies over them. (Optional) Top each fillet with a slice of mozzarella cheese, cook at 350 degrees for twenty minutes.

Pheasant and bananas. Place two pheasants in roasting pan, lave with butter, dust with salt and pepper and place in a 450 oven for about ten minutes or until the birds are seared. Reduce heat to 350 and add one bottle of beer, cover and cook until tender. Meanwhile slit an opening on the side of a half-dozen bananas, and slip a teaspoon of clear honey in each banana. Add the bananas to the roasting pan just before you are ready to serve; remove the birds and bananas after five minutes. Use care in lifting the bananas out so you don't break them. Place the birds in the center of serving platter and space the bananas around them. Thicken the gravy remaining in roaster with a tablespoon of buckwheat or corn flour and spoon over the whole birds on the platter. The gravy will have just the delicate trace of banana flavor. This is a dish for those of your friends who lean toward exotic foods.

Press your electric frying pan into service for those game birds that are quite badly shot up. Cut the birds into serving pieces, season well with coarse black pepper and salt, dredge in flour, melt three tablespoons of sweet butter in electric skillet, turn heat dial to 360 and brown pheasant or game birds pieces. Turn dial down to 200, submerge pieces in one pint of heavy sweet cream, cover and cook about 2½ hours or until tender. This recipe can be varied in many ways. Instead of adding the sweet cream make it sour, or substitute a big cup of dry red wine, then 45 minutes before the birds are ready, throw in a handful of fresh mushrooms and some baby onions; or turn the whole business into a game bird stew or salmi by adding halved small potatoes, hearts of celery, carrots, and a couple of leeks. The flour browned on the birds, together with the addition of tne red wine, will make a delicious gravy. If necessary you can thicken this by stirring in a tablespoon of flour, mixed into a smooth consistency in cold water, then strain the finished gravy and serve over the pieces of game bird, or just serve the whole thing right in the electric frying pan on the table. Plug it in, turn dial to warm, and there it will be at your elbow ready for second servings without a dash to the kitchen.

Quail is the only game bird I know (unless the other may be very young doves, almost squabs) that should be eaten soon after shooting, the one game bird that doesn't need hanging for several days to improve its flavor. Quail, dove, band-tailed pigeon, duck, grouse, all can be substituted for pheasant in the above recipes. But I would like to throw in my own special quail number that I think you will like.

Arrange six dressed bobwhite quail in roasting pan with two tablespoons of butter and rub the birds well with salt and coarse-ground black pepper and coat generously with soft butter. Place six peeled white grapes in each cavity, then truss legs and wings of birds. Wrap each bird with thin slices of salt pork. Most quail don't take a great deal of cooking. A half hour in a 450 degree oven should be sufficient. Remove them to a heated platter, keep them warm. Pour excess fat from roasting pan and add a ½ cup of Chablis wine, reducing this to half by cooking over a moderate flame, and scraping the brown drippings well into the wine as it cooks down. Then add a cup of rich chicken or beef stock and bring to a boil. Reduce heat until the sauce has stopped boiling and place in about 4 dozen peeled white grapes until they are heated through. Season the whole with more coarse black pepper, divide the grapes equally between the birds and pour the sauce over the quail on the serving platter. We like to serve this with ordinary cooked brown rice mixed with the livers of the quail which have been chopped and sauteed in butter.

Duck and geese are excellent cooked in a 450 degree oven and stuffed with raw apples and celery. The latter half of the cooking time should be done with the cover of the roasting pan removed so the excess fat cooks off the birds; and they get the desired crusty skin. Discard the apple and celery stuffing.

I like braised wild duck done in casserole and served with a nice burgundy. Line the casserole with 2 chopped leeks, 2 small carrots, one celery stalk, a few small onions, all chopped, one clove, a sprig of chopped parsley, a bay leaf, a cupful of sliced fresh mushrooms. Cover this with two cups of rich chicken

stock. I take four mallards that have hung for four days and
stuff them with their own livers and two nice extra chicken
livers per bird. To this stuffing I add calf sweetbreads, blanched
and cubed, the whole well seasoned with salt, pepper and
sprinkled with sherry. In all of my seasonings you will note
that I frequently mention coarse-ground black pepper. I get
tellicherry peppercorns, which were introduced to me by my
good friend, Liesl Laugseth-Christensen, a gourmet of the
highest type, and are available in this country mail-ordered
from White Flower Farm, Litchfield, Connecticut, and put them
through a coarse-cut grinder. This kind of pepper picks up the
flavor of wild game. I then skewer up the openings in the duck
cavities, season and place the birds over the vegetables in the
casserole. I then pour a full cup of brandy over the birds, seal
them with buttered parchment paper, place the top tightly on
the casserole, and cook for about 45 minutes in a 450 degree
oven.

A good point to remember in cooking game birds is that the
white-fleshed birds are better cooked longer; fowl like ducks
and doves can be served medium-rare and be at their best.
Grouse and quail are tender and usually cook through quickly,
so it improves flavor and adds juiciness if you lard the breasts.

The legs of the larger game birds are usually uneaten, so
before serving I disjoint them and put aside for what has
come to be called "Scott Game Hash." I chop the meat
from these legs into small cubes, about two cupfuls, then take
2 cups of cold boiled potatoes, ½ cup of onions (uncooked)
chopped very finely, ½ cup of drained canned tomatoes, and a
sprig of minced parsley. I mix all these ingredients in a bowl,
moisten to bind with a cup of heavy cream. I then place the
mixture in a copper skillet with melted butter, season with salt
and pepper and stir slowly until thoroughly heated. This is
then removed and arranged in a buttered casserole. Four thin
slices of New York State cheese are arranged on top and the
whole business cooked uncovered in a 300 degree oven until
it is golden brown. Good served with steins of cold beer and
hunt talk.

The ways of cooking venison are infinite, but if you remember
to age the meat and broil or roast the tender cuts medium-rare,
you will be well on your way.

One venison roast I remember in particular was cooked for
me by an old Maine guide. He must have been at least seventy
at the time he gave me the recipe and served a hunk of a big

buck that he had had hanging in his shed for almost a month. It was the leg portion, about an eight pound piece, with the bone removed and the meat cut so that it could be stuffed, tied and roasted. He spread the meat out, arranged about 15 anchovy fillets on it, sprinkled the whole with black pepper, rolled it and tied it together in a neat roast. He rubbed the outside with bacon fat left over in our frying pan from breakfast, dusted on more black pepper and popped the whole piece in a roasting pan. In places on the roast where the tied cord left openings he stuck in a clove of garlic cut in four pieces. He had preheated his oven to 500 and shoved the pan in uncovered and browned the roast on all sides. Then he stuck four large carrots in the pan, took a pint of Riseling wine from his cupboard and added the whole thing. He covered the pan, turned the heat down to 350 and cooked the whole business about 2½ hours which worked out to about 20 minutes per pound. I've never forgotten the guide nor the meal.

Young cottontail rabbit is good hung for two or three days, the kernels or glands removed from under the legs and along the spine, cut into serving pieces and soaked in salted ice water overnight. Then take at least ¼ pound of butter, melt it in the electric frying pan and turn the dial to 360. Place the rabbit pieces in, sprinkle them liberally with oregano and salt and pepper and brown. Turn the dial to 200, squeeze the juice of one lemon over the rabbit, cover the pan and cook until the meat is tender. Serve with broad noodles, and spoon the pan gravy over the rabbit and noodles and add a dollop of chopped fresh parsley.

Vary this by browning the rabbit in olive oil and garlic then cover with a large can of tomatoes and cook at a reduced heat until the meat is tender. For another change of pace lift the lowly rabbit into the upper culinary stratosphere by roasting just the loin in butter for a half hour at 400 degrees covered, then uncover and pour on two cups of champagne. Cook at reduced heat until the wine has evaporated and the loin is tender. Or place the loin in a casserole and cover it completely with sour cream, cover the casserole and cook at 350 degrees until done.

That's about all there is to it. Cooking your game can be as much fun and relaxation as bagging it. But if you really want to be successful, the first step in any kind of game cookery is to ask your wife to step out of the kitchen. Kindly, of course. But firmly.

CHAPTER 19

Outdoor Notebook

WRITING a column never becomes a chore if you can always keep your readers in mind. And during the years I have written the outdoor column for the *American Legion Magazine,* my readers have never permitted me to forget them for an instant. Hardly a day goes by that I don't receive letters postmarked anywhere from Atlanta, Georgia, to Accra, on the Gold Coast of Africa, giving me the writers' favorite method of catching anything from a sea turtle to a cottontail rabbit. "Reader-participation," this helpful attitude of passing information on to the column is called. I'm grateful for the interest these American sportsmen and women have taken, and the help they have given me in making my column of some value. This chapter is possible because of them. My outdoor notebook is filled with their helpful hints. I hope some of the following is worthy of inclusion in *your* outdoor notebook. Help yourself.

FISHING

John G. King, 19 Warner Street, Springfield, Massachusetts, has a gimmick that gets them: "If you are an early trout fisherman and use garden hackle worms or night crawlers," he says, "then bear with me and I'll show you how to put trout in the creel. About 25 yards above a likely looking hole where you think there are fish, with as little noise as possible, crumple a section of the bank into the stream until the flow of water is muddy. Then let your bait drift down with the roiled water. If a trout is in the hole you'll get a fast strike. In addition to worms, a variety of bait such as crickets, white grubs and grasshoppers will turn the trick."

"Do you consider it a worthwhile effort to wipe a fishline dry and make it ready for use in a single operation?" asks Robert Benson, Lincoln Street, Holden, Massachusetts. "Sure do," we answer. "Then," says Benson, "fill a fired shotgun shell with melted tallow. Cut a slit through the side of the shell and into the wax about one-third the way. Then insert the fishing line in the slit. As the line is rolled in, water is squeezed out and the wax is applied."

Elmer Ermatinger, 800 4th Street North, St. Petersburg, Florida, down in the country where fishing is a year-round, shirt-sleeve proposition, sends his less fortunate brethren a sure-fire way of taking bass. Here's the way he tells it:

"If you want to take bass in heavily fished water, go to the swampy or mucky part of the lake or river, particularly where there are water hyacinths or lilies. Take a hay fork, turn them over and look for eels from six to 10 inches long. Put them in any container with wet moss, shaded from the sun. Go back to your bass spot; use the regular bass hook, a three-foot, six-pound test gut leader, and a bobber. Use any kind of rod you want. This goes on any rig. The eel is the liveliest thing you can put on a hook. His constant wiggling action is 25 times that of the best worms. After your bobber disappears on a strike, take five seconds before setting the hook. It takes about that long for the bass to get the eel in his mouth. This method gets them when they can't be got."

A really good item from Harold Thomsen, 523-5th Avenue North, Clinton, Iowa. "When dunking a line from a boat," he says, "try using a gallon glass jug, filled with water and several very lively minnows. Punch small holes in the metal lid so the bottle will sink to the bottom. Tie a rope through the handle and drop overboard. Fish are curious critters. They'll spot the imprisoned minnows quickly, will fin in to leer at them. That's the time for you to drop your baited line and start fishing."

Martin Leber, 599 East 18th Street, Brooklyn 26, New York, has enthusiasm that's catching. "Here's a great idea for catching pan fish in a strange body of water," he says. "Cast a large, bright-colored, wobbling plug as far as you can. Retrieve it at a moderate speed, giving it a little jerk every few feet. The big pan fish will follow the plug right up to the boat or dock. After this, throw in a line baited with a worm or any fish-taking bait. Before you know it you'll have a stringer full of fish."

Simon J. Freymuth, 309 North 22nd, Mattoon, Illinois, offers: "Just before you get ready to wet that line," he advises, "lift the hood of your car and take a good look at the screen in front of your radiator. You'll find it covered with insects. Now you know what kind of bugs are flying. The rest is simple. Duplicate as nearly as you can the winged things on your radiator and you'll fill that creel to the brim."

Snowy Crisco has another unsuspected use. Mrs. James E. Mc-
Donald, Tazewell, Tennessee, says: "Soak your fishing line in
melted Crisco. I've found that fish love the smell of it and
come flocking around your line and bait."

Mr. Frank Ashbrook of the Fish and Wildlife Service in
Washington, D. C. seems to have a hobby of unearthing items
and gadgets that will aid the sportsman. Recently he called to
our attention the fact that a good bait bucket has been invented
that will really keep your live bait alive. As most of you live-
bait-users know, the great problem is transporting the minnows,
worms, crawfish, hellgrammites or what have you to the fishing
destination. Metal buckets are all right, but where minnows
are concerned, even if you do change the water, the midget
fish become logey, sluggish and hardly the best morsel for
attracting the big ones.

Well, it seems that the Animal Trap Company of Lititz,
Pennsylvania, has come out with the Victor Long Life Bait
Bucket. It is made of porous molded pulp which allows the
life giving oxygen to enter but doesn't permit water to leak
out. It is light and only costs $1.19 in 8¼" x 9" size.

Blood-red worms seem to be favored by fish over other worms,
so make your worms red. Beat up a red brick and mix the
dust with three times as much soil. Worms in this mixture
will be blood-red within a week. Feed them coffee grounds,
crumbs of moistened cornmeal. Keep the brick-and-dirt mixture
damp.

A handy measuring rule you always carry can be your hand.
Measure the spread of your hand, between the tip of thumb
and the little finger. Then you can easily measure things
instantly.

Jack Richardson of Clinton, Missouri notes: "If you are
fresh out of sinkers, cut in appropriate strips empty tooth-paste
or shaving cream tubes and wrap around line. For that offensive
and lingering odor of fish on pans and hands, rinse either or
both with vinegar." Tony Sallazzo from Bolivar, New York,
says, "It is important that all of your tackle be in good shape.
Look it over carefully for defects, such as missing or sharp tops
and guides on rods. Be sure line wear hasn't caused razor
sharp edges which will cut your line. Also check your line for
bad or weakened spots. Many prize winning fish have been lost
because these things were not taken care of."

More from Tony: Hint for worm dunkers. "Carry the

wigglers in a glass, wood or plastic container. You'll find they'll end up much livelier and be greater fish-getters, than if you tote them around in the old tin can."

Earl W. Capper, Sr., of Letts, Indiana, advises:

"A new treatment of an old technique, the variations of which are quickly and easily adaptable to many conditions and situations can be had by using materials at hand in most any fishing kit. Remove the gangs or single hooks from any old floating plug that fits your casting or spinning style. Attach 1 foot of 4 pound gut leader to the dummy plug, adding a small snap swivel to the end of the leader. To the end of your line, attach in the order named, 18 inches of leader, a #0 silver or gold spinner, hook or gang removed from plug. Bait with worms, night crawlers or pork rind.

"For any depth fishing, 4 feet for example, make a simple finger loop in line 3 feet above bait, and attach plug by means of snap on end of leader (3 feet of line and 1 foot leader on plug give 4 feet).

"The rig can be cast or tossed effectively into moving water at the lower end of pools and potholes, allowed to drift into swift water, then retrieved slowly by reeling in. Wet flies, in combination with a couple of small split shot will also produce. By varying proportions of line and leader this arrangement with a little experimenting provides a method of getting light baits in desirable spots and working them presentably."

Remember the *Pelican* disaster off Long Island a few years ago? That party fishing boat that was pathetically overloaded with Sunday fishermen and went down with a loss of many lives? As a result of that tragic sinking, legislation has been introduced specifically limiting the number of fishermen passengers on small party fishing boats. This act hasn't been passed as yet and has met strong opposition from commercial fishermen.

Respected oldtime seadogs like Joseph and Frank Dolan, of Guilford, Connecticut, put it this way: "We've been running out commercial craft from these shores for twenty-five years, and never has a boat of ours been overloaded. No one gets any fish and you spend all of your time untangling lines and hooks, with the result that nobody is satisfied.

"Take a tuna fishing boat. Six men should be tops. Maybe eight if they take turns. No more. We troll with overhead rigs and it's impossible to get more than a couple of them in action. And bottom fishing for black: Put no more than eight people in a boat, with a captain to run the boat and a mate to bait hooks and take care of the paying customers." Joe Dolan shakes his head. "I'm not sure any legislation could turn the trick now. Seems to me it's up to the people themselves. If they see a captain has so little concern for them that he'll jam up the boat, then they should get off that boat."

Benny Leonard, who has something to do with Grace Lake in Bemidji, Minnesota, has an idea that may make fishing a little easier. It's a float that will mark the spot in a lake where you had a strike or where fishing has been good. Mr. Leonard says to empty two beer cans of the cap variety the easy way. Then place the cans neck to neck and tape them with friction or adhesive tape so that they are as waterproof as possible. Better yet, solder them together. Now take a cord that is longer than the distance in depth that you want to mark and tie one end around the neck of the beer can; on the other end attach a heavy lead weight. Wrap the cord around the neck until you are up to the weight. Place the whole business on the boat seat beside you and toss it overboard when you have a strike. The weight will go to the bottom; the cans will float. For plainer marking, paint the can contraption a bright red or orange so it can be seen from a distance.

Night fishermen should be interested in the discovery of Henry Laidler of 46 Chelsea Street, Charlestown, Massachusetts. "In daylight," he says, "fit your rod sections together so that the guides match perfectly. Then take a small brush and paint a white line lengthwise over the point where the sections join. After that, simply watch for white lines when putting the rod together in the dark. I find that luminous paint works even better than plain white."

Carl E. Mohn of 3308 Salena Street, St. Louis, Missouri remarks: "With some of us not so spry as we used to be, a wrinkle on how to catch fish and not be at your pole all the time, comes in handy. I take a small cork, just big enough to hold up the line, and set it at the depth I want to fish. Then I take a large cork and place it about three feet, polewise, from the small cork. When the fish takes the bait and starts to run with it, the large cork will act as a tug on the line and set the hook."

If you want to take that fishing rod out for a once-over before the season starts but seem to have sticky-ferrule trouble, W. F. Wood, from Savannah, Georgia, has news for you.

He suggests that corroded or sticky ferrules can be easily

separated by applying a few drops of carbon tetrachloride in and around the joint. Allow it to penetrate for about 20 minutes, twist the ferrule, then with a light pull it's out. It's also a good idea while inspecting the rod to go over any rust spots with a fine piece of emery cloth; then before putting the sections back together coat the ferrules with a light oil.

Norman Stava, 3923 W. 58th Place, Chicago 29, Illinois, has help for us. "If hooks used for trout fishing and other smaller fish are dulled against stream rocks and other obstacles," he says, "try rubbing them against the scratching surface of a book of matches. Points will reappear quickly." He adds another pearl: "A satisfactory hook disgorger can be easily made from an old tooth brush. File off the butt end of the handle, leaving about half of the hole which was used for hanging it up. Cut off the bristle end. Smooth off all edges and you'll have a small and efficient hook extractor."

For those fishermen lucky enough to have a use for a landing net, Paul Penquite, 1522 Alberta Street, Dayton, Ohio, says: "Attach about 3/4 ounce of lead weight to the end of the net. This helps get a dry net under your fish more quickly."

"A couple of years ago," says George Bartholomaeus, 422 East 63rd Terrace, Kansas City, Missouri, "my fishing partner and I lost several of our fine catch to the appetite of turtles. It was not my first experience, but these fish were dandies and I was angry at myself for allowing them to hang in the water off my stringer. After that trip I began thinking: "A minnow bucket for minnows, why not a minnow bucket for fish? Actually a portable live trap."

"I constructed one out of half-inch mesh wire, about 2' x 14" x 9"—with a small trap door at the top and a length of rope for tying to a handy limb or to the boat. Already it has saved me plenty of nice fish."

F. E. Sharpe, P. O. Box 374, Monterey Park, California, has a tip for us given him by a guide. "On a fishing trip to Norwalk Lake, Mountain Home, Arkansas," he says, "my guide showed me a new and very efficient way to scale fish. His scaler was a curry comb, which is even better on fish than on horses."

Mrs. Reuben Pulkinen of Buhl, Minnesota, has something for the pikers among us. "With the walleye pike season upon us, I want to pass on some information that has worked wonders for me. If the walleyes aren't biting on a plain minnow add a large nightcrawler just above the minnow and fish about six inches to a foot from the bottom. We pulled out about 26 pike, ranging from 1½ to 3½ pounds that way. Those long-nosed fish also like a spinner with the spinner removed and just the colored beads remaining."

Charles G. Ridlou, a guide living in Naples, Maine, offers this: "When fishing a lake, try working the shoreline where the wind seems to be heading. The reason: there are flies and bugs on top of the water, and the fish swim along with the wind feeding on the wind-borne bugs or what-ever may be floating. I find this 'following the wind' fishing really pays."

Tony Daniels, 53 New Street, Hudson, Pennsylvania (Wilkes-Barre, P. O.), pops up with a new wrinkle. "There are certain days when the water is crystal clear," he says. "Fish should be biting, but they're not. They follow your lure half-heartedly, never strike. I light a match and hold it just far enough away from my chrome spoon lure so that the smoke will darken the bright metal. This subdues the flash, and there are certain occasions when fish will go for the darkened lure and won't touch the bright one. It has worked for me often."

Bernard I. Rabin, a dentist of 4753 Broadway, Chicago 40, Illinois lists two items that he feels may be helpful to his fellow anglers.

1. "I always carry a small tube of lather type shaving cream in my fishing tackle box," he advises. "It comes in handy when used in place of bar soap to wash up prior to a shore lunch."

2. "To clean and remove fish odor from the cork portion of any fishing rod, use a small amount of any cleaning fluid or cigarette lighter fluid on a piece of cloth or cotton. It will make the rod look neater and smell sweeter."

Sam Underberger, 736 N. W. 1st Street, Miami, Florida, tells us that if we want to keep fishing supplies from rusting in the tackle box, just to drop in a couple of moth balls. Says they do the job in tool boxes and gun cases, too.

Herman P. Hoehler, 910 2nd Street, N. W., Grand Rapids, Michigan finds: "A handy gaff-hook can be made for inland lake fishing," he says, "by using a broken hoe handle, or any round hardwood handle. Saw the handle off to the length wanted, then screw in the bottom end a large clothesline hook. Sharpen the point of the hook to needle sharpness (filing will accomplish this) then sandpaper the whole thing smooth and deck it out with a couple of coats of varnish and you've got a gaff that will cost practically nothing except a little of your time."

And Lt. Col. H. H. Hearfield, 2000 Magowan Drive, Santa Rosa, California, informs us that most fishermen don't know how to use a landing net. In case you are one of those, here's how:

"Some try to approach the head end of the fish and thereby invariably hit the line and often disengage the hook or at least excite the fish and lose him," the colonel says. "Others try the tail end, touching him and sending him off on another run. Not good. The net should be placed *under the fish* and brought up evenly, one side of the net circle frame touching the fish forward on the body, the other side touching the rear of the fish. If this method is used fish will always bend into the net to resist contact with the frame . . ."

Live-bait fishermen take note: Fred M. Asbury, 4000 Bamberger Avenue, St. Louis 16, Missouri, has a thought: "The correct method of setting a minnow trap," he says, "is to place it in fast water parallel to the current flow. Reach down to the trap, place your forefinger on one end of it, against the current. When the water flows evenly on both sides of your finger, the trap is parallel to the current and ready to take the tiny fish. I keep them alive in an old-style minnow bucket by lifting the inner bucket up to almost the top of the outer bucket, then gently forcing it back into position. Done every 15 minutes, it will aerate the water sufficiently to keep minnows alive for hours."

Dick Fox of Arlington Heights, Illinois, sends in a good idea for fishermen camping on the water. Dick says, "Before leaving camp we put up three or four pie plates (tin is best) on sticks or branches, horizontally along the shore line, about ten feet apart. Returning in the dark, we watch for these markers with our flashlight. When the beam picks them up, we know we're home."

Victor Toth, 443 Oxford Avenue, Elyria, Ohio, has decided to give up one of his fishing secrets: "Cut off the small piece of loose white gristle on the underside of a pickerel's jaw," he confides. "It has a frog-leg action when retrieved in short jerks, and is a real killer for both bass and pickerel. It has proven much better than perch belly or pork rind."

Two quick ones: E. C. Mangione, 187 4th Street, Troy, New York, finds that when he's at streamside and has lost his last sinker, an old house key does the trick. He says it is always either nickle or brass, won't rust, and sinks better than sinkers.

Ray Schmidt, 321 Cumnor Road, Downer's Grove, Illinois, suggests that when you take your fishing reel apart for cleaning or inspection, you do it over an empty pie tin. This prevents loss of those tiny screws.

Russell Rhoads, Sr., Box 282, Stanwood, Iowa, doesn't believe in keeping minnows alive. "Pack them in a shallow pan," he advises. "Cover lightly with a mixture, half salt, half sugar, then add a screen and set pan in the sun until minnows are completely dried. Thus cured they are easily carried in a wrapper. I say that these tasty little fellows are more effective than live bait. They will not be expelled by game fish like formalin-preserved minnows before you have a chance to set the hook."

Lawrence Calder, Apt. 7, Keyes Building, International Falls, Minnesota, has a hint for you when you have a fish all ready for the freezer. "Here's an idea that will preserve your fresh-caught fish for an unlimited time. Fillet them and put them in used milk cartons, then fill the cartons with water so that the fish are completely covered. Place them in your freezer and freeze solid at below-zero temperature. This prevents moisture from evaporating or being frozen out of your fish."

Mrs. Philip J. Deneau, Route 1, Rapid River, Michigan tells us that she's passing on tried and true outdoor gimmicks that should save headaches. She reports: "String your fish hooks on a safety pin before placing them in tackle box, makes them easier to handle and keep track of . . . just a little old kitchen tea strainer is handy for dipping minnows out of buckets, hands stay dry and minnows live longer when caught this way . . . Losing my boat key in the water once was a lesson to me. Now I attach a little cork bobber to the key chain; keeps it afloat if dropped overboard."

Mr. James F. Gannon has a tip that will be of help to fishermen who are getting their rods in shape.

He says, "When overhauling your fishing rod, if you find that it needs new silk wrapping, here's a way to make the job easy. Place the guides where you want them and wrap scotch tape around one end of the guide. This will hold it steady and in place while you wrap one end, wrapping the other end will be a cinch.

"When finishing a light bamboo rod use a good varnish and dip your finger tips in the varnish, then run your fingers evenly over the rod. This leaves an even coat without bumps or bubbles. I also suggest using a fine camel's hair brush for working around the guides."

Ever catch a friend when you were angling for a fish? It's a harrowing experience, and the tricky maneuvering necessary to force the hook out of the flesh is enough to make a strong man shake. Rush E. Castelaw, a fish-catching M. D., has a few words of advice.

"If a fish hook is caught," he says, "in any part of the body and has penetrated past the barb, remove it by pushing the hook forward, on through the tissue until the barb is exposed. Then cut the barb off and back the remainder of the hook out of the flesh tissue.

"Be sure to clean and sterilize the field, both where the hook entered and where it was pushed through. Iodine or alcohol is suitable for sterilization. Then dress the wound with a clean dry or wet dressing." The treble-type hook is a nastier problem and may call for more expert attention.

Harry H. Hammer of 121 West 21st Street, Los Angeles 7, California has submitted an idea for baiting with live fish that looks awfully good. Here it is:

The system is to use rubber bands. You apply the rubber band around the fish and you put the hook between the fish and the rubber band . . . The method of putting the hook through the fish causes them to bleed and in a short time they lose their pep and die . . . "For anchovies, herring, minnows, or any other live bait, my friends and I have had great success with this method, as it keeps them alive for a long time, with plenty of action."

For easy application we recommend that you twist the band around the 1st and 2nd fingers; then spread the fingers apart wide enough so you can slip the band over the bait. With a little practice you can regulate the tension of the rubber band so it will fit snug but not tight around the tail, gills or lower jaw.

This last is best because it exposes the white belly of the bait to fish approaching from above. It will not work with *all* bait fish.

Want a surefire method for finding fish? Ben Tepe thinks he has it. "When fishing for crappies, or any school fish," Ben says, "tie a string about fifteen feet long through the gills of the first fish caught. Then tie an inflated balloon to the other end of string and release the fish. It will find a school of fish and stop. All you have to do is watch the balloon, stop your boat nearby and start hauling them in."

Dick Fox, Arlington Heights, Illinois, sounds a warning that carp should be cleaned out of gamefish waters. He says they are top battlers on light tackle and that he has discovered the bait they like best is marshmallow. Just pinch off enough to cover the hook, says Fox. Carp are wary and suspicious of a weighted line. So he also uses a six-foot light leader with a split shot about one foot from the hook. Fox also says that for camping and eating outdoors, he finds the best way to carry fresh eggs is to break them in a long olive bottle. They stay separated and can be poured in the frying pan as needed.

William P. Jacobsen, 2525 S. Coral Street, Sioux City, Iowa, thinks he has the fish-scaling solution. He takes a pan of water with just enough in it to submerge the fish. Then when he works the fish over, the sticky scales are caught in the water instead of flying in 70 directions . . . M. L. Belot, 720 Mississippi Street, Lawrence, Kansas, uses small forceps or tweezers (such as stamp tongs used by philatelists) for lifting those delicate and small flies from a fly-box . . . Gerald Belter, Baraboo, Wisconsin, has discovered that wet fishing boots are quickly dried with the home vacuum cleaner by simply inserting the nozzle in the boot. Either the blower or suction end of the cleaner does the job.

Mrs. H. Egner of 3731 E. 63rd Street, Cleveland, Ohio, suggests that you use a discarded tooth brush to clean the zippers in your fishing jacket. And husband Mat says, "A coating of ordinary cold paraffin wax will revitalize the finish of a nylon fly line, help the line to shoot through the rod guides and keep it soft and pliable. Run the line out under a straight tension if possible. Put on plenty of cold paraffin, rub it well with a soft cloth. The friction will soften the paraffin and work it into the finish." And William Woodward of 1923 Laurel Street, Pottsville, Pennsylvania, whips out an idea that may save a fishing day for you. "If you lose a small screw from your fishing reel," he says, "don't give up. Shave a lead sinker down to the same size as the screw and sort of wind it into the screw hole. The soft lead won't damage the reel threads and it will keep you fishing until you can replace the original screw."

A. H. Cansey, Johnson City, Tennessee, imparts this tart bit:

"This idea might stink, but it works. When fishing, try placing a couple of cloves of garlic in your can of worms to eliminate the mouldy scent."

Blake Anderson, Jr., feels that the opening of the fishing season is always chilly. He says, "I find that if I clean my fishing reel with gasoline and then use vaseline as a lubricant, it works well in cold weather."

Thomas H. Newton of Camden, Arkansas has a thought about keeping your tackle box in shape:

"March is the time to start tinkering with your tackle box," he says. "First remove rust and dead paint with steel wool and apply a high-grade enamel both inside and out. After the enamel has dried, cut a rubber mat from an old inner tube to fit the inside bottom. This prevents tools and heavy items from scratching the enamel and the mat can be removed for cleaning.

"Next, mask off a strip about one inch from the bottom—around all four sides. Have the bottom and the sides below the tape sprayed with undercoating at your car dealer's. This can be done at nominal cost and will add years of service to your tackle box."

Kendall Green who carries his tackle box to the lakes of Wisconsin has a simple but useful addition to the above. "It's quite a job to fumble around in your tackle box looking for a certain lure or plug in the dark of early dawn or the dim light after sunset. I painted the inside of my box with a white paint and it makes a world of difference. It gives a nice bright background for tackle and makes those lures recognizable even in poor light."

Paul Davis of Pell City, Alabama pens the following: "Mark the butt end of your fish pole in inches so you can measure the length of your catch." Another idea for handy storage of small gear follows. "Bore a hole in the butt end of your fishing rod and you have a convenient place for extra hooks, sinkers, and swivels. Use a cork to close it. And a rubber band stretched on cup hooks on the ribs of your boat is handy for holding spare baits, and a box swinging from the bottom of the boat seat can be a neat tackle box—one you won't put your foot in."

W. F. Butler speaks up: "When fishing with minnows I want to fish close to the bottom but know for sure that my bait isn't lying directly on the bottom. I use a small cork, attached to my line about fourteen inches above the hook. The sinker should be placed on the end of the line; the hook with a ten-inch leader is fastened to the line about eighteen inches above the sinker. Then the cork one-half inch in diameter is placed about one foot or fourteen inches above the hook.

"Arranged this way, the cork has buoyancy enough to lift your hook and bait clear of the bottom, and if you are using live minnows or crabs, their action will attract many more fish."

Fellow with the complicated name of Elwood Berkebile has an uncomplicated suggestion:

"Even with all the new-fangled gadgets the fisherman still has trouble keeping loose hooks in a safe place. Here's one method that works: Use strips of scotch tape one inch wide and lay your loose hooks on the sticky side and cover with another strip the same size. Use a separate strip for each size and style of hook. With this rig, you can keep dozens of loose hooks in an envelope with points protected and the entire hook waterproofed. Also you can see at a glance exactly what hooks you have and what you need."

John Donahue feels that April is likely to be a cold and wet month for fishermen and worries about damp feet.

"No matter how good a fisherman you are," he says, "five will get you ten that you come home with wet feet at the end of the day. If you're planning on going out again the next day, it's mighty uncomfortable to climb in soggy boots of an early morning.

"I've found that a quart of ordinary oats will dry out a pair of boots very nicely. Put the oats in an open pan and heat them, then pour half in one boot, half in the other. Next morning simply pour the oats out and you'll find the boots are completely dry."

Flounder fishermen, be of good cheer. William A. Harris of Reading, Pennsylvania, has words for you: "A lot of anglers fish our bays and inlets of New Jersey and other points for summer flounder or fluke without much success. Their method, drifting for flounder, dragging a 4-ounce sinker over the bottom and catching nothing but kelp, sea robins and crabs, is discouraging.

"I fish the edges of the channel back to even three feet of water and use a 4-foot, 1-pound leader and two hooks baited with minnows. A ¼-ounce clinch sinker fastened on the leader between the hooks holds the minnows down. I also use a small, adjustable, plastic bobber or cork. If the edge of the channel water is eight feet deep, I adjust the leader accordingly and wind-drift over the flats. Many, many times I've taken up to 100 flatties in a few hours. No weeds, or trash fish either."

Are you a tip guide breaker? Many of us are, and L. R. Pat-

tison of 1828 Adams Street, Pinehurst, Washington, thinks he
has the answer for our clumsy clan.

"Take an ordinary safety pin, secure it to the tip section
with scotch tape, adhesive tape or even a piece of fishing line.
Bend the loop end of the pin to the desired angle to give
smooth action to the line."

A fisherman with the appropriate name of Allan Learn from
Bismarck, North Dakota, has a snag item for us: "Many times
in the process of casting my lure," he writes, "it has become
snagged near the bottom of the river or lake and I haven't
been able to retrieve it. Now I carry with me a large weight
with a good-sized snap on it. My hook snags, and I snap my
weight, which is free sliding, on the line, working the weight
down close to the snagged lure by raising my rod as far above
my head as possible. When the weight reaches the lure, a few
light tugs on the line, plus the weight, will dislodge the hooks."

If you like tasty fried crab, then don't let your wife throw
away her old nylon stockings. From Brisbane, Australia, comes
word that fishermen there are using discarded stockings to great
advantage. They fill an old stocking with decaying meat and
fish heads, tie a line to the stocking and dump it overboard.
Crabs tangle their claws in the fine mesh of the nylon trying
to get at their meal, can't get untangled; all you have to do is
hoist them into the boat. Better yet, net them when you get
them near the top of the water.

Richard E. Herd, Bath, Pennsylvania, offers the following:
"When using a rowboat to fish lakes or rivers, be sure to take
along several good burlap bags and place them on the deck
of the boat. They help prevent undue noises made by movement of feet, bait and tackle boxes—folded they make a comfortable seat cushion. And if you have forgotten your fish bag
or box, just grab a piece of wire leader from your tackle box
and string it through the top of a burlap bag. You can then
attach this to the boat so that it is suspended in the water. It's
a good way to keep your catch alive so you can sort the fish,
returning those to the water (in good condition) that you
aren't taking with you."

Here's a cute one from LeRoy J. Smith, Morrisville, New
York: "If you're fishing on a stream that has culverts, bridges,
or heavy cover such as tag alders and willows," he says "and
you want to place a baited hook in a certain spot; (worm or
piece of crab) just put it on a light piece of bark or wood and

let it float down until it reaches the precise spot where you want it. Then you give your line a little jerk and the baited hook will drop in that hard-to-reach pool."

D. G. Simmonds, Omaha, Nebraska, claims that pipe cleaners make good fly bodies. Colored ink can be used to work the fly body into any hue desired.

We heard an apt fisherman's prayer the other day:
"God grant that I may live to fish until my dying day.
And when it comes to my last cast, I then most humbly pray,
When in the Lord's safe landing net, and peacefully asleep,
That in His mercy I be judged as good enough to keep . . ."

There's another use for glass gallon jugs—this time empty—and that's to use them as floats in catching big river fish. Many river fishermen, going after big catfish or carp, tie a well baited hook to an empty glass jug and cast it loose in a current where the fish may be feeding. The rig calls for a sinker heavy enough to hold bottom at the end of a heavy line. The fisherman may throw over a dozen or more such jugs, and then remain in the vicinity in an outboard driven motor boat. When he sees one of the jugs bouncing on the water or moving, he figures there's a fish on the hook and takes after it in the boat.

All that's needed from then on is a gaff hook or a big net. Big cans will do in place of the glass jugs and may be better for smaller fish.

Clayton A. Locker, Fremont, Wisconsin, believes in warmth while dropping a line through a hole in the ice. "For ice fishing," he says, "get a five-gallon can with an open top, and fill it 1/3rd full of sand, the remainder with charcoal. With no holes or outlets in the pail except the top, the charcoal will last several hours, will warm up your fishing hut and will even give off enough heat to broil or fry those fresh-caught fish."

L. Nagle, St. Paul, Minnesota, remarks: "Fishermen won't have any trouble keeping their fish during these winter months, because the meat is usually quick-frozen on the spot. However, if you want to keep frozen fish any length of time, give it this added treatment: After your fish has frozen naturally, dip it in the water two or three times to get a thick coating of ice over it. This means there's little loss of moisture and you don't have to worry about the fish defrosting during a brief thaw."

Wilbert Wright, Munice, Indiana, feels that fishing through the ice gives plenty of time for thought. While ice-dunking, he devised a method for mathematically computing a fish's weight

—without scales. "Simply multiply the square of the girth 'A' in inches by the length of 'B' in inches and divide by 800, he says. "For example: A bass measures 21 inches in girth and 22 inches in length, 21 X 21 equals 441 and 22 X 441 equals 9702; 9702 divided by 800 equals 12 pounds." Wright claims he has confounded many a fishing buddy with his system and he's always right on the button.

This is going to come as a shock to some advertising copy writers, but we have it on the good word of Earl Taylor, 247 Dublin Street, San Francisco 12, California, that it really works. "If you want fishing worms without spade work, take a detergent such as Vel or Tide or any of the others, and place a big dollop of it in a bucket, then fill with hot water. Take this bucket of suds, pour it on your lawn or any grassy spot—then wait. In three or four minutes the worms will come popping out of the ground. Be sure to wash the worms off with clean, cool water before using."

Joseph Ray Nash, Route 2, Box 23, Brandan, Mississippi, has a simple fishing philosophy that seems to pay dividends for him. "Try not to pull the fish out of water where he is hooked," he advises. "If you do he causes a commotion and may scare away a good catch. Just move him in the water to a reasonable distance from where he took the bait. Then when he comes thrashing out of the water on the end of your line, he won't confuse and terrify his cousins."

HUNTING AND GUNS

Frank Jones, Milan, Tennessee, suggests:

"Save your empty shotgun shells when hunting in cold weather. The paper case is soaked in oil. Slit the shell a couple of times, light it; it will burn long enough to warm stiff fingers, and start fires when fuel is damp.

"Patience is the best insurance for a clean kill. Wait until the game is within range, and, above all, be absolutely sure it's game before you shoot.

"Never put a shotgun in storage for any considerable length of time without releasing the trigger spring tension. Prolonged tension on any gun spring will weaken it and impair its resilience.

"Burn the ends of your rawhide boot laces with a match. The hardened ends will help you thread through eyelets easier.

"A good way to be sure of having a pair of warm, dry socks

to wear in the morning is to put them inside your undershirt before retiring at night.

"Ducks are like airplanes. They usually come in to the decoys with their noses in the wind. Always keep the wind at your back, decoys in front, the birds are more apt to come toward you where you can get a clean shot, not surprise you from behind."

"The barrels of guns in which black powder or blank cartridges are used can be effectively cleaned with ordinary household ammonia," says Sergeant Dean D. Fish of the Quentin Roosevelt Post in Washington, D. C. The bore should be thoroughly swabbed with patches saturated in the solution, flushed well with hot water, carefully dried and oiled. Ammonia works better than most commercial powder solvents which are intended for guns using the up-to-date smokeless ammunition. Remember to do the cleaning outdoors or in some place where there is good ventilation, as there is an accumulation of fumes resulting from this procedure. Legion firing squads using black powder blanks in drill and ceremonies will find the ammonia method of bore cleaning will remove the residue of burnt powder salts in the barrel. These salts draw moisture into the barrel and cause a fast rust.

Sergeant Fish suggests that small gun parts such as butt-plates, floorplates, barrel bands, sights, screws, can be reblued by polishing bright with an emery cloth, degreasing with carbon tetrachloride or gasoline and placing the objects on the broiler rack of your stove. The heat should be at the highest temperature and your rebluing subjects should be exposed to the heat for fifteen minutes—or until the metal turns bark blue in color. The parts that contain alloys or are likely to lose temper can be quickly reblued with a commercial *cold rebluing solution*.

Dewey Walton, Route 2, Milan, Tennessee, in the heart of the squirrel country, offers: "When I go squirrel hunting, especially when the leaves are off the trees, I carry about 50 feet of strong cord. When I see a bushy-tail some distance away, I go to that tree, find a small bush or tree near the squirrel tree, tie my cord to it, then go back to the tree where the squirrel is hiding. I walk to the opposite side from where the bush is, stand against the tree, and give the cord a few jerks. The bush moves; the squirrel comes around and starts down my side of the tree."

Leroy Cooper, South 15th Street, Coshocton, Ohio, says:

"When looking for a hidden, treed coon, try taking a small limb and rubbing or beating the tree with it. Thinking something is coming up after him, Mister Coon will look at your light and move around on the tree. This also works on tree-hidden squirrels."

Miles Harden, Box 86, Casey, Iowa, speaks for the shotgunner classified as the non-expert. "Good basic training for trap-shooting or for hunting this year can be had without the aid of a handtrap. All you need is a hill for backstop and a tin can. Put the can in an easily visible spot on the side of the hill and walk back to mid-range for your particular gauge gun. Then, after turning 90 degrees away from the target, snap the gun to your shoulder and swing around *fast,* shooting as your gun lines up on the tin-can target, then continue to follow-through. Do not slow down or stop your swing to take aim; the trigger pull should be part of the swing and follow-through. This is basic practice to develop speed and timing needed to get your shot away fast on moving game. When you score a hit almost every time, you are ready to graduate to moving targets. This 'still' shooting is valuable, for by watching where your shot hits, you can see exactly how much you are leading or undershooting the target—something it is impossible to see while you are blasting at a moving target."

If you're in a state permitting only the use of shotguns with rifled slugs, the following facts may help you bag your buck. At 100 yards, the shotgun will shoot from 11 to 16 inches low. At 50 yards, the slug will drop 3 inches. Shot groups at 100 yards will have spreads of 15 inches. You should have no trouble keeping 50-yard shots in an 8-inch group. But remember, not all shotguns shoot alike. So before you start off after your buck, fire a few shots to check on accuracy. As soon as you slip a slug in your shotgun you are converting it into a high-powered rifle that will kill up to 600 yards.

"Some rifles are equipped with a white dot front sight," remarks Alan Littman of 4th and Broadway, Greensville, Ohio. "The white dot works well in hunting when the light is bad, but if you're shooting in bright sun it is somewhat less than helpful. I carry a small bottle of red fingernail polish and, when the occasion demands, I just dab the white dot with the red polish. The result, especially when hunting across snow-covered ground, is very good and the red polish can be removed with a simple flick of the fingernail."

Henry Pitts, Gardiner, Maine, has a cold-weather gimmick: "I've found through experience and from other sportsmen, that in below-zero weather, freezing rain or snow, some automatic rifles and shotguns have a tendency to freeze, *not* jam," he says. "I have found that drying the gun then lubricating it with a good grade permanent anti-freeze eliminates this condition."

John King, Springfield, Massachusetts, is concerned about hunters who get lost in the woods: He says, "It's important to know what you are about when in the woods. If you get lost, haven't a compass but do have some daylight, keep working *downhill* until you come to a brook or any kind of running water. Then follow in the direction of the flow. Once you've hit a road your troubles are over."

Eugene L. Foehner, of 1417 7th Street, Bay City, Texas, has a do-it-yourself duck blind. It goes like this:

"An effective duck blind, adaptable to almost any terrain, can be made from a roll of chicken wire and 3 or 4 sharply pointed stakes," he says. "Arrange wire in a circle large enough to enclose your partner and yourself, leaving a narrow opening for entrance and exit. Then pin the wire in place with the sharp stakes. It's a simple matter then to thatch the wire with nearby natural cover. The portability of the chicken wire blind can often mean the difference between success and failure, particularly when duck flights are erratic and the birds are not decoying well. In this case you actually do pull up stakes and move."

If you're thinking of doing a little rifle shooting, Robert J. Kindley of 3220 Palomas Drive, N. E., Albuquerque, New Mexico, has this to offer:

"One of the most common reasons why rifles fail to hold their zero is that the small screw attaching either scope mounts or receiver sights to the rifle works loose with recoil. To remedy this, dip each screw in a good grade of shellac before screwing it in place. The shellac will set up and insure good tight mounts on the heaviest of calibers."

Earl Taylor, 247 Dublin Street, San Francisco, California, says: "I have an idea I use in early morning or at dusk when I'm hunting and it has improved my shooting and increased my bag of game. I take a small piece of white cloth and tie it around the end of my gun muzzle. In indistinct light, instead of trying to sight down a dark barrel, you have the flash of white to help in lining the gun up."

Mrs. B. Franks, 7512 Union Avenue, Cleveland, Ohio, says that one way she avoids corrosion on her shooting iron is to remove the gun from its case after a hunting trip so that the moisture that collects can evaporate.

Like wild turkey?* The state of West Virginia gives the happy word that the bronze beauties are on the upswing in the mountain country. They say that 879 wild turkeys were tagged and landed on lucky platters last year; the year before the total kill was only 419. The West Virginia conservation officials don't believe that hunters are becoming better shots. The answer is that turkey population is really growing. If you're thinking of bagging a wild tom, try the mountain areas of Tucker, Randolph, Pocahontas, Greenbrier, and Webster. If you want more information drop a line to C. F. McClintic, Conservation Commission, Charleston, West Virginia.

It is suggested that you use a dog on the gobblers. Not in the ordinary sense; a turkey will not lie for a dog like other game birds. The birds are wild and wary, fly swiftly, for two miles if necessary, and can outrun Man O' War. Look for turkey sign; droppings, etc.; hide in or near the locality and send the dog out to flush the birds. After the dog has flushed, bring him to your side and put your turkey call to work. The bronzes will walk or fly back to congregate at the spot where they were flushed. IF—if your turkey calling technique is up to par. When they fly in, put the shotgun into action and sub the dog in as a retriever. Make sure you use 2s in one barrel and 4s in the other. This heavy shot is a must unless shooting for the head and neck of walking or standing birds. The turkey is a powerful bird and hard to kill. And if you just wound him, even if you hunt with a dog, he can run and hide and you'll never get him. Check your sporting goods stores on turkey calls and read the technique in Rog Latham's book, The Wild Turkey, on calling and hunting this proud bird. It's a great sport and seems to be coming back.

Old gun trader Mac McHaley from Lafayette, Indiana, passes on a neat one for all of you who like to keep that high polish on your gun wood.

"Here's a good idea on stocks, butts and nuts," says Mac. "The problem of removing briar and wire scratches on gun butts can be solved quickly and economically by using the nut meat of

---

* For unusual sports in *all* states see Chapter 5.

black walnuts (or English) as the polishing and cleaning medium."

And F. M. Stevens from the Buckeye state has a simple one that may make taking your gun apart a trifle easier: "When cleaning and oiling my gun," he says, "I put all small parts in sequence on a strip of cellophane or Scotch tape. That way you can't go wrong in replacing the parts or losing them down a warm-air register."

Charles R. Steitz, Jr., of Pennsylvania, has a simple but useful tip for December hunters. "It's quite a job to keep matches dry in wet winter weather," he says, "I've found that by inserting an empty 16 gauge shotgun shell into an empty 12 gauge shell these sizes just naturally fit tightly together. The cases are heavily waxed and completely waterproof. My homemade match-box holds about ten "strike anywhere" matches. Simple, but it works."

"For a novel and rustic appearance, hang your guns on crotches cut from trees. I cut a number of crotches and left them to dry for six months in the garage. Then I peeled the bark off with a knife and cut a flat surface on the back side with a saw. Drilling two holes for screws, I varnished them and later put them in place." So says Ted Keller of Seaford, Delaware.

Rifles can be as complicated as women so we're going to keep it simple and recommend the following. Keep this in mind: In deer hunting, the bullet you use should be heavy enough to stop, have sufficient shocking power to halt the animal in its tracks, but not the terrific velocity that damages and tears meat.

30.06 Springfield with 150 or 180 grain bullet

30.06 Winchester model 70 with 150 or 180 grain bullet

.30 Remington with 150 or 170 grain bullet

.32 Remington or Winchester Special with 170 grain bullet

.35 Savage, Marlin or Remington with 150 or even 200 grain bullet.

Some states specify that only a shotgun can be used. Stick to the 12 gauge with the rifled slug, or 00 buck shot.

Remember the old argument about correct deer hunting methods? Well, there are three: Still hunting, Stalking, Driving. The method depends upon terrain. If it's open country, stalk; if the cover is thick and heavy, still hunting is wise; if the forests and woodlands aren't too thick, driving can be worked successfully although it is the least interesting of the methods and requires at least a dozen hunters.

Jack Dunfee of Olathe, Ohio, claims that if you can get your young son to cooperate, he has an idea that will save many a weary mile of lugging.

"When you are packing for that long awaited hunting trip," he says, "slip in your son's snow sled. When hunting in the snow there is no better way to get game back to camp. Just plunk it on the sled and stop your worrying about skinning or bruising the meat. The sled runners offer no resistance on the snow and a heavy buck can be pulled with little effort—also you can ride down many of the small hills you normally would have to walk."

"Scratches disappear from gun stocks when they are colored with burnt umber," says Mrs. M. Sulaz, of 3684 E. 63rd Street, Cleveland, Ohio. "Let the color set for five minutes, then wipe and polish with a clean, soft rag. Finish the job with a touch-up of varnish, sand it smooth, then wax."

Do you own one of those sheepskin-lined gun sheaths or carrying cases? They're swell for lugging your gun into the field, but if you leave the gun in them for any length of time, moisture collects or condensation occurs laying a quick film of rust on the important parts of your gun. Remember to grease your gun barrel and to spray oil in the working parts before and after using and put the weapon to rest in the gun rack after the hunt. Here's some energy saving news: According to the big arms and ammunition manufacturers it isn't necessary to clean your gun after even a hard day's shooting. The new types of gun powder are supposed to be of a cleansing nature. Every time you fire your gun you're doing right by it.

"What about shotguns and patterns," a sportsman writes. "Most of the outdoor magazines and others that handle the subject make it so complicated that I don't know if I'm reading or looking at a problem in calculus."

First, let me say that a shotgun is so-called because it fires a shell containing a quantity of lead shot. It is made with a smooth-bore barrel.

Shotguns are made in several well-known gauges, 10, 12, 16, 20, 28 and 410. Other gauges have been made in the past but are not in common use. These include 4, 8, 14, 24 and 32 gauges.

The unit of gauge measurement is based on numbers of lead balls weighing one pound. 12 gauge is approximately the diameter of a lead ball of which 12 weigh one pound, 16 gauge is the diameter of a lead ball of which 16 weigh one pound, etc. The one exception is 410 gauge, which is actually .410 caliber. In terms of gauge, it would be 36 gauge.

Bore diameters in thousandths of inches are as follows:

10 ga.—.780″	20 ga.—.624″
12 ga.—.730″	28 ga.—.553″
16 ga.—.678″	410 ga.—.410″

Shell length is measured in inches; in terms of the overall length of fired shell, with the crimp open. A 2¾″ shell measures about 2½″ to 2⅝″ before it is fired, but 2¾″ overall after firing. This method of measuring has been adopted to conform to standard chamber lengths of shotguns. A gun with a 2¾″ chamber will thus handle shells of the proper gauge up to 2¾″ length.

If you want to know the number of pellets in any given shotgun size, or what the sizes mean here's a handy and simple chart.

Shot size	Pellet diameter in inches	Approximate average number of pellets in one ounce
No. 12	.05	2385
No. 11	.06	1380
No. 10	.07	870
No. 9	.08	585
No. 8	.09	410
No. 7½	.095	350
No. 7	.10	300
No. 6	.11	225
No. 5	.12	170
No. 4	.13	135
No. 2	.15	90
No. BB	.18	50

If your automatic pistol jams, here's a tip that may help. A close inspection of the magazine itself will probably show that the lips have been slightly spread or pried. A thin line or crack appears on the rear of the lip. This leads to a further spread of the lip and causes the jam.

Don't stick your guns away in the summer and forget them. Clean the exterior of the gun with a solvent like carbon tetrachloride and oil the inside of the barrel and action as usual. Then use the neat Silicote Cloth which costs under a buck for keeping the rust off the exterior. This also gives a beautiful finish on both stock and gun barrel. Tieing up your firearms in plastic bags made for the purpose is good. Make a practice of taking your guns out and inspecting them periodically. Don't neglect them.

The brains in most of the state agencies claim that one out of every four ducks shot is crippled and not bagged. A couple of solutions: Try waiting the birds out until they are within killing range, never out over 40 yards. Thirty-five yards is even better. Also plan hunting with a dog. The trained retriever is still the best answer for cripples. Young William Simpson, Jr. has a gimmick that could be of help if you're forced to hunt ducks without a dog. He takes along his casting rod, uses a plug with gang hooks and when a duck is downed, flips the plug out, hooks the duck and reels in.

Ashton Burrowes tells you how to call a squirrel within shooting distance. "Take two half dollars," he says, "place one in the semi-circle formed at the base of your thumb and forefinger. Then take the other half dollar and, holding it in the other hand, hit the flat face of coin number 1 with the edge of coin number 2. By cupping hand in and out with the rhythm of tapping (using the cadence of the squirrel chatter), a sound not unlike a gray squirrel is emitted and you'll find they answer."

MISCELLANEOUS

Wet feet cause discomfort afield. Stephen A. Oellerich has a suggestion to take the damp out of clodhoppers. "A simple and fast way to dry the wet inside area of any hunting or fishing boot," he says, "is accomplished by using an ordinary electric light. Even a 40- or 60-watt bulb will generate enough heat to dry the inside of a boot. Lower it to the bottom of the boot; careful not to leave it in overlong or it will burn or scorch the lining. Slowly move the lighted bulb up and down inside the boot. You'll be pleasantly surprised with results."

John Schaeffer slides in and out with a minimum of wordage. "An old barracks bag makes a good cover for your outdoor motor," he says.

And Sid Kleinberg of Catskill, New York throws out these tips:

"If you have an old nylon casting line past its prime, don't throw it away. It makes excellent thread for reinforcing seams and sewing rips in fishing and hunting clothing.

"Have trouble carrying split shot sinkers? An old fountain pen with nib and sac removed makes a fine carrier—clips to your fishing shirt or jacket.

"For keeping fish fresh while astream, make a lining for your creel out of light canvas or muslin. Soak the lining with water. Natural evaporation will keep the fish cool and moist.

"Do porcupines give your cabin the business in their prowl for salt? A salt block in a protected spot under or near the cabin will save damage and big hunks of temper.

"Don't clutter your camp area with tin cans. Throw them in the fire when empty, crush them flat when cool and put them in a shallow hole in the ground. Oxidation will be rapid with the tin plating burned off, soon leaving nothing but a little pile of rust."

Going camping? Remember then you are going to spend at least one-third of that camping trip in bed. So the making of a comfortable bed is important. Here are a few facts that will add to your comfort.

Heavy wool blankets aren't what they are cracked up to be. They're too heavy in proportion to the warmth they retain. Two light blankets will do the trick nicely. They're easier to pack and will place a layer of dead air between them which is the secret of warmth.

M. E. Egner, 3218 Tampa Avenue, Cleveland, Ohio, warns that when traveling the woods, even though you may have a compass, unless you keep it away from iron you may throw it off its true north and render it worthless. Avoid carrying it in the same pocket with your keys or knife.

A few items from Eddie Thurman, 1007 W. Rose, Stockton, California: A newspaper folded under your tackle box keeps down vibrations and noise in your boat. A rubber band around the soles of hip boots makes for easy hanging in the proper, upside-down way. Use a safety pin for storing swivels and snap swivels. Carry those precious dry flies in a tooth brush holder. This season put your name and address on your duck blind as both a claimer and as identification, should someone be there when you arrive.

Dick Fox of Arlington Heights, Illinois has a quick and helpful hint for boat owners: Dick suggests using an old chair. Remove the legs from it, make two angle irons and screw them in so that entire chair hooks right over the regular boat seat. Simple and comfortable.

Harry E. Chrisman, Scottsbluff, Nebraska, offers the following for use on a hunting trip: If you are camping where it's apt to be windy, always collapse the tent when leaving it for the day, especially if it is an umbrella type. A gust of wind may blow it down, tear it or break a pole. If there are signs of a storm, loosen the guy ropes or spreader arms to allow shrinkage. If this should happen, the wet tent may get torn and pull loose from the supports. If the tent is wet when you get home, set it up so it can dry completely, otherwise it will get mildewed and the fabric will rot. A final tip for the camp cook: To remove that unpleasant odor of onions from your hands, rub them with salt.

The cold months are the time of year your dog needs plenty of fat in his food. Not only does it improve his health and the looks of his coat, but it provides warmth for cold winter nights. Ask your butcher for fresh suet, cut it up bite-size and mix it with his meat and meal. Bacon drippings, animal lard, even the clean cooking grease is a good mixer.

On duck cleaning John C. Chilton, 7793 Rolland Street, Castro Valley, California has a word: "When cleaning wild duck," he says, "I remove the pin feathers without use of the old hot water bath or the wax treatment. I remove the large feathers by plucking by hand. Then I use an art gum eraser, and, moving over the skin from rear toward the neck, simply rub those stubborn pin feathers right off. Be careful to make the erasing movement brisk, but don't force the rubber into the skin too hard or you'll tear it."

Afield this year maybe some of you have downed your deer, started to clean him and noticed large white spots on the liver. Now deer liver, as all of you know, is a delicacy, one of the delights of the hunt, and it is disappointing to have to discard it. That white spot is commonly called a liver fluke; it's a parasite with the imposing Latin name *Fascioloides magna*. But unless the infestation is an especially heavy one, it is harmless to the deer—and you. Just cut the white fluke out, then make sure you broil or fry the liver thoroughly and the meat will be perfectly safe.

Readers living in rural areas and interested in more abundant wildlife and game bird propagation should write for the following free booklets published by the Wildlife Management Institute, Wire Building, Washington 5, D. C.: "The Farmer and Wildlife," "Waterfowl Management on Small Areas," "Quail and Pheasant Propagation," and "Upland Game Management."

They are all hefty, illustrated booklets running about 80 pages and cover. I guarantee they treat the subjects well, and you will find them interesting reading for the long winter evenings. If you write, please address your communication to James B. Trefethen, Director of Publications.

Ervin W. Mitchell, Roswell, New Mexico, has a wrinkle for camp cooks. "Along about now," he says, "many nimrods will hit the brush to hunt the deer and other animals. They will carry assorted cooking equipment including many skillets for frying, the hardest things to clean after frying anything in camp—especially a dry camp where water has to be hauled.

"As a suggestion to these many folks, why not line the bottom and sides of these utensils with a complete sheet of aluminum foil before using? After cooking, simply peel the foil off. Very, very painless and a clean skillet!"

"I've found it's a simple matter to get burrs from a dog's hair," writes Charles G. Love, 1431 Oberlin Avenue, Lorain, Ohio. "Try rubbing linseed oil on the burr. It will then come off without any trouble at all."

On the same subject, Harry E. Chrisman remarks: "Foxtail and prickly burrs are troublesome to the hunting dog. Rub a little white vaseline on the dog's outer ears. Burrs will then stick to the vaseline, won't work into the ear or get embedded in the dog's hair."

If you're a trapper, Chrisman has a word. "New traps often smell of grease or perspiration from the hands, caused by contact with merchandise in shipping. If you want that fox or whatever you're trapping to come romping in, it's a good idea to boil the traps in a mixture of sage leaves or leaves from native trees. Or bury them underground for a while. Never burn traps to remove odor—it ruins the temper of the springs."

Did you realize that the wild goose has been known to live for seventy years? Only vultures and parrots are said to have longer life spans in the bird family.

Smoke from a green pine needle smudge is said to remove the friend-killing odor of skunk from clothing.

James Combs, 809 East 10th Street, El Dorado, Kansas, feels he has a suggestion that will increase the life of your foot leather. "Rub a good coating of common white vaseline on your leather hunting boots or shoes for keeping them dry," he says. "If it gets warm, the vaseline softens and works into the leather, conditioning it."

A character named Pete Rickard over in Cobleskill, New York, claims he has a system that beats them all. Pete manufactures scents to help the hunter accomplish everything from training his dog to enticing the brain-heavy fox into a trap. Now he says that he has perfected a deer scent. All you do is rub it on a convenient tree, hide and, quicker than you can say whitetail, the deer comes walking in to investigate.

If you've had lost-dog trouble while hunting this year, here's a little trick to remember: Walk into the center of the area where you were hunting and where you believe the dog may be lost. Scuff your feet around the ground. This helps impart your scent to the ground. Then remove an article of clothing, place it on the ground and continue to scuff the general area thereabouts. Continue to call your dog. If he still doesn't return, go back there early the following morning. In nine cases out of ten you'll find your lost dog curled up on the article of clothing you left behind. He found your scent and stayed there, hoping you would turn up.

Landis Blake slides in with a tasty item: "Rabbits seem to be on the upgrade. If you had a full bag of them this year, try a cooking tip that will make them your favorite game food. Stuff that cottontail with a good tangy sausage and bake in a slow oven. The rabbit will emerge from the oven a golden brown and will hit the table juicy and delicious."*

Fred Nichols of Lathrop, California, has one for the deer slayer. "If you have ever decided to give away your venison because it tasted too gamey," advised Fred, "or ever wondered what to do to hype up the flavor of bear meat or fresh salmon, it may be well to know that plain everyday French-type dressing (How 'everyday' can that be?), with young garlic buds cut up in it, is the perfect solution to marinate wild game or fowl. In addition to improving flavor, it aids in making the meat tender and helps it retain a good color."

Don't waste those deer hides. Do your planning for the season now. They can be converted into many types of usable jackets and clothing. I've found that the Midwestern Sports Togs, Berlin, Wisconsin, does a top job. If you're interested, drop them a line and ask for their catalog. It contains full instructions: tells how much hide is needed for various articles, gives color samples, even sketches of patterns used in making the actual garments. A couple of tanned deer hides and a few bucks and you can trot out looking like ole Dan'l Boone himself.

---

* See chapter 18 for detail on game cookery.

Friends of ours came over toting a dead porcupine and an idea. "Long been interested in how many barbed spikes this critter has in his tail," he said. "Let's make a count." The count took three hours. Result: this porky, a big one, had 1,600 tail spikes.

Don't bag your deer then spoil the delicious meat by doing all the wrong things. It's a good idea to take along a small ax, a dozen feet of 1/4-inch rope and a sharp knife. After you shoot the deer, approach cautiously to make sure he's dead. The body then should be drained of blood as soon as possible. Insert your knife five inches at base of the neck and chest and cut sideways to sever blood vessels.

The deer should be placed on its left side or on its back with hind quarters down hill. Make a shallow cut through the abdominal wall, just above sexual organs. Turn knife, sharp side facing up and cut right up to the ribs. Then cut out the muscular sheet separating the lungs from the abdominal cavity, reaching into chest to sever the windpipe and food pipe. Remove lungs, heart, liver, stomach and intestines from the body. Cut around the anus so that it will easily pull out with the intestines. Save the eatable heart and liver and bury the remainder.

Cut off all bloodshot meat, prop chest and abdomen open to aid in cooling, and hang the body in a shaded spot. Wipe the entire body cavity dry with cloth, paper or dried leaves. *Never* wash it out with water. Let the carcass cool at 40 degrees for a full week before storing it. Above all, do *not* let it freeze, then thaw, then freeze again. This ruins the meat.

Dr. Wilson M. Blatz, 608 Livingston Building, Bloomington, Illinois, feels that a trick he learned will be of help.

"It's no job at all," he says, "to be able to tell how soon the sun will set when out fishing on a lake or hunting in the woods. Hold hand at arm's length, palm towards face, with fingers parallel with horizon. Hold hand so the top edge of first finger just touches bottom of sun. Count the fingers necessary to cover distance from bottom of sun to horizon. Let each finger represent 15 minutes, two fingers 30 minutes, etc., until the sun goes down. If horizon is hidden by timber or mountain range, consider a line at eye level as the horizon."

Gerald E. Brown, Box 369, Stuttgart, Arkansas, tells us that having done plenty of camping out, he'd like to suggest an item he learned that might make life easier.

"To reflect heat from your campfire toward you while you're sitting around exchanging chitchat before bedtime, drive a few stakes in a semicircle behind the fire and stretch aluminum foil over them—bright side toward the fire. This will throw the heat where it will do the most good."

E. E. Paddock has a hint about ticks that should be helpful to your dog and maybe yourself. He points out, "When one goes afield and accumulates several tick bites, it is helpful to have a simple remedy to stop the almost unbearable itching caused by the tick.

"Wring out a rag or sponge in piping hot water, apply to the bite for two or three minutes. The itching will stop and not return.

"Also if you try to extract a tick from the body of your dog, yet the tenacious head remains, try applying a few drops of iodine directly on the tick's head. It will drop off in a few minutes."

Sound advice from Jess L. Gurley:

Like campfire baked potatoes? Place small piece of salt pork or bacon with potato and roll up in metal foil (or wet paper) and drop them on the coals. Especially good if your fishing camp is short on seasoning materials.

John Hudson, Conservation Officer from Union City, Tennessee, states that many times when he has been in the woods and had occasion to use his pocket knife and found it dull, he simply took a smooth piece of wood, rubbed a little soil on it and found that it made an excellent knife-sharpening stone.

If you want a new taste sensation this fishing season, try a fresh-caught trout broiled over coals that have first been sprinkled with a few hickory nut hulls. Make certain that you use the outer hulls; these give broiled fish a delicate hickory-smoked flavor.

If you like to tinker, have a boat and like to fish, maybe W. C. Rush's design for a light boat anchor that you can make with little trouble will appeal.

Rush says that you need three or four (depending upon your choice) short automobile spring leaves approximately twenty inches long, one piece of iron rod about twenty-four inches long and threaded two inches on one end, and two nuts to fit the threaded end of the rod.

The anchor is assembled by placing the spring leaves on top of each other, running one nut up on the threads of the rod and then putting the rod through the center holes of the spring leaves. The second nut is then placed on the rod. While in transport, the leaves of the anchor are lined up and this makes the whole thing into a light, compact anchor, easily stored in your car or boat. When in use, the spring leaves are spread so as to form the spokes of a circle.

While walking in the woods this past hunting season exercising my dogs and trying to work an inch or so off the midriff, I noticed a couple of characters leaning against a tree, rifles in hand. They appeared to be listening intently. As I got closer, I noticed ear plugs peeking out of their flappers, and started thinking about the number of hearing aids I had noticed hunters wearing during the last season. This, I reasoned, could be because they had got too close to the blast of a twelve-gauge, or else the auditory nerve of the average American was rapidly going to hell.

As I got closer they threw me a disgusted look, took the hearing aids out and said, "Well, Buster, you gonna be around here long? We're trying for some bushy tails."

It ended up with me asking them about the ear plugs. It seems that science has again chalked up a score against the wild animal. Hearing aids are being used to magnify woodland sounds. The scamper of a squirrel or the thump of a rabbit picked up on the hearing aid device gives the hunter almost the same auditory range and ability as the woods creatures.

R. J. Christiansen believes in comfort for sportsmen. "A pleasant way to make your noon ten-minute break in the field more productive," he says, "is to carry an extra pair of socks along in your hunting coat. After you've eaten lunch, change your socks and give your feet a break. During these cold months, you know that the action of walking makes your feet perspire. Toward the end of the day, it's the men who wear the same pair of socks who become footsore. The two-pair-man is still going strong."

He also suggests that the man leaving on an extended deer-hunting trip have his teeth checked by his dentist before taking off. There's nothing like a painful toothache to botch up a trip in the woods.

Providing you are lucky during the shooting months ahead, George H. Soule, coach of high school athletics in Geraldine, Montana, has two suggestions that may improve the taste of your game. "If you are cooking liver from wild meat like deer, antelope or elk," he recommends, "pour boiling water over the liver in a pan and wait until it turns a little white. Pour off the water, add butter and fry as you would ordinary beef or calf liver and there will be no wild taste at all.

"If you want to take that extra gamey flavor out of bear, deer, even hare or rabbit, sprinkle the meat a couple of hours before cooking with ginger. With a nice piece of bear meat you won't be able to tell it from beef steak. Try it."

Ever been attacked by a woodchuck? Bitten by a squirrel? Chased by a skunk? No fooling! These three are supposed to be among the most timid of animals, but within the last six months reports have arrived telling where a man was attacked by a woodchuck and severely bitten. One hunter had a squirrel run boldly up his leg and bite him on the thigh. A motorist reported that a skunk had attacked his slowly moving car and levied great assault on his left front tire.

When things like this happen, you can almost be certain that the animal has rabies. This can be dangerous and may result in death to yourself, if you are bitten, or imminent danger to other people and domestic animals. If you are bitten, wash the wound immediately with a strong soap and water. Then quickly see a doctor or go to your nearest health department. If possible try to capture the animal that bit you—alive. If you can't get the animal alive, take great care that the head isn't injured. An examination of the brain by a competent veterinarian will determine whether the animal in question had rabies or was merely a bold one. In any event, don't take chances with animals that are overly bold and aggressive. Take it for granted that they are mad and full of rabies and steer clear of them.

Johnny Crooks of Odessa, Texas, thinks that fall is the time to think about camp stoves—hot coffee and comfort in the woods. Here fresh from his pen is his invention:

"This is an idea for a camp stove to use with a wood fire. I got a piece of ¼-inch steel plate, 18 x 26 inches. Drilled a ¼-inch hole in the center of each end so that I could handle the plate with a hook when it was hot. On two sides I tapped the edges with a hammer to give me a little ridge, then ground, or rather filed off the rough edges. The plate is mounted on top of four steel rods, about 18 inches long so they can be driven into the ground about eight or ten inches. The corner where the two ridged edges come together is set a trifle lower than the other three, allowing the grease to drip off into a jar or can, to be used later in frying the fish or game."

Victor Moench, famous dog breeder and trainer, from Orchard Park Road, Buffalo, New York, has a tip for dog owners that is worth passing on. It has to do with dogs and skunks—a combination that cause trouble around the house, and put both you and the dog in bad with the little woman for a few smelly days.

"If your dog does tangle with one of the striped critters," Victor says, "bathe him well with soap and water, then wash the dog again using nothing except strong black coffee—the stronger the better. After he's been well coffeed, wash him with soap and water again and the skunk smell will disappear." Victor also says that one of the giant cans of tomato juice will do the trick. The method is identical.

Allen LeLande suggests that you place in your gun cabinet a small can, punctured with holes (½-pound or small can will do the trick) and fill it with anhydrous calcium chloride which is available in drug stores. Allen says that the chemical is 100 per cent effective as a moisture inhibitor and will keep the interior of the cabinet dry, thereby eliminating the old bugaboo rust.

David Blade reminds you to dip your matches in paraffin before going on the hunting, fishing or camping trip. Then if they get wet, they'll still strike and produce a flame. He also says that he has found it handy to crack eggs in an extra thermos bottle. This naturally protects them from getting broken and wasted en route; when you want them you merely have to pour them from the thermos.

An idea that will be of use to the thousands of you who plink at small game with a .22 rifle during the summer months, was sent along by Robert D. Osmondson, North Pacific Avenue, Chicago, Illinois.

"From a drug or cigar store," he writes, "obtain a plain leather tobacco pouch with a zipper opening. Take this to a shoemaker and have a sturdy pair of belt loops sewn on the reverse side, so that it can be worn on a belt.

"The pouch will hold three boxes of .22 long rifles, and is almost completely dust and waterproof. Its virtue is that it permits reloading without fumbling around in your pockets."

And don't throw away those woodchucks you shoot. Those

cagey creatures are worth more than mere targets for your .22, Hornet or Swift. Skin them, remove the hard white kernels from under the forearms, cut the animal into pieces, soak in vinegar or red wine and peppercorns overnight. Remove, drain and either roast or fry and you'll have a meal that will make your taste buds dance for days.

Worn hip boots can still serve useful purposes. Cut off the leaky feet, pull the leg portion over your hunting boots and they will keep your legs dry in wet underbrush or on rainy days. Slit open, the rubber will serve as a dry seat when still hunting in damp weather or to drape over wet boat seats.

Have Fun. ALL OUTDOORS is yours.